Kleist's Female Leading Characters and the Subversion of Idealist Discourse

Studies on Themes and Motifs in Literature

Horst S. Daemmrich
General Editor

Vol. 75

PETER LANG
New York • Washington, D.C./Baltimore • Bern
Frankfurt am Main • Berlin • Brussels • Vienna • Oxford

Grant Profant McAllister, Jr.

Kleist's Female Leading Characters and the Subversion of Idealist Discourse

PETER LANG
New York • Washington, D.C./Baltimore • Bern
Frankfurt am Main • Berlin • Brussels • Vienna • Oxford

Library of Congress Cataloging-in-Publication Data

McAllister, Grant P. (Grant Profant)
Kleist's female leading characters and the subversion of idealist discourse /
Grant P. McAllister, Jr.
p. cm. — (Studies on themes and motifs in literature; v. 75)
Includes bibliographical references and index.
1. Kleist, Heinrich von, 1777–1811—Characters—Women. 2. Kleist, Heinrich von,
1777–1811—Views on women. 3. Women in literature. I. Title. II. Series.
PT2379.Z5M368 838'.609—dc22 2004018812
ISBN 0-8204-7486-X
ISSN 1056-3970

Bibliographic information published by **Die Deutsche Bibliothek**.
Die Deutsche Bibliothek lists this publication in the "Deutsche
Nationalbibliografie"; detailed bibliographic data is available
on the Internet at http://dnb.ddb.de/.

The paper in this book meets the guidelines for permanence and durability
of the Committee on Production Guidelines for Book Longevity
of the Council of Library Resources.

275 Seventh Avenue, 28th Floor, New York, NY 10001
www.peterlangusa.com

Printed in Germany

Table of Contents

Acknowledgments

This study would have not been possible without the help and support of family, friends, and colleagues. I am especially thankful to Martha Helfer for her inspiring intellect, her unwavering support and friendship throughout graduate school and academia, and for her tireless critical feedback on this project. I would also like to extend my gratitude to Marcia Klotz, whose careful commentary and suggestions provided new perspectives. I owe a special thanks to Judy Hunt for reading countless drafts of this manuscript, our many conversations, and her editorial skills. I would also like to extend my gratitude to Horst Daemmrich, Heidi Burns, and Maria Amoroso for their support and editorial suggestions and assistance. I am very grateful to my friends and colleagues in the German and Russian department at Wake Forest University, whose magnanimous support and encouragement helped bring this study to completion. I would also like to thank Wake Forest University for its financial support through the Publication and Research Fund. I owe special thanks to my family: my parents, Kristy, Brooke and Nicole, whose love and humor provided me with comfort, laughter and the necessary respites from frustration. I am very thankful to Opa for reminding me to take those necessary breaks and to occasionally "sheet in." Finally, I am especially thankful to Marci for her consistent support, love, indefatigable belief in my ability to succeed, and of course for G3, my greatest joy.

Introduction

Kleist's Sexual and Textual Tropes of Ambiguity: A Deconstruction of Idealist Discourse

Throughout Kleist's oeuvre, a theme of contradiction constructs a literary world of ambiguity and uncertainty, a world in which gender absolutes are as rare as "truth" and self-certainty. By examining textual images of unstable sexuality and shifting gender boundaries within the context of Kleist's own personal experiences and judgments about sexuality, one sees that Kleist's concept of gender is, like his overall "Weltanschauung," unstable.

The destabilizing gender problematic that informs Kleist's texts and correspondence encourages critics to attribute a postmodern status to his poetic production. Paglia blatantly claims Kleist presents a discourse of femininity women seldom match: "Women have rarely spoken so boldly for themselves as Kleist speaks for them here [*in Penthesilea*]" (265). However, Kleist's definition of gender eludes monolithic methodological categorizing. In fact, Kleist's personal views on women often appear misogynist. In a letter to his cousin Marie von Kleist he overtly blames women for the failure of "German Theater": "Wenn man es recht untersucht, so sind zuletzt die Frauen an dem ganzen Verfall unsrer Bühne schuld" (796).[1] In a letter to his fiancée, Wilhelmine von Zenge, he chauvinistically preaches the roles and duties of man and woman in a marriage: "Der Mann ist nicht bloß der Mann seiner Frau, er ist auch ein Bürger des Staates; die Frau hingegen ist nichts, als die Frau ihres Mannes" (506).[2] He then maintains the sexist position that the man's happiness is the goal of both partners: "Das Glück des Mannes hingegen ist *der einzige* Gegenstand der Frau" (my emphasis, 507). In this light, Kleist can hardly be defined as the proto-feminist Paglia describes.

However, Kleist's relationship with his half-sister Ulrike undoubtedly influenced his view of gender, and possibly led him to adopt a largely opposite definition of sexuality. His sister was a woman known to cross dress frequently for the privileges and freedom it afforded, and she also never married.[3] At first his sister's refusal to accept the feminine role society expected of women troubled Kleist. He calls his sister's refusal to marry a crime:

> Du wärst entschieden, Deine höchste Bestimmung nicht zu erfüllen, Deine heiligste Pflicht nicht zu vollziehen? [. . .]Ich bin wahrlich begierig die Gründe zu hören, die Du für diesen höchst strafbaren und verbrecherischen Entschluß aufzuweisen haben kannst. (493)

A month later in a New Year's "Wish" to Ulrike, Kleist pleads with her to conform to a normative sexual identity: "Amphibion Du, das in zwei Elementen stets lebet, / Schwanke nicht länger und wähle Dir endlich ein sichres Geschlecht. / Schwimmen und fliegen geht nicht zugleich, drum verlasse das Wasser, / Versuch es einmal in der Luft, schüttle die Schwingen und fleuch!" (44).[4] However, Kleist's rigorous attempts to persuade Ulrike to conform to a specific, stable gender ultimately fail.

In fact, it is possible Kleist's own dissatisfaction with his sister's shifting gender reflected his own troubled and unstable sexuality. In a letter to Ernst von Pfuel, Kleist unveils an unquestionably homoerotic desire.[5] The letter's language teems with allusions to homosexuality.[6] For Kleist, Pfuel presents "the age of the Greeks" (*das Zeitalter der Griechen*), a clear code word for homosexuality.[7] Kleist then proceeds to pronounce his glowing admiration of Pfuel's physique, and openly asks Pfuel to marry him, so that they can form a symbolic all-inclusive family complete with children and grandchildren. The homoerotic inclinations of this letter certainly undercut the Rousseauean definition of gender he preaches to his fiancée, and highlights an irreconcilable contradiction within Kleist's gender discourse.

MacLeod argues Kleist's unstable sexuality can be defined in terms of a "third sex," androgyny:

> Actualized as an equivocal, sensual compound, the figure of the androgyne evokes monstrosity (in the case of the amphibian Ulrike) and a nomadic aestheticism (in the case of male homoeroticism), in both cases denaturalizing binaristic heterosexual norms and provoking gender trouble. (213)

For MacLeod Kleist's homoeroticism instantiates a type of "nomadic aestheticism," whereas feminine androgyny manifests itself as a "monstrosity." Although Kleist's letters to his male friends (Pfuel) are written in a literary register, employing intertextual imagery, metaphor, and prose, he by no means excludes "androgynous" women from his world of aesthetics. In fact, women, like Ulrike and his cousin Marie von Kleist, appear to be very influential in his aesthetic production. The idea of a "third sex" finds its inception in the amorphous female, a variant of the feminine that destabilizes normative gender definitions as well as traditional Western aesthetics. This type of woman differs from his fiancée and the women he derides in his tirade about the failure of German theater in that they do not conform to normative, Idealist gender categories. In life he finds this image of the amorphous female in his half-sister Ulrike and in his cousin Marie von Kleist;[8] in his writing, he locates this alternate femininity in his female heroines, who represent a destabilizing aesthetic in Idealist philosophy.

This destabilizing aesthetic is largely influenced by and critical of Kantian philosophy, the impetus for Idealist thought. Kleist's "Kantkrise" is frequently identified as the existential and philosophical influence that shattered his previous eudaemonistic philosophy and, I propose, his Rousseauean definitions of gender. However, Kleist's own gender and philosophical background was not entirely without schism or contradiction before his "Kantkrise." Helbling proposes Kleist's philosophical crisis was impending well before he read Kant:

> Although, superficially, it looked as though one philosophy had destroyed another in his inner world, the 'newest Kantian philosophy' almost certainly did not create his despair but rather furnished him with the linguistic means to express it. (8)[9]

The "Kantkrise" provided Kleist with a philosophical justification to question not only the limits of scientific investigations, but also the limits of socially constructed definitions of gender.

Importantly, the "Kantkrise" furnished Kleist with a "linguistic means" of expression, a critical aesthetic. Following the crisis Kleist's literary career bloomed. Notably, this literary explosion directly coincides with an apparent reassessment of gender. Rather than propounding Rousseauean models of masculine and feminine roles, Kleist now seems to praise his sister Ulrike and revel in her ability to resist a normative sexuality: "Sie ist eine weibliche Heldenseele, die von ihrem Geschlechte nichts hat, als die Hüften, ein Mädchen, das orthographisch schreibt und handelt, nach dem Takte spielt und denkt — — Doch still davon. Auch der leiseste Tadel ist zu bitter für ein Wesen, das keinen Fehler hat, als diesen, zu groß zu sein für ihr Geschlecht" (664). Ulrike's sexuality clearly extends beyond biologically and socially gendered limits (*zu groß für ihr Geschlecht*), as she deceptively plays by society's rules to constitute a socially unrecognized definition of femininity that transcends biology (*von ihrem Geschlechte nichts hat, als die Hüften)* and fixed borders of subjectivity (*sie ist eine weibliche Heldenseele*). Kleist's female title heroines (the Bettelweib, the Marquise, Käthchen, and Penthesilea) all enact a similar transgression of physiology and binary structures of Idealist knowledge, subjectivity and most importantly gender.

Kleist's "Kantkrise" freed him from the normative definitions of morality, ethics, and gender, resulting in a frantic, fruitful ten years of literary production. Pfeiffer argues aesthetics provided Kleist with an escape, a means to explore his subjectivity and gender beyond socially prescriptive categories: "Because, for Kleist, all pregiven models of socialization were threatening, literature remained for him the only escape; it allowed him to place an aesthetically constructed subjectivity in the place of socially mediated identity" (227). Significantly, Ulrike was paramount to Kleist's construction of this aesthetic. She is the model of the oppositional theory of aesthetics Kleist's four female title characters represent in *Das Bettelweib von Locarno, Die Marquise von O . . ., Das Käthchen von Heilbronn,* and *Penthesilea.* Each character represents an alternative aesthetic that extends beyond traditional Idealist definitions of woman and simultaneously undercuts the Idealist mode for constructing knowledge, subjectivity, and gender: namely representation—*Darstellung*.

My study analyzes these four female title characters as representatives of an amorphous feminine theory of representation. By calling into question the Jena Romantics' reliance on *Darstellung* as a guarantor of effective representation, Kleist's female title characters call into question androcentric theories of self-definition and the establishment of knowledge and truth. Each female title character deconstructs Idealist theories of *Darstellung* by exposing the tenuous relationship between truth and representation. In the process, the women figures present their own oppositional theory of representation that strives not for the absolute reproduction of truth, self-definition, and absolute knowledge, but rather for the reproduction of deception, confusion, and the utter lack of knowledge. Through these means the female characters undermine the epistemological basis of fixed gender differentiation. Kleist's female title characters share the representational task of portraying Kleist's aesthetic theory within the text, and at the same time symbolizing the body of the text itself. Kleist portrays female characters in other texts who achieve the same controversial status as the title figures I examine, yet no other female characters identify (as title) and perform (as character) Kleist's aesthetic theory.

The order of texts I analyze does not correlate to their chronological publication; rather the order reflects the level to which each text engages various Idealist theories of representation. My study interprets Kleist's theory of representation from various philosophical vantage points. In each chapter the relationship between Kleist's theory of feminine representation and Idealist discourse is structured within the context of Kantian aesthetics, engaging Idealist and Jena Romantic discourses ranging from Hegel, Schlegel, Novalis, and Fichte, to Nietzsche.

In Chapter I, I argue the title figure of *Das Bettelweib von Locarno* symbolizes an audible theory of negative representation that undermines Kant's theory of *negative Darstellung*. The Bettelweib represents, much like *negative Darstellung*, that which is phenomenally not present. However, she represents audibly, not visually like Kant's figure. The Bettelweib presents an alternative theory of *negative Darstellung* through a nontraditional medium of sound; she also symbolizes an alternative discourse of feminine verbal representation. In so doing, Kleist's figure of feminine negative representation questions the long philosophical tradition of representation based on patriarchal, visual models. Rather than being a guarantor of reason and effective representation, Kleist's feminine representation effects a total destruction of Idealist reason, epitomized by a conflagration that ultimately kills the male subject, his self-definition, and any possibility for knowledge.

Chapter II focuses on *Die Marquise von O . . .*, arguing the Marquise represents a deceptive figure who directly confronts a patriarchy's demand for paternal "truth" with her own theory of representation that provides nothing but artistic illusion as a means of transcending the Idealist notion of truth. The search for the child's real father rewrites the transcendental struggle for absolute knowledge and truth through a progressive critique and scientific-like investigation. Yet this search is impeded by the Marquise and her theory of representation, encapsulated succinctly in her statement: "Ich will nichts wissen" (129). She refuses knowledge and substitutes unknowledge or "nichts" in place of truth. Even though she produces an ad that implies a search for truth, her ad is a fictional construct that strives to expose how "truth" itself is nothing more than a subjective construction. The Marquise and her representation, the ad, do not reveal the "true" father, but rather leave it to the reader of the ad to establish the true father. Truth becomes an arbitrary production, dependent upon society for its existence and definition; otherwise it is, as the Marquise exclaims, "nichts."

Chapter III analyzes *Das Käthchen von Heilbronn* as a critique of Romantic male writers and their predilection for artificially appropriating female voice as a vehicle for *Poesie*, "truthful" aesthetic representation. Through the juxtaposition of Käthchen and Kunigunde, the text also explores the fragile limits of gender, and the role gender traditionally plays in the aesthetic theories of Romanticism, in particular the idealization of the woman as the epitome of *Poesie*. Käthchen represents the intangible concept, the a priori ideal woman. Kunigunde represents the physical embodiment of androcentric artistic creation. Both figures adhere completely to male projections of the ideal female. Whereas Kunigunde's artificial appearance represents a grotesque physical exaggeration of this male projection, Käthchen represents an equally grotesque psychological exaggeration of the devoted female to her male "master." In the end both characters become parodic examples of male Romantic authors' images of feminine voice and aesthetic creation. Even though the text appears to conclude with an affirmation of androcentric aesthetics, the male figure fails to possess "pure" female voice. In the end, Käthchen pointedly sinks into oblivion, or nothingness, during the marriage ceremony and fails to provide the male subject with a viable self-definition.

Chapter IV examines the construction of female subjectivity within male discourse in *Penthesilea*. I argue Penthesilea represents neither a definitively "feminine," polemical inversion of a patriarchal definition of woman nor a simple reflection of masculine imagery. Rather, Penthesilea presents a plural definition of the subject, a literal and metaphorical definition: her literal physical body becomes the locus for and signifier of a metaphorical linguistic definition of the subject. Penthesilea's physical body becomes the parchment for masculine discourse, inscribing its dominance upon her through physical scars, cuts, and wounds. Ironically, Achilles' attempt to limit and define Penthesilea's physical definition literally through a physical confrontation effects a metaphorical definition of Penthesilea, momentarily giving her authorial control of the text. Within the play's structure, itself a product of masculine discourse, Penthesilea becomes a metaphorical presence who, in turn, inverts metaphorical language and transforms it into an actual agent of physical destruction. In the end, Penthesilea's discourse actually devours and destroys itself as the boundaries between reality and language fuse together into metaphorical nihilism. Ultimately, Penthesilea represents a fractured definition of the subject. She is neither entirely antipatriarchal nor entirely passively constructed through a masculine gaze. Penthesilea creates a space between both antipatriarchal and patriarchal discourses in which an interplay of competing dichotomies creates an ironic mode of language that perpetually defers absolute textual closure and epistemological and gender stability.

In *Penthesilea* Kleist strips representation of its Enlightenment moral and ideological façade and presents a controversial female character whose desire for ultimate self-destruction represents a theory of "Unbildung" or "Abbildung." Similar to the destructiveness of the Bettelweib, the subversive aesthetic of the Marquise von O..., and the parodic pageantry of Käthchen and Kunigunde, Penthesilea deconstructs, if not destroys, Idealist notions of knowledge, gender, and self-definition.

Kleist's undermining of Idealist discourse through these four sexually and textually ambiguous female characters creates a mode of criticism strikingly similar to Postmodernism. Long before Saussure and Derrida, it seems Kleist understood that hierarchical structures of knowledge, value, and socially accepted norms depend upon imperfect representation, a trope these four female figures repeatedly call into question. In place of harmonious signifieds and signifiers Kleist's title heroines offer infinite pluralities and ambiguities, a set of contradictions that strives to render representation and normative definitions of knowledge, truth, and gender more fluid and diverse. Azade Seyhan identifies Romanticism as a Postmodern discourse: "Perhaps deconstruction needs to relive its past through the restless spirit of Romanticism to exorcise its demons" (21). Although Kleist is traditionally not considered a Romantic and generally resists literary categorization, he arguably personifies this Postmodern "restless spirit of Romanticism" Seyhan mentions more closely than do Schlegel, Novalis, Hoffmann, or Fichte. For unlike the Romantics', Kleist's aesthetic is defined by a pervasive and persistent lack of closure, meaning, and absolute understanding that never resolves in the Idealist notion of infinite progressivity and development. Perhaps deconstruction could better "exorcise its demons" through a critical reassessment of Kleist's female title figures, four restless spirits of an apocalyptic aesthetic.

Chapter I

Das Bettelweib von Locarno: An Audible Poetics of *negative Darstellung*

A year and approximately two months before Kleist committed suicide at the Wannsee in Berlin, he published Das Bettelweib von Locarno in his own journal, *Die Berliner Abendblätter*. Although this is his shortest novella,[1] its brevity neither limits nor facilitates interpretation. In his review in the *Zeitung für die elegante Welt*, Wilhelm Grimm succinctly summarizes the text's narrative quality that distinguishes it from typical ghost stories:

> Von jener erkünstelten Zusammenhäufung gespenstlicher Apparate und von jener alle Wirkung wieder aufhebenden, inkonsequenten Ungläubigkeit, die den Aberglauben zu befördern fürchtet, und in manchen beliebten und bekannten Gespenstergeschichten sich so possierlich ausnimmt, ist hier nicht die geringste Spur. Die Sage ist schlicht erzählt, und gibt sich wie ein *rätselhaftes Faktum*, das man dahin gestellt sein läßt. (my emphasis, Lebensspuren, 434)[2]

Rather than employing all the textual devices one typically finds in spook stories, *Das Bettelweib von Locarno* creates greater intrigue precisely because its narrative fabricates the impression of believability or probability (*Wahrhaftigkeit*) out of an otherwise improbable or uncanny subject matter. Through the "puzzling" nature of the text's central theme, the text establishes a rich and inexhaustible hermeneutic challenge for critics.

This challenge is undoubtedly enhanced by the text's brevity. The story begins with a straightforward—if not linguistically verbose and syntactically complex—image of a castle in ruins. This image, encompassed in the text's first sentence, tells the reader how the story will end. Thus, the text no longer depends on a chronologically linear plot for suspense and intrigue; rather the story's intrigue is created by a desire to understand how and why the castle came to be decimated. Although the text suggests a probable cause for the castle's destruction, the nature of that cause (a ghost) remains inexplicable.

By all reasonable assumption, the castle's demise originates with an old sick woman, who is found begging at the castle door. Rather than alms, the castle's sympathetic Marquise gives her shelter in one of the castle rooms on a bed of straw. As the woman lies sleeping on the floor in a corner of this room, the castle's owner, a marchese, enters the room to store his rifle following a hunt, and orders her to move. As she gets up to reposition herself behind the oven, according to the marchese's order, the old woman slips with her crutch on the slick floor and severely injures her back. Moaning and groaning from the pain of her injury, she somehow still manages, with great effort, to rise and cross the room to settle down behind the oven, where she dies shortly thereafter.

After this incident the Marchese's life drastically changes for the worse. Due to wars and bad harvests, his financial security is severely jeopardized. Coincidentally, a Florentine knight offers to purchase the castle from the Marchese because of its beautiful location, and presents the Marchese with a solution to his financial problems. However, the deal fails to be finalized. Ironically, the Marchese decides to put up the knight in the same room where the old woman had died earlier. Around midnight the knight is abruptly awakened by what appears to be the old woman's ghost: the sounds of someone rising with great pain, moaning and groaning, then arduously walking from one corner to the other and finally dying behind the oven. Aghast, the knight runs out of the room, and informs the Marchese the room is haunted, and pleads with him to stay the remainder of the night in his room. Needless to say, the frightened knight chooses not to buy the castle and leaves the next day.

Troubled by the rumors this incident created among his servants, which subsequently continues to frighten away other potential buyers, the Marchese decides to investigate the nature of these hauntings himself. He prepares a bed in the haunted room, and is shocked to discover that the room is indeed haunted. He hears the exact same sounds that frightened away the Florentine knight. The next morning, he reluctantly informs his wife that the rumors are true. After hearing this, the Marquise implores her husband to allow her to investigate the room herself. Agreeing to her demands, the Marchese takes his wife and a servant and inspects the room. Not surprisingly, they encounter the same sounds heard by the knight and the Marchese. They are both horrified; however, because the Marchese and his wife are so desperate to sell the castle, they manage to control their emotion and fear in front of their servant and prevent further rumors.

To solve this problem once and for all, the couple decides to engage the ghost again. They prepare two beds in the room, light some candles, bring in a dog they found in front of the room, and await the ghost. As expected, around midnight the haunting sounds return. However, this time the ghost's sounds are accompanied with a visual reference: the dog not only makes the sounds of the old woman's ghost, but he also reenacts her death. He rises, yelps and moans, and finally cowers behind the oven. The sight terrifies the couple. The Marquise bursts out of the castle and readies her horses for immediate departure. However, the Marchese stays in the room, and, like a madman, begins thrusting his dagger into the air, shadowboxing with the supposed ghost. Completely enraged by the ghost's presence, which he fails to kill, comprehend, or explain, the Marchese takes a candle and sets the castle on fire. The Marquise sends in servants to try to rescue him, but it is too late. He dies in the flames. In the process of trying to destroy the old woman's ghost, the Marchese destroys the castle and himself.

In the end, the story's last sentence returns to the imagery of the castle in ruins at the text's beginning. The narrative explains how the villagers (*Landleute*) gathered the Marchese's bones and laid them to rest in the same corner of the room from which the Marchese initially ordered the old woman to rise. Ironically, this final sentence is the first time the old woman is called the beggar woman (*das Bettelweib*). The narrator waits until the story's conclusion to identify the old woman. Through this belated identification and the structural self-reflexive nature of the text's beginning and end, the story reveals a metaphysical subtext about representation and the definition of the subject. The Bettelweib's ghost symbolizes a figure of negative representation that creates a linguistic deconstruction of the subject, not a constructive definition (*Bildung*).[3]

Through the narrative plot of an invisible ghost, *Das Bettelweib von Locarno focuses* on the paradoxical role vision plays in the theoretical foundation of representation in transcendental Idealism.[4] Specifically, Kleist's Bettelweib rewrites the Kantian sublime, exposing a visual lapse at the heart of *negative Darstellung*. Whereas Kant (indirectly) and the Romantics (directly) rely on sight as a necessary element in their theories of *negative Darstellung*, Kleist experiments with the fallibility of vision. The Bettelweib's ghost represents analogously to Kant's figure of *negative Darstellung*; however, she represents audibly. Her medium of representation is acoustic not visual. Through this audible signification, the ghost paradoxically creates a sensible but invisible negative representation and, in this way, exaggerates Kant's own suppression of the visual in his figure of *negative Darstellung*.[5] Through this exaggeration, Kleist presents a critique of Idealism that calls into question the very foundation of *negative Darstellung*, and constructs a poetics of the sublime based on sound, rather than vision.

Moreover, the representative figure of this new poetics is female. The Bettelweib not only represents a controversial theory of *negative Darstellung* through a non-traditional medium of sound, but she also symbolizes an alternative discourse of feminine verbal representation. Throughout the text, her audible discourse remains beyond the signifying capabilities of the Marchese's patriarchal linguistic system. This anomalous female discourse creates a sublime chaos the Marchese fails to comprehend and represent through his visual (masculine) means of signification. Ultimately, his urge to subdue and subjugate this "other" discourse that has infiltrated his castle, his linguistic structure, results in the castle's and his mutual destruction. He destroys his own subject.

Out of this chaotic and violent acoustic poetics of the sublime, Kleist creates a problematic mode of self-definition. Like Kant's figure of *negative Darstellung*, which permits the subject to momentarily transcend sensible limits and define him- or herself as a supersensible subject,[6] the Bettelweib's audible *negative Darstellung* also allows the subject to construct a self-definition. However, this definition is not a constructive definition (*Bildung*). I argue the Bettelweib, as a figure of a controversial feminine theory of audible representation, constructs a deconstructive definition of the subject. Kleist's theory of representation actualizes an inherent danger of *negative Darstellung*: "the danger of succumbing to fanatic vision, which is the death of all philosophy" (Helfer 49). Rather than lifting or "expanding the subject's soul" (*die Seele erweitern*),[7] Kleist's negative representation reduces the subject to bones. Ironically, this reduction of the subject constructs a definition of subject as metaphor. As the Marchese's bones are laid in same location as the Bettelweib's original death, the locus of her invisible yet audible representation, his bones become a visual referent of the Bettelweib's sounds. Together they construct a sign and signify a reading of the text *Das Bettelweib von Locarno*.

My analysis begins with a short summary of recent scholarship. Due to the rich interpretive quality of the text's narrative, the interpretations are equally diverse. My purpose in reviewing past criticism is to establish how the majority of scholarship ignores the Bettelweib's function as an alternative form of representation. Specifically, I will illustrate how critics overlook the importance of her gender, which I argue presents a decidedly alternative mode of signification to patriarchal discourse. Next I will explain the Bettelweib's analogous relationship with the Kantian sublime, and illustrate how she functions as a negative representation akin to Kant's figure of *negative Darstellung*, however through an audible feminine medium. The final section of my analysis concentrates on the Marchese's problematic self-definition, which is confounded by the Bettelweib's visually unrepresentable presence. This problematic self-definition leads the Marchese through episodes of homoeroticism, autoeroticism, and finally a self-masochistic desire for self-destruction. Ultimately, my analysis illustrates how Kleist's theory of *negative Darstellung* constructs a self-definition that is realized not in absolute terms of truth, but rather in illusive nondiscursive terms of aesthetic language.

Recent Scholarship

Traditional scholarship (Staiger, Werlich, Pastor and Leroy) focuses primarily on the overt contradictions and chaotic nature of the text, which present a cognitive impossibility not only for the reader, but also for the fictional reader, the Marchese.[8] These interpretations ultimately view such discrepancies and contradictions as a reflection of Kleist's pessimistic view of the world, infused with chaotic, uncontrollable circumstance and destiny. In their analysis "Die Brüchigkeit als Erzählprinzip in Kleists 'Bettelweib von Locarno'," Pastor and Leroy closely examine several inconsistencies and textual contradictions. They argue the sheer number of discrepancies cannot be due to writer error or neglect, as critics like Staiger argue:[9] "Tauchen diese Unebenheiten indessen dermaßen häufig auf wie in unserer Novelle, dann sollte man doch vielleicht dem 'großen Dichter' eine Absicht zutrauen und dieser nachfragen" (166). Instead of interpreting the many disparities as accidental, they argue this is part of Kleist's narrative technique. The goal of this technique, they maintain, is to bring the reader into the protagonist's own point of view: "Im Medium eines gebrochenen Erzählens wird eine hoffnungslos gebrochene Welt gestaltet, und im Munde eines im wahrsten Sinne des Wortes fassungslosen Erzählers wird eine unfaßbare Wirklichkeit gegeben [. . .]" (175). According to their analysis, all the contradictions point to a "broken world" (*gebrochene Welt*). This is a gloss on "die gebrechliche Einrichtung der Welt"[10]—a commonly employed hermeneutic key to interpret Kleist's paradoxical world as a reflection of his own existential crises, trapped in a world of circumstance and destiny.

Lilian Furst also examines the overwhelming number of inconsistencies and contradictions and constructs a similar argument. However, she maintains even the tentative conclusion Leroy and Pastor present is textually impossible to support. According to Furst, the text is beyond interpretation. The text's syntactical structure creates a veil of continuity that leads critics and readers alike to establish a sense of causality and reason. However, this causality, Furst suggests, ultimately leads to further questions: "Questions of motivation, responsibility, and causation are inevitably raised in our minds, but remain forever without answer" (109). The text is defined by paradoxes that simultaneously support interpretations, but at the same time undercut these same readings. As Furst states in her conclusion, the only textually indisputable interpretation is one of indeterminacy:

> If, as Todorov insists, "A text always contains within itself directions for its own consumption," then those directions in The Beggarwoman of Locarno are patently self-contradictory. Our interpretive processes are repeatedly thwarted by the absence of assured exegetic models within the text. [. . .] Through his eschewal of definiteness within the text Kleist withholds from us reliable prototypes to guide our meta-exegetic tactics. Or rather, the system into which readers are initiated is essentially one of indeterminacy. (110)

Ironically, Furst's argument that no interpretation of the text is valid includes her own. In trying to "eschew" definitive interpretation in order to escape the text's contradictory nature, Furst paradoxically constructs a negative exegesis: that the text cannot be understood. Moreover, she advances the same argument Leroy and Pastor present: "Again our position as readers is very similar to that of the Marchese in his role as a fictive reader of his predicament" (110). Unwittingly, it appears Furst does establish an unambiguous interpretation, a type of consensus she previously argues is impossible to reach.

In her structural analysis "Kleist's 'Bettelweib von Locarno': A Propositional Analysis," Katherine M. Arens constructs a reader-response interpretation that, in some regards, resembles Furst's argument. Like the previously discussed interpretations, Arens focuses on textual inconsistencies and contradictions. She argues Kleist's syntactic structure is modeled after a Kantian model of the mind, and illustrates how Kleist's narrative mirrors Kant's theory of communication, which is dependent upon the notion that all "human minds could communicate with each other, since they were constituted on similar patterns, and with the world" (453). According to Arens, Kleist employs this idea of "common patterns" for communication in the syntactical structure of *Das Bettelweib von Locarno*. Kleist's use of a Kantian framework of cognition within his linguistic structure attempts to establish a similar pattern of narrator-reader communication. However, as Arens argues, this communication is designed to manipulate the reader's perception. Kleist presents propositional information in his subordinate clauses, which are typically used for supportive information about the plot. The result of this inversion of typical langue, as Arens calls it, results in an inversion of how humans react to situations, or how their reaction appears to cause a situation:

> Such a manipulation on the part of Kleist, moving a reaction into the grammatical position reserved for events, corresponds to a statement about the ways in which humans and the world may interact: that emotions cause series of events to happen as efficiently as do other causes. (463)

Ironically, it appears Kleist's text creates the possibility for characters to control their destiny, but what Arens's analysis reveals is that Kleist constructs a text which places the reader, not the characters, in a position to create textual meaning:

> The propositional structure of the tale which he [Kleist] established reflects an absence of absolute standards for judgment [. . .]. All the "facts" are presented which render certain moral judgments almost inevitable for the reader, but which also require the reader to draw these conclusions actively. (468)

Basically, Arens interprets the text as creating a "judge" out of the reader.

Thus, Arens's analysis begins to resemble the Kantian aesthetic framework I argue is at work in Kleist's text. Arens engages Kant's *Kritik der Urteilskraft*, which specifically examines the limits of aesthetical judgments, judgments Kleist's readers also make. Unfortunately, Arens's analysis remains within its structuralist framework and does not consider the intertextual significance of "judging" I argue Kleist's text explicitly engages. Like Furst, Arens concludes that the text's structure is infinitely diverse, leaving ultimate interpretation up to the reader.

Kevin Hilliard's analysis presents a fresh divergence from traditional analyses by introducing a psychoanalytic reading of the text and interpreting the Bettelweib's symbolic importance. Whereas the critics I have examined thus far do not delve deeply into the Bettelweib's symbolic importance, Hilliard argues the Bettelweib presents a psychological figure of repressed guilt. Hilliard focuses, as did Werlich before him, on a small detail most critics fail to notice: that each haunting fails to reenact the Bettelweib's fall: "But as Egon Werlich has argued, it is not so much the Marchese's initial command to the beggarwoman which would constitute his crime, but his failure to intervene after she *slips*" (my emphasis, 282). Hilliard maintains this lack of representation of the slips in subsequent hauntings reveals a repressed guilt, a locus of blame or cause: "What he [the Marchese] is really defending himself against here are the prerational stirrings of a thought in his own mind, a memory of something important laboring to emerge from the penumbra of his subconsciousness" (287). Thus, like a repressed trauma that manifests itself in neurosis or some other pathological anomaly, the Bettelweib's recurrent hauntings are metaphorical manifestations of the Marchese's repressed guilt repeatedly emerging until he takes his own life.

Although Hilliard does not make direct reference to representation or Kantian aesthetics, he does define the Bettelweib's hauntings in terms of *negative Darstellung*: "If it [the text] has secrets, it conceals them in full view: the incriminating action passes in front of our eyes no fewer than five times in the course of the story" (288). What "passes in front of our eyes" is ironically an absence, a nonrepresentation, a *negative Darstellung*. The Bettelweib's recurrent hauntings (representations) are defined by an inherent lack (the missing slip) which ironically represents, according to Hilliard, the nature of the Marchese's crime and the reason for the Bettelweib's mysterious haunting.

Gero von Wilpert's analysis of the relationship between the Marchese and the Bettelweib reveals yet another aspect of the Bettelweib's function previously overlooked by Kleist scholarship. Wilpert proposes the Bettelweib is in fact the Marchese's sexual partner. Grounding his analysis in Schulz' argument that the text is in fact a story about a failed marriage,[11] Wilpert suggests the Marchese actually sleeps with the Bettelweib and that the Marquise instigates this sexual liaison by purposely positioning the Bettelweib in a room the Marchese most certainly would enter following his hunt. To substantiate his argument, Wilpert highlights many of the narrative contradictions other critics have addressed, interpreting these contradictions as suggestions of a hidden, subtextual discourse:

> Doch warum so viel Aufhebens um Anzahl, Lage und Stil der Betten und um das Gebettetwerden, das selbst als anschauliches Bild adliger Gastlichkeit übertrieben erscheint? Wäre es gar zu abwegig, eine unterschwellige Assoziation zwischen "betteln" und "betten" anzunehmen, nach der das Bettelweib gebettet werden muß, auf daß aus dem Bettelweib ein Bettweib werde? Gleichviel! (287)

Wilpert further justifies his argument by comparing other scenes throughout Kleist's work where suspected sexual activity takes place behind closed doors (*Die Marquise von O . . .*, *Der zerbrochne Krug*, *Der*

Findling, Die Verlobung in San Domingo) and between couples with stark social differentiation (*Das Erdbeben in Chile, Das Käthchen von Heilbronn*). He also notes the presence of phallic symbolism throughout Das Bettelweib von Locarno: "Büchsen, Kerzen, Degen, Pistolen und selbst Krücken" (288). Ultimately, Wilpert states his argument merely tries to further Kleist scholarship by pointing out some of the erotic underpinnings of the text. Like Wilpert, I interpret the Bettelweib as a sexual figure. However, my analysis moves beyond Wilpert's in that I attribute the Bettelweib's sexuality to an underlying motif of self-definition that instantiates a Romantic model of subject-object reflection.

At first reading it appears Thomas Dutoit's analysis of the text offers an interpretation similar to my own. Dutoit argues Kleist's text is a redaction of the Kantian sublime: ";*Das Bettelweib von Locarno* can be read in terms of both the sublime/Geist and natural/supernatural pairs, in a way that dramatizes the fantastic as well as the schema" (226). Dutoit focuses on Kleist's rhetoric, which mirrors to a large extent Kant's in his discussion of the sublime. Moreover, Dutoit also affords the Bettelweib representational importance. He argues the visually imperceptible nature of the Bettelweib presents a negative representation similar to Kant's: "Indeed, 'Das Bettelweib von Locarno' foregrounds negative presentation and negative perception in a number of ways" (227). Dutoit's reading thematically resembles mine, but we differ in our approach to analyzing the importance or significance of *negative Darstellung* as a means for self-definition. Moreover, Dutoit's analysis does not consider the paradoxical nature of *negative Darstellung,* which ironically dissolves limits and simultaneously draws limits. Dutoit merely focuses on the drawing of limits: "In the 'Analytik des Erhabenen' what Kant calls a 'bloße negative Darstellung' is articulated precisely in terms of limits: it guards against 'über alle Grenzen der Sinnlichkeit hinaus etwas sehen . . . zu wollen'" (232). *Negative Darstellung* does draw a limit and its primary function is to guard against the notions of visual limitlessness Detoit mentions, but *negative Darstellung* also removes limits.

Detoit's analysis offers an insightful reading into Kleist's text that no other critic has presented. Moreover, his comparison of the Bettelweib's ghost to *negative Darstellung* also engages another level of interpretation other critics have failed to perceive. However, Detoit does not examine the primary function of *Darstellung* or of the sublime itself, which Kant indirectly associates with the definition of the subject. Moreover, he does not afford the Bettelweib's acoustical form of negative representation the significance it demands, namely its function as an alternative form of feminine discourse. This discourse is not only negative in its import, but also negative in its implications for male self-definition. What follows will illustrate how Kleist's text rewrites the Kantian sublime with an audible form of *negative Darstellung* that first violently deconstructs the subject, and then reconstructs that subject within an indeterminate discourse of fictional language.

Text as a Redaction of the Kantian Sublime

That Kleist experimented with the poetics of the sublime is well established. In his article "Das Beben der Darstellung," Hamacher draws an incisive parallel between Kleist's *Das Erdbeben in Chile* and the Kantian sublime:[12]

> Das gesamte Wortfeld von 'Fall' und 'Erhebung' und die korrespondierenden antithetischen Bewegungen, die Kleist in seiner Erzählung ausbreitet, folgen in ihrer Organisation dem dynamischen Prinzip, daß etwas erst da steigt, wo es fällt, und stürzt, wo es den Gipfel seiner Erhebung erreicht hat. Dieses Prinzip permanenter Peripetie, das Vokabular und Ereignisfolge der Erzählung vom ersten bis zum letzen Satz reguliert, ist dem des Dynamisch-Erhabenen in der Natur nachgebildet, das Kant in der *Kritik der Urteilskraft* analysiert. (158)

Hamacher identifies a theme of *permanenter Peripetie,* a theme of sudden reversals that informs the text. This "permanent peripetia" is defined by the paradox of *Fall* and *Erhebung,* and corresponds to the same paradox found in Kant's discussion of the "dynamically sublime."

In her book *The Retreat of Representation,* Helfer constructs a similar analysis of *Über das Marionettentheater.* She focuses on the marionettes' movements, which are also defined by a theme of *Fall* and *Erheben.* The marionettes' movements are perpetuated by their momentary contact (*Fall*) with gravity, which in turn lifts (*erhebt*) them in a seemingly weightless manner (*antigrav*): "This second attribute literally elevates the puppets to the sublime: *erheben*, to lift, is the etymological root of *das Erhabene*, the sublime" (131). Thus, Helfer argues the text constructs a redaction of the sublime: "*On the Marionette Theater* couples a critique of reflection with a redaction and revision of the Kantian sublime" (130).

Kleist formulates a similar aesthetic and theoretical structure of the sublime in *Das Bettelweib von Locarno*.[13] Significantly, the text's language and structure reflect the theme of *Fall* and *Erhebung*. In German das *Erhabene* is the word for the sublime, and, more so than the English, the German word denotes height and elevation. In the first sentence of Kleist's text, allusions to elevation and descriptions of immeasurable greatness abound, suggesting the text does construct a redaction of the Kantian sublime:

> Am Fuße *der Alpen*, bei Locarno im *oberen* Italien, befand sich ein altes, einem Marchese gehöriges Schloß, das man jetzt, wenn man vom *St. Gotthard* kommt, in Schutt und Trümmern *liegen* sieht: ein Schloß mit *hohen* und *weitläufigen* Zimmern, in deren einem einst, auf Stroh, das man ihr *unterschüttete*, eine alte kranke Frau, die sich bettelnd vor der Tür eingefunden hatte, von der Hausfrau aus Mitleiden *gebettet* worden war. (my emphasis, 163)

The Castle is located in upper Italy, at the foothills of the Alps, mountainous heights. It is approached only after going through a foreboding pass, whose name, St. Gotthard, reflects a divine nature (*Gott*), emphasizing the castle's sublime context. Moreover, it is only by going through this pass that a subject "sees" the castle.[14] It appears the castle can be experienced only within a sublime context. Additionally, the Bettelweib is offered a second-story room described later in the text as decidedly above the rest (*die Treppe zu dem Fremdenzimmer bestiegen* [197]) and here as being large (*weitläufig*) with high (*hohen*) ceilings. One also notices here the polemic differences between descriptions of heights and descriptions of depths, corresponding to the paradoxical interplay of subjugation and elevation present in Kant's discussion of the sublime. Every instance of raising, erheben, is countered by a repression, a return to earthly bounds. The allusions to sublime heights and violent repressions of such heights continue throughout the text. The phrases *sich erheben*, *sich heben*, and *aufstehen* are repeated several times and are countered in each instance with a metaphor of subjugation: *unterkommen*, *legen*, *niederschlagen, untersuchen, niedersinken, unterwerfen,* or *unterdrücken.* This polemic reflects the *Fall* and *Erheben* paradox in Kant's discourse, which Hamacher also finds in *Das Erdbeben in Chile.*

Kleist's text emphasizes another fundamental element of the sublime: its paradoxical nature to simultaneously repel and attract.[15] Each haunting is frightfully repulsive, yet curiously attractive at the same time. The Marchese's desire to rid himself of the unbearable and paralyzing fear evoked by the Bettelweib is similar to the Kantian subject's need to measure himself against an immense object of nature, which is at the same time powerfully repulsive. Each frightening encounter with the Bettelweib is ironic in that it results in a heightened need on the part of the subject to see, or rather hear, her again. Why does the Marchese demand that his guest, the knight, occupy the exact room in which the Bettelweib died—a room previously unfit for guests one wishes to impress, but which now is beautifully decorated and designed to attract? The Marchese consciously or unconsciously fosters the possibility of a repeated encounter with the Bettelweib. This room, both immensely foreboding (sublime) and beautiful, becomes the mystical vortex to which the Marchese is repeatedly drawn, satisfying an enigmatic need within himself to encounter (hear) the Bettelweib's horrifying metaphysical essence, her sound. A polemical oscillation is constructed, which appears can only be resolved in the violent destruction of the subject.

Each time subjects confront the presence of the Bettelweib's ghost—her sounds that eerily recall her death—they retreat back down the stairs and away from the haunted room. The subjects and their consistent downward retreating metaphorically reenact the Bettelweib's original deadly fall. Ironically, the structure of authority is inverted. It is no longer the Graf who stands in an authoritative position, ordering the Bettelweib to move and inadvertently fall. Rather, the Bettelweib's ghost now holds the position of authority and repels each visitor downward: The knight "verstört und bleich, . . . herunterkam" (196), the Marchese "am anderen Morgen . . . herunterkam" (197), and finally the Marquise "stürzt mit sträubenden Haaren, aus dem Zimmer" (198). In the end the Marchese is in a state of permanent stagnation as his bones lie in the corner of the burnt, crumbling castle which also lies in a state of ruin, "in Schutt und Trümmern *liegen*" (my emphasis, 196). Unlike the Bettelweib, who through death is revitalized in an invisible medium, sound, through which her existence transcends the sensual limits of vision, the Marchese is silenced and suppressed into the visual imagery of decay and bones. This image underlines the Marchese's metaphysical limitations.

According to Kant, a successful experience of the sublime depends on the subject's reason first imposing limits, and then prompting creative contemplation. This process spurs one's active imagination to produce a representation, a negative Darstellung. By creating such a representation, the subject becomes aware of "the idea of humantity in our own subject"[16] (*die Idee der Menschheit in unserm Subjekte* [154]). In other words, the subject elevates him- or herself through a sublime experience and constructs a self-definition. In *Das Erdbeben in Chili,* Hamacher argues Kleist creates a similar type of negative representation in the form of a metaphor: "Und in der Tat schien, mitten in diesen gräßlichen Augenblicken, in welchen alle irdischen Güter der Menschen zu Grunde gingen, und die ganze Nautur verschüttet zu werden drohte, der *menschliche Geist selbst, wie eine schöne Blume, aufzugehn* (my emphasis, Kleist qtd. in Hamacher 159). Moreover, this metaphor of *negative Darstellung*—a flower—is responsible for elevating the subject's soul: "Die Metapher [die Blume] des 'menschlichen Geistes' ist zugleich Metapher der Darstellung" (Hamacher 159).

I argue *Das Bettelweib von Locarno* also creates a theory of *negative Darstellung* akin to the Kantian model. From the very beginning, the reader recognizes the text resembles a specular structure: a type of structural representation. The text's beginning reflects the status of events at the end of the novella and the end refers back to the beginning by naming the figure for whom the text is titled, "Das Bettelweib." The beginning reads: "Am Fuße der Alpen, bei Locarno im oberen Italien, befand sich ein altes einem Marchese gehöriges Schloß, das man *jetzt,* wenn man vom St. Gotthard kommt, in Schutt und Trümmern liegen sieht" (my emphasis, 196); and the end: "[. . .] noch jetzt liegen, von den Landleuten zusammengetragen, seine weißen Gebeine *in dem Winkel des Zimmers,* von welchem er das Bettelweib von Locarno hatte aufstehen heißen" (my emphasis, 198). Thematically, the Graf's and the Bettelweib's roles are also inverted. Initially the Bettelweib is homeless and poor; she finds shelter in a room at the Graf's castle; she is forced to move and, because of this, dies in a corner of the room. By the end of the text, the Graf loses financial security (*in bedenkliche Vermögensumstände geraten* [196]); he tries to rid himself of his home (*das Schloß, es koste was es wolle, los zu werden* [197]); he eventually destroys his house (*das Schloß ringsum in Flammen aufgehen* [198]); and he finally dies and assumes the same position in the corner of the room the Bettelweib had originally occupied in the novella's beginning: "und noch jetzt liegen, von den Landleuten zusammengetragen, seine weißen Gebeine *in dem Winkel des Zimmers,* von welchem er das Bettelweib von Locarno hatte aufstehen heißen" (my emphasis, 198). Structurally and thematically, the text creates a specular inversion, and presents itself as a representation. However, the representational structure of the text does not coincide with a successful definition of the textual subject, the Marchese, as it would in Kant's figure of *negative Darstellung*.

In contrast, Kleist presents a model of *Darstellung* in which a subject's self-definition is undermined by a sublime experience that refuses to be given to the eyes: the Bettelweib's ghost becomes an invisible yet audible *negative Darstellung*. In the text, the Bettelweib's ghost and its mysterious sounds create a state of intrigue, chaos, and confusion that demands causality, an answer, knowledge—a representation: "dem Vorfall irgend eine gleichgültige und zufällige Ursache, sich entdecken lassen müsse, unterzuschieben" (164). *Entdecken* appeals to the eyes, bringing something hidden or invisible within visual reach. Yet the mystery, or rather the referent, of the metaphor (*das Bettelweib*) remains hidden, or at best illusory. Like *negative Darstellung,* the Bettelweib becomes a paradoxical representation. And this is the cause of the Marchese's demise—his suicide and confused self-definition. The repeated occurrences of the Bettelweib's death, present now only as audible signification, are never "entdeckt," never represented in the Kantian (visual) sense of the word. Such impure (avisual) representation, placed within a system of visual codification (Kantian aesthetics), is the cause of the deadly "fanaticism" which eventually destroys the Marchese's chances for self-definition as well as his mortal life.

Das Bettelweib's Sublime Transformation into an audible *negative Darstellung*

The Marchese's initial encounter with the Bettelweib is reminiscent of a subject's experience with the sublime: the Marchese is paralyzed and rendered temporarily impotent. He is "durch Krieg und Mißwachs, in bedenkliche Vermögensumstände geraten" (163). In Kant's discussion of the sublime the subject encounters a similar experience of impotence and paralysis, which, however, is followed by a period of calm contemplation, measurement, and mental activity, i.e., movement. The Marchese encounters the Bettelweib and subsequently experiences a state of stagnation and obvious lack of productive capabilities (*in bedenkliche Vermögensumstände geraten).* The narrator claims that such paralyzing times resulted from a war (*Krieg*) and a bad harvest (*Mißwachs*), yet the only event the narrator mentions before this unfortunate state is the Marchese's encounter with the Bettelweib. Kant explains in paragraph 28 of *Kritik der Urteilskraft* that war has something sublime about it:

> Selbst der Krieg, wenn er mit Ordunung und Heiligachtung der bürgerlichen Rechte geführt wird, hat etwas Erhabenes an sich, und macht zugleich die Denkungsart des Volks, welches ihn auf diese Art führt, nur um desto erhabener, je mehreren Gefahren es ausgesetzt war, und sich mutig darunter hat behaupten können: da hingegen ein langer Frieden den bloßen *Handelsgeist*, mit ihm aber den niedrigen Eigennutz, Feigheit und Weichlichkeit herrschend zu machen, und die Denkungsart des Volks zu erniedrigen pflegt. (my emphasis, 163)

Could the Marchese's encounter with the Bettelweib be the war (*Krieg* [196]), inciting a sublime experience? The language describing the scene does resemble that of a war, with its discussion of weapons, a disputed piece of property, a demand, and a death, not to mention that the Marchese is returning from a hunt, "[. . .] bei der Rückkehr von der Jagd [. . .]" (163). Moreover, as the words *Mißwachs* and *Vermögensumstände* suggest, the economic situation of the Marchese's castle represents Kant's "commercial spirit"[17] (*Handelsgeist*) negatively: there is no peace to secure a fortuitous "commercial spirit." The Marchese is engaged in a war. Even though the Marchese desires such a "commercial spirit" (*dem viel an dem Handel gelegen war* [196]), the Bettelweib's ghost prevents him from achieving "peace" and an atmosphere conducive to trade. Without question, the Marchese's encounter with the Bettelweib is warlike and awakes a feeling of the sublime within him. Yet unlike Kant's subject, who recovers from the sublime and rebounds into mental contemplation and movement, Kleist's subject is paralyzed, leaving him and his imagination stagnant.

The Marchese's war-like experience with the Bettelweib certainly does not create a more sublime disposition (*Denkungsart*) within the Marchese, as in the Kantian sublime. Rather, the Marchese's experience creates the exact opposite of what the sublime is supposed to evoke: "niedrigen Eigennutz, Feigheit und Weichlichkeit herrschend zu machen, und die Denkungsart des Volks zu erniedrigen pflegt" (Kant 163). Similarly, the Marchese develops such "low selfishness" (*niedrigen Eigennutz*) that he takes his own life (*müde seines Lebens* [198]); at times he appears "coward-like" (*feig*) and "timid" (*weichlich*) (*da er sich, mit scheuen und ungewissen Blicken, umsah* [197]); and finally his "disposition" (*Denkungsart*) is "diminished" (*erniedrigt*) to that of a madman (*gleich einem Rasenden* [198]).

The irony in this inversion is that the Bettelweib first occupies a position lower than the Marchese, a subordinate position the Marchese demands she forfeit in his first encounter with her. After the Marchese orders the Bettelweib (*befahl der Frau* [196]) to move from the center to the corner of the room, she slips, breaks her spine, and dies. In elevating herself, she falls. Yet in doing so her existence, her Geist, becomes elevated beyond the sensible comprehension of the Marchese; she becomes "ein unbegreifliches Geräusch." The tables have turned on the Marchese. Once free and able to transcend the limits of his own castle, the Marchese is from this point on locked up in his own castle and never again transcends its walls. The Marchese is literally trapped within the figurative word game Kleist repeatedly plays within the text. The German word for castle (*das Schloß*) also means "lock." This suggests that the nature of the "Schloß" is less a means of protection against outside foreign forces than a textual prison for entrapping subjects, specifically the Marchese, linguistically and internally. Following his next encounter with the Bettelweib's Geist, it is significant that he and his wife are described as "trodden" (*aber wie betreten war das Ehepaar* [196]). He not only is limited by the Bettelweib's limitless sound, he also is trodden underneath her elevated state. In his attempt to subjugate her, he becomes the subjugated. The Bettelweib's invisibility and her audible signification, illimitable and elusive, appear to cause a representational dilemma that leads to an inversion of power structures, which the Marchese and his wife fail to reverse.

This inversion of authority takes place immediately following the Marchese's first encounter with the Bettelweib. Subtextually, this first encounter suggests another level of competing discourses, namely a sexual discourse. The scene is introduced by images of weaponry, a metaphor Kleist frequently employs as an allusion to sex:[18] "Der Marchese, der, bei der Rückkehr von der Jagd, *zufällig* in das Zimmer trat, wo er seine *Büchse abzusetzen pflegte,* befahl der Frau unwillig, aus dem Winkel, in welchem sie lag, aufzustehen, und sich hinter den Ofen zu verfügen" (my emphasis, 163). The *Büchse,* like other weapons in Kleist's oeuvre, is a sexual, if not a phallic, symbol. That the rifle signifies more than a literal weapon is further substantiated by a key narrative contradiction in this passage. Ironically, the Marchese just happens to enter the room where he habitually deposits his weapon. Why does he enter the room after his hunt *zufällig,* if indeed this is where he habitually deposits his gun? Would it not be expected that he enter the room after his hunt? What the paradox calls into question is the nature of this room. It seems the room is not for his literal *Büchse,* but rather for a euphemistic rifle—a sexual encounter.

The location of the Bettelweib's bed and the type of bed she is given also raise some important questions. Why is the Bettelweib offered a bed of straw instead of one of the two beds that supposedly already stand in the room? In his article "Der Ausrutscher des Bettelweibes von Locarno: 'Capriccio con fuoco', Gero von Wilpert constructs a convincing argument, explaining the hidden sexual implications of the straw:

> Daß er die Stelle bestzt finden sollte, und zwar mit einer Frau, die bewußt nicht im Bettenpaar, sondern ausdrücklich und, um im Bilde zu bleiben, gewissermaßen "außerehelich" außerhalb desselben auf einem Strohlager liegt und wehrlos dem Willen des bewaffneten Mannes sich fügen muß? Es bedarf fast gar nicht des Hinweises darauf, welche Konnotationen Stroh oder Heu für die galant-erotische Bildkunst des 18. Jahrhunderts, etwa bei Boucher oder Fragonard, als der Ort außerehelicher "Begegnungen" haben. (288–9)

Wilpert argues the bed of straw not only recalls the erotic paintings of Boucher or Fragonard, informing the scene with a clearly sexual subtext, but that the Bettelweib's position on the floor signifies a certain "extramarital" transgression the Marchese only too gladly exploits. Moreover, Wilpert argues the Marquise purposely places the "woman" (*die "außereheliche" Frau*) in a room the Marchese most certainly would enter following his hunt (*bei der Rückkehr von der Jagd*), a traditionally masculine expression of "potency":

> Ist es angesichts der vielen Leerstellen und Motivationslücken im einführenden Absatz allzu abwegig, die Vermutung zu äußern, die Marquise habe ungeachtet der damit verbundenen Mühen und Gefahren mit voller Absicht eine andere Frau im Innersten ihres Heimes gebettet, und zwar mit vollem Bewußtsein genau an die Stelle, wo ihr Gatte, der während dieser Vorbereitungen der männlichen Ersatzhandlung der Jagd huldigt, bei seiner Rückkehr eben eines dieser männlichen Potenzsymbole, seine Büchse, zu entladen und abzulanden pflegte? (289)

Certainly, the Marquise's actions appear rather suspect, and Wilpert's study provides a controversial, yet viable explanation for her actions. The Marchese's and Marquise's marriage is anything but exemplary. Moreover, Wilpert's analysis highlights the subtextual sexual current informing this scene. However, Wilpert's examination does not explore the subtextual implications of this sexual scene in enough detail. The passage presents much more than a simple sexual encounter. It presents a subtextual confrontation between two discourses, where one clearly subjugates (rapes) the other.

At first the Marchese's masculine discourse certainly enjoys a privileged status over the Bettelweib's. This is illustrated when he orders the Bettelweib to reposition herself behind the oven, and she unwillingly (*unwillig*) concedes to his demands. His demand results in a painful fall, damages her spine, and finally splits her being:

> Die Frau, da sie sich erhob, glitschte mit der Krücke auf dem glatten Boden aus, und beschädigte sich, auf eine gefährliche Weise, das Kreuz; dergestalt, daß sie zwar noch mit unsäglicher Mühe aufstand und quer, wie es vorgeschrieben war, über das Zimmer ging, hinter den Ofen aber, unter Stöhnen und Ächzen, niedersank und verschied. (163)

Verschied is the past tense of *verscheiden*, meaning "to die." Additionally, *verscheiden* is derived from *scheiden*, meaning "to split."[19] This linguistic relationship between *verscheiden* and *scheiden* is thematically reflected in the scene, which portrays the Bettelweib's death (*verscheiden*) through a series of crossings and splitting (*scheiden*). The word "cross" (*Kreuz*) figures prominently in the scene: she injures her lower back (*das Kreuz*) and she crosses the room diagonally (*quer*), metaphorically splitting the room into two halves. Whereas the Bettelweib figuratively splits the room in two, the Marchese's order literally causes the Bettelweib to injure (*beschädigt*) her own spine (*Kreuz*), the dividing line in human physiology. He splits her in two.

Through this interplay of *scheiden* and *verscheiden* the text suggests that, along with physical limits (*das Kreuz* and life and death), linguistic borders are transgressed and crossed. *Verscheiden* extends beyond its usual syntactic "limits" and evokes a larger linguistic register and now refers to multiple signifieds. Therefore it is possible to read the Bettelweib's death (*verschied*) as much more than a simple death: it is a transcendence of empirical perception; a transcendence of linguistic representation; and it is a violent expression of authority of one discourse over another. Moreover, the scene is couched in a sexual context, suggested by the words *Büchse* and *verscheiden*, which is also etymologically linked to "*Scheide*," "vagina."[20] The Marchese's discourse forces the Bettelweib's essence, her linguistic representation, to split. Metaphorically, the Marchese's linguistic order (*Befehl*) instigates a linguistic rape.

Ironically, this linguistic rape figuratively castrates the Marchese, rendering him physically, authoritatively, and mentally impotent, as his state of financial capabilities (*bedenkliche Vermögensumstände*) suggests. The Marchese never regains dominance, sexually, socially, or linguistically. Instead he occupies a subordinate position: he is trodden (*betreten*). In every instance, he must climb or rise, returning repeatedly to the high room in which the original encounter occurred (*zu dem Fremdenzimmer bestiegen*) in order to attempt to overthrow the Bettelweib's rumor-inciting ghost: "das Gerücht erhob, daß es in dem Zimmer, zur Mitternachtsstunde, umgehe, er, *um es mit einem entscheidenen Verfahren niederschlagen*, beschloß, die Sache in der nächsten Nacht selbst zu untersuchen" (my emphasis, 197). Not only does the Marchese desire to subjugate the Bettelweib and regain his authority, but it appears he wants to do this by "un-splitting" (*entscheiden*) her fragmented essence. *Entscheiden* is related to *scheiden* "to split," and evokes all the previously discussed etymological possibilities this word presents: a physical and metaphorical split, and a rape. However, this time the *ent* implies a reversal, an undoing.[21] Unfortunately for the Marchese, this regressive "un-splitting" is defined as a *Verfahren*, a mistake.[22] Moreover, his (visual) mode of linguistic signification is unable to comprehend the Bettelweib's (avisual) signification. By evading his visual dependency, she continuously eludes any attempts to thwart her linguistic dominance; she never is relegated to a subordinate linguistic position. The Marchese and the Marquise try but fail to substitute (*unterschieben*) the Bettelweib's mysterious presence with their own linguistic explanation that is as equally valid (*gleichgültig*)[23] as the Bettelweib's elusive mode of signification: "[. . .] dem Vorfall irgend eine *gleichgültige* und zufällige Ursache, die sich entdecken lassen müsse, *unterzuschieben*" (my emphasis, 197). Ironically, through such misguided efforts (*Verfahren*), the Bettelweib manages to achieve total linguistic control in her (negative) signification in the text. She is the symbolic figure of an audible theory of aesthetic representation.

The Marchese is unwittingly responsible for transforming the Bettelweib's textual signification. His order, his discourse, names at once the text and the identity of the woman, *das Bettelweib von Locarno*: "[. . .] in dem Winkel des Zimmers, von welchem er *das Bettelweib von Locarno* hatte aufstehen *heißen*" (my emphasis, 165). This last sentence not only encapsulates the entire text by functioning as the title (*Das Bettelweib von Locarno*) but also names, for the first time, the identity of the Bettelweib (*das Bettelweib*). Up to the end, the Bettelweib is a nameless woman and is given only audible attributes. The Marchese's earlier order, demanding the Bettelweib (then only a nameless woman) to move and reposition herself according to his own needs, actually calls the Bettelweib into the linguistic realm. He orders her to reposition herself into his visual symbolic order of language. The Marchese's name mirrors his linguistic "marking" of the Bettelweib. *Marchese* is derived from *Markgraf*, which is related to the Latin *marca* (*Grenze* / border / an artificially drawn limit). The Marchese's order seems to epitomize what Butler calls the marking of the female body "within masculine discourse" (12): "Instead of a self-limiting linguistic gesture that grants alterity or difference to women, phallogocentrism offers a name to eclipse the feminine and take its place" (Butler 13). Yet this artificial visual demarcation of limits, itself a representation of the Marchese's hegemonic domination, violently backfires. The Bettelweib is in fact defined by a male gaze: she achieves self-definition, and the Marchese becomes objectified. In the end the Bettelweib is named and the Marchese is stripped of his title—his self-definition—and objectified as bones, "weiße Gebeine" (165). In his demarcation of the Bettelweib he comes to remove his own marking and limits, which socially define his identity. Similar to Hegel's "master-slave" dialectic, the role of subject and object are reversed.

Naming, or calling, the Bettelweib into language is the key to Kleist's redaction of the sublime. At the point where the Marchese orders the Bettelweib to erect herself (*aufstehen*), and calls her (*heißen*) into language, the Bettelweib ceases to exist and signify visually. Ironically, her entrance into language is also her exclusion from it. Again the Bettelweib's problematic relationship to language reflects the concerns of Butler's argument regarding the phallogocentric definition of "women":

> Irigaray would maintain . . . that the feminine "sex" is a point of linguistic absence, the impossibility of a grammatically denoted substance, and, hence, the point of view that exposes that substance as an abiding and foundational illusion of a masculinist discourse. (10)

Likewise, the Bettelweib is described as an "unbegreifliche[s] Geräusch." She has become a non-conceptual noise. She is inconceivable, visually vacuous, and only appears with "vernehmlichen Schritten." Not she, but rather her steps, her traces, are heard. Finally, she is described as *entsetzlich*. Kluge defines the word *entsetzlich* in an etymological sense as "ausser Fassung bringen" (168). Literally, the definition correlates with the Bettelweib's nature, which is beyond grasp (*unbegreiflich, ausser Fassung*). The adjective *entsetzlich* also implies a syntactic removal. *Ent* implies an elimination and a negation, and *setzen* meaning to place, is etymological related to *Satz* "sentence." She is linguistically, syntactically, implacable. The Bettelweib's description as *entsetzlich* encapsulates her terrifying presence, and suggests she belongs outside the boundaries of a linguistic system, outside the limits of a sentence (*ent-setzlich*). Thus, the Bettelweib is not only inconceivable and invisible, but she is also linguistically incompatible.

Because of her invisibility and linguistic incompatibility, the Bettelweib questions (male) vision and linguistic comprehension. Kleist's critique thus introduces a major shift in aesthetic modes of representation. Kleist substitutes the Bettelweib's (female) audible and invisible form of signification for the (male) visual system. This explains the Bettelweib's "entsetzlich" (incompatible) yet ironically dominant nature within the text. She is the embodiment of an audible poetics within his own text, and thereby constitutes and signifies the text itself. She becomes a free-floating signifier, a reflection, or in this case, an echo that has no visual image. Yet she signifies the text, making visible via audible sounds not a picture or image of the Bettelweib, but rather a subjective—to the eyes invisible but to the ears recognizable—image created by the imagination. She symbolizes a reading of the text.

Through this nonvisual representation, Kleist develops not only an alternative audible aesthetic, but also an alternative nonmale (nonvisual) aesthetic. Kuzniar identifies a similar juxtaposition between female language (nonvisual and yet audible) and male language in Novalis' *Heinrich von Ofterdingen*. Kuzniar illustrates how Novalis privileges the "female voice" over male language due to its poetic nature: "Woman's language, in fact, establishes a regulatory paradigm in the novel: it not only corresponds to but grounds a self-referential theory of poetry" (1197). Similarly, Kleist uses the Bettelweib as a metaphor of an audible aesthetics to define his text. She is the poetic utterance throughout Kleist's text that, much like Novalis' female characters, offers a "non-visual, hence dephallicized system of signification" (Kuzniar 1200). Kleist emphasizes the Bettleweib's dephallicizing power by opposing the Marchese's visual dependency to the Bettelweib's audible and visually elusive, unbegreifliche nature. Not only is the Marchese figuratively castrated, but so too is the visual linguistic system he personifies. In contrast, the Bettelweib's audible representation signifies—gives birth to—the text. Although the Bettelweib does not speak or sing like Novalis' female characters, she does make sounds and it is the sound of her breath (*Stöhnen und Ächzen, Geseufz und Geröchel*) that completes each haunting scene. The "female voice" is defined by the overall sound of the female—the sound she makes either through music, song, and even breath.[24] Clearly the Bettelweib's sounds are more similar to primal gurglings and raptures of death than to the beautiful melody of an instrument or song, yet we must not forget the nature of the Bettelweib and that which she audibly represents. The Bettelweib is born out of a Kleistian redaction of the *Analytic of the Sublime*, not the *Analytic of the Beautiful*. She is destructive, life threatening, and fearfully repulsive. She is an audible poetics of *negative Darstellung*. She embodies negativity—not through outwardly visual physical appearance, but rather through a hidden, physically vacant echo.

The Bettelweib's ghost signifies only negatively. She is not the image of the Bettelweib; she is what the Bettelweib was not. She represents the negative space or sound left by the Bettelweib's death, a process that changed her from an "objective" being to an invisible, *unbegreifliche*, representation. In life she is a visual entity, *eine Frau*. In death she is a figure of sound and negative space: "dem Blick unsichtbar" (196); "das unbegreifliche, gespenstartige [. . .] und entsetzliche Geräusch [. . .], [das] kein Mensch mit Augen sehen kann" (197–198). And she is the negative embodiment of a linguistic text, *Das Bettelweib von Locarno*.

That the Bettelweib functions as a text is further suggested by the conjunction *als ob*, which precedes each haunting. This conjunction identifies an additional negative aspect of the Bettelweib—a certain (un)knowability or illusory limit that fails to be unambiguously understood. *Als ob* means "as if," and emphasizes an uncertain ambiguity: it is not positive that the Bettelweib's representations truly represent the Bettelweib's death, it is only *as if* they could be considered such. It is left up to the reader to define such representation as the Bettelweib. In other words, Kleist has created a text based on negative, illusory knowledge (hearsay), which is infinitely indeterminate and readily open to reader interpretation. Kleist invites textual interpretation through *als ob*, a textual device deferring hermeneutic closure.

Negative Darstellung also creates a subreption, an illusion: "Kant invariably chooses expressions like *as it were* and *as if* to explicate his definitions, and his entire discussion of *Darstellung* is predicated on the notion of illusion or appearance" (Helfer 48). The language with which Kleist constructs his metaphor for *negative Darstellung* is "tentative," much like Kant's own language about the sublime and *Darstellung*: "*als ob* es auf Stroh gelegen, im Zimmerwinkel aufgestanden, mit vernehmlichen Schritten . . . ," "*als ob* ein Mensch sich von Stroh, das unter ihm knisterte, erhob . . . ," and finally "*als ob* ein Mensch auf ihn eingeschritten käme . . ." (197–8). Taking into consideration the figurative and linguistic semblance of the text to Kant's discussion of the sublime, and the Bettelweib's illusory, ironical, invisible and life-threatening signification throughout the text, it seems the Bettelweib functions as a cipher for *negative Darstellung* from within a completely different—I propose, even more negative—mode of signification. What Kleist's example of audible *negative Darstellung* produces is exactly the opposite, i.e. negative, of what Kant had planned for *negative Darstellung*: the defense against illusory knowledge. Kleist's cipher for *negative* Darstellung resides within dark corners of the Kantian sublime, the Dionysian space unwilling (*unwillig*) to resolve into Apollonian form and limitation. And as such the Bettelweib evokes a chaotic state of confusion that destroys the subject in order to construct a definition of the subject as metaphor.

Deadly Fanaticism and the Definition of the Subject

The Bettelweib's internal, rather than external, audible signification contributes to the Marchese's paradoxical self-definition. After the Marchese's initial—implicitly sexual—encounter with the Bettelweib, he no longer is the aggressive, order-giving patriarch. In his linguistic-sexual rape of the Bettelweib the Marchese's phallic and visual dominance is not so much castrated as it is consumed by the Bettelweib's cacophonous noise. Moreover, her audible representation is perceived internally. Unlike vision that is gathered and comprehended with outwardly, aggressive gazing eyes, themselves apparent to vision, sound is gathered and comprehended passively and internally; the ear's receptive properties are hidden, much like the female reproductive organs.

In her interpretation of sexual ambiguity throughout Romanticism, Paglia argues a male's masculinity is diminished through sexual intercourse: "Every male copulating with a woman returns to his origins in the womb. Goethe postponed intercourse until he was forty. This must be related to his self-imposed distance from his forceful mother.

To refuse phallic penetration is to refuse surrender to the female matrix" (Paglia 257). When the Marchese orders the Bettelweib to surrender her position for one which he prefers, he appears to dominate when in fact he actually surrenders to her "female matrix," her internally oriented invisibility. He willingly, yet unknowingly, diminishes his own phallic dominance, physically and linguistically.

Even though this sexual transgression is implicit, a sexual atmosphere is suggested through the euphemism *Büchse* and the linguistic relationship between *Verschied* and *scheiden* (to split) and *Scheide* (vagina). The allusion to sexual penetration is figurative, not explicit. Certainly the Marchese invades the Bettelweib's private space and individual will by imposing himself and substituting her wishes to lie where she wants with his own desire that she move. Her moving—her subjugation—results in the "fall"[25] that ultimately breaks her back and takes her life. The Marchese's initial order which presents through a visual matrix a displacement of locus (from the corner of the room to the back of the oven) is a visual intrusion, piercing and usurping the Bettelweib's own will, expressed through the word "unwillig" (196). Following the Marchese's visual penetration, he never again visually grasps, i.e., penetrates, the Bettelweib's "lack" of physical presence. The Bettelweib's sound and presence clearly penetrate everyone, most importantly the Marchese. One cannot prevent the penetration simply by closing an ear; the ear is passive and eternally receptive. The Bettelweib is no longer the penetrated; she is now the penetrator. And the figure whose sanity she destroys and whose sexual security she threatens is the Marchese. He becomes a passive and receptive androgyne, sexually submitting service to anyone willing to dominate him—to limit his freedom, define his identity.

The first incident that illustrates a passive submission is the Marchese's dubious and obscure offer to spend the night with the Florentine knight. In the *Goethezeit*, "Florentine" and "Florenzen" were often code words for homosexuality.[26] Even though the story takes place in Italy, where it is not inconceivable for a "Florentine" knight to appear, the fact Kleist chooses a "Florentine" and not a "Genoese," "Venetian," or "Roman" is noteworthy. This "Florentine" knight's symbolism extends beyond simple nationality. The knight is given the same upstairs room where the Bettelweib had died for his lodging. Ironically, it appears the room has also been aesthetically remodeled:

"Der Marchese, dem viel and dem Handel gelegen war, gab seiner Frau auf, den Fremden in dem obererwähnten, leerstehenden Zimmer, das sehr *schön* und *prächtig* eingerichtet war, unterzubringen" (my emphasis, 196). Obviously, the room is decorated in a manner to incite aesthetic pleasure. However, this aesthetic proves to be a mere deceptive veil to conceal the otherwise terrifying sublime fear the room creates. For in the middle of the night the knight hears the haunting sounds of the Bettelweib's ghost and immediately runs back downstairs to the Marchese and his wife. Following the knight's rapid exodus from the deceptively beautiful, but fearfully sublime, room, the Marchese offers to ease the knight's heightened emotional state by staying with him for the remainder of the night. Two aspects of the Marchese's proposition throw a shadow of suspicion upon an ordinarily innocent proposal. First, the Marchese's language betrays a sexual intent. He says, "er wolle *sogleich aufstehen,* und die Nacht zu seiner Beruhigung, *mit ihm* in dem Zimmer zubringen" (my emphasis, 163). Within the context of sleeping or staying with someone, the word *mit* conveys sexual intent. Rather than a platonic *bei ihm* that conveys simply sharing the same space or room with someone void of sexual implication, the *mit,* usually reserved for intimate relations, here suggests sexual intentions. He offers to substitute himself for the Bettelweib, take on her feminine gender, and in the same manner as the Bettelweib before him, "sogleich," surrender his will to the knight. The word *sogleich* reveals more than just the immediacy with which he wishes to serve the knight. "Sogleich" can mean "quickly" but also means "just the same," or "in the same way." To be precise, the Marchese wishes to (re)present (*sogleich aufstehen*) the events which so drastically changed his physical, psychological, and economic state years earlier ([*der Marchese*] *befahl der Frau* [. . .] *aufzustehen*), but within a reversed paradigm of dominance: he wants to receive the knight's will. Second, the Marchese's behavior surrounding the offer is suspect and reveals a tenuous, if not grotesque, deception at the heart of his proposal. Before the Marchese presents his dubious offer he suspiciously laughs with feigned amusement; "[er] lachte den Ritter mit *erkünstelter* Heiterkeit aus . . ." (my emphasis, 163).[27] Clearly the Marchese is hiding a hidden agenda behind his proposal. This deceptive behavior begs the question: what is the Marchese trying to hide? And from whom is he hiding his intentions? Whether he is hiding his intentions from his wife or from the knight, the outcome is the same: he appears to be seducing the knight. Yet the knight refuses the questionable offer and requests a position within the Marchese's and the Marquise's room upon a chair, and the Marchese's desires remain unfulfilled. His troubled state fails to be rectified and in fact worsens.

After his homoerotic exchange with the knight, events within the castle become even more chaotic. Following the encounter with the knight the Marchese becomes considerably more passive and increasingly finds himself an object passively affected by events outside his control. He no longer controls the goings-on within his castle. He is repeatedly shocked or shaken by the Bettelweib's hauntings; he awaits the Bettelweib's return rather than actively pursuing her; and he eventually allows servants and his wife to take over the investigation into the Bettelweib's troubling hauntings. He has become a pawn unable to direct the course of events in his own life. In terms of his gender confusion, he becomes even more sexually confused.

In the second haunting the Marchese actually appears to engage in an act of autoeroticism. Whereas he was unable to serve the knight in a manner similar, if not equal, to the Bettelweib's earlier service to him (*sogleich aufstehen*),[28] he now focuses his attention on himself:

> [. . .] Er, um es mit einem entscheidenden Verfahren niederzuschlagen, beschloß, die Sache in der nächsten Nacht *selbst* zu untersuchen. Demnach ließ er, beim Einbruch der Dämmerung, sein Bett in dem besagten Zimmer aufschlagen, und erharrte, ohne zu schlafen, die Mitternacht. Aber wie erschüttert war er, als er in der Tat, mit dem Schlage der Geisterstunde, das unbegreifliche Geräusch *wahrnahm*. (my emphasis, 197)

Clearly the Marchese is planning to investigate the nature of the haunting himself (*selbst*), alone. It is an autoerotic scene largely unnarrated in the novella, yet textually implied through negativity. There is also a major gap in the narrative from the time when the Marchese hears the Bettelweib's sound to the time when he returns to his wife in the morning:

> Es war, als ob ein Mensch sich von Stroh, das unter ihm knisterte, erhob, quer über das Zimmer ging, und hinter dem Ofen, unter Geseufz und Geröchel niedersank. Die Marquise, am andern Morgen, da er herunter kam, fragte ihn, wie die Untersuchung abgelaufen. (197)

We do not know exactly what happened between the time the ghost collapses (*niedersinkt*) and the following morning (*am andern Morgen*). Yet we know what did not happen: the Marchese did not flee the room in fear. Every other haunting ends in a hasty exodus. This time he slept/stayed there with himself for the remainder of the night. The significance of the scene becomes clearer by examining the Marchese's mysterious behavior not in the scene itself (which is missing from the narrative), but rather following the scene, when his wife questions him about his night alone.

The Marchese's repeated dubious and sly behavior following the scene betrays a guilty conscience. He appears ashamed of the "deed" which he performed the night before and shyly, with uncertain glances, hesitates before neurotically locking all the doors to reveal to his wife the "truth" (*die Richtigkeit*) about the ghost and "his" (*seine*) hauntings. "Da er sich, mit *scheuen* und *ungewissen Blicken*, umsah, und, nachdem er die Tür verriegelt, versicherte, daß es mit *dem Spuk seine* Richtigkeit habe . . . " (my emphasis, 164). Again the Marchese is caught in the act of trying to hide something. The shyness and uncertain glances betray a deception and cast doubt upon the degree of "truth" or "correctness" that the Marchese tells. Moreover, the shy and uncertain glances could suggest shame. This shame could be attributed either to his inability to explain or exorcise the Bettelweib's ghost, or to an unmentioned sexual encounter with himself. The use of a masculine noun, *der Spuk*, and its masculine possessive, *sein*, in place of a feminine noun—which would better parallel the linguistic gender of the Bettelweib—reveals that the Marchese either fails to draw the logical comparison between the haunting sounds and his first encounter with the old, sick woman—then physically and linguistically feminine—or that he projects his own gender onto the Bettelweib's ghost in the process of trying to understand, investigate, and come to grips with the ghost's purpose. It appears the night was dedicated to investigating himself, rather than a "feminine" ghost.

In fact the Bettelweib rarely appears with pure feminine signification after her "*Verschied.*" Following her fragmentation, her gender also becomes fragmented and less apparent, and is most often expressed through neuter or masculine signification, "*das* Geräusch" or "*der* Mensch." Only when the Marquise is present are feminine nouns used to refer to the Bettelweib, e.g., "*die* Sache" and "*die* Ursache." It appears the Bettelweib's gender closely mirrors the gender of the subject who senses her sound. Or by turning things around, it appears that each subject projects his or her own gender onto the Bettelweib in a narcissistic auto-projection of the "I" onto the "not-I" in order to remove the inconceivable (*unbegreifliche*) nature of the Bettelweib.

This aspect of self-projection is also found within the self-reflexive structure of the text itself. Tellingly, this self-reflexivity is mirrored on the linguistic level of the text. The castle, located at the foothills of immeasurable mountain peaks, literally "finds itself"—"Am Fuße der Alpen, bei Locarno im oberen Italien, *befand sich* ein altes, einem Marchese gehöriges Schloß . . ." (my emphasis, 196). This sentence sets up a whole series of self-reflexive phrases: "eine alte kranke Frau, die *sich bettelnd vor der Tür eingefunden* hatte" (196); "mehrere Jahre nachher . . . *fand sich* ein florentinischer Ritter bei ihm ein [. . .]" (196); "die Sache in der nächsten Nacht *selbst zu untersuchen* [. . .]" (197); "er *sah sich* mit scheuen und ungewissen Blicken um" (197); ". . . eine Ursache, die *sich entdecken* lassen müsse [. . .]" (197); and finally "Am abend des dritten Tages . . . *fand sich* der Haushund, den man von der Kette losgelassen hatte, vor der Tür desselben ein [. . .]" (198). Throughout the text self-reflexive language dominates, underscoring a self-investigative theme. Yet it appears that each subject finds nothing other than his or her own projection, as the Bettelweib reflects the person's gender experiencing her sound. This reflexivity is illustrated best at the end of the novella, when the Bettelweib's sound is reflected through the dog's action: "und mit dem ersten Schritt: tapp! tapp! erwacht der Hund, hebt sich plötzlich, die Ohren spitzend, vom Boden empor, und knurrend und bellend, grad als ob ein Mensch auf ihn eingeschritten käme, rückwärts gegen den Ofen weicht er aus" (198). This passage indicates the Bettelweib's representation reflects the subject's features, who is experiencing her sound. Thus, the "truth" (*seine Richtigkeit* [197]) that the Marchese claims about the nature of the ghost and its hauntings is essentially his own subjective fabrication of the sound he perceives. The illusive nature of the Bettelweib evades subjects and only allows them to discover that which they seek. In the end the Bettelweib's gender resolves into linguistic neutrality, "*das* Bettelweib." The Bettelweib is the nexus of the sexual and identity confusion within the text and thus reflects her "cultural" construction. She consists of both her own noumenal value, imperceptible, and each subject's problematic (phenomenal) perception of her.

Unlike the Marchese, the Marquise appears to be more adept in objectively defining and understanding the puzzling nature of the Bettelweib's ghost. Perhaps as a female herself, she is better able to understand the essence of the Bettelweib. This could also explain her enthusiasm and zeal in clarifying the Bettelweib matter. Like other female characters in Romanticism (specifically the female figures in F. Schlegel's *Das Gespräch über die Poesie*),[29] the Marquise appears to have a privileged grasp of reason. It is then no surprise she takes over the investigation and role of judge: "die Sache [. . .] in ihrer Gesellschaft, einer kaltblütigen Prüfung zu unterwerfen" (197). She says to her husband that she wishes to judge the matter before he announces it: "die Sache verlauten ließ" (197). And with "verlauten" she identifies the major problem: subjects are apparently mis-sounding the Bettelweib. The word *verlauten* means to announce. However, the prefix *ver* can also be used to imply a mistake or error.[30] In this way, *verlauten* is a type of mis-placement or mis-hearing. Conceivably, the self-reflective process subjects use in their attempts to understand the Bettelweib's ghost is the crux of the problem. They fail to correctly identify and hear the Bettelweib because they confuse her sound with projections of themselves.

This sexual and identity confusion reaches its climax in the most sexually implicit and fanatically violent scene in the text, the last or fourth haunting. The sexual tone of the scene is first set by the polar juxtaposition of the Marquise and the Marchese in their own distinct beds. The Marquise is given no description other than that she is still dressed. Having no other character distinction than this, her "dressed" state is emphasized in opposition to the Marchese. The narrator never mentions when the Marchese is dressed or not, yet one may infer through his statement that he is not: "Der Marchese Degen und Pistolen, die er aus dem Schrank genommen [hatte]" (164). Again we have weapons functioning as male genitalia. Moreover, the dressed or undressed state of the Marchese is hinted at by "aus dem Schrank genommen" (198). The *Schrank* alludes to the Marquise and the reference of clothing. Literally, the Marchese has removed his weapons (genitalia) from the closet (*aus dem Schrank*) in apparent anticipation of a confrontation, a sexual encounter.[31] The possibility of intercourse between the Marchese and the Marquise is, however, rather doubtful. Not only is she clothed, but they also are sitting on separate beds. In harmony with the text drawing parallels between sexual and linguistic intercourse, their difficult linguistic communication prefigures on a subtextual level their sexual incommunicability: "[. . .] während sie sich mit *Gesprächen*, so gut sie *vermögen*, zu unterhalten suchen . . ." (my emphasis, 198). Intercourse (sexual and linguistic) is something both have un-learned or for which they are now disabled. The verb "vermögen" does mean "to be able to," yet the prefix *ver* again draws the certainty of this ability into question, a question affirmed by the juxtaposition of each character and his or her clothed or unclothed state.

Once the sound of the Bettelweib is again heard, the chaos, sexual confusion, and violent fanaticism explode in a giant conflagration consuming the Marchese's life, castle, and self-definition. What really sets off this explosion of sexual lust and fanatic violence is a visual depiction of the Bettelweib's audible representation. The dog—expressly free (*von der Kette losgelassen* [198]) in opposition to the Marchese's and Marquise's imprisoned state within the "Schloß"—visually performs the sound of the Bettelweib's movement, moans, and death: "[. . .] Der Hund *hebt sich* plötzlich, die Ohren spitzend, vom Boden empor, und *knurrend und bellend*, grad als ob *ein Mensch auf ihn eingeschritten käme*, rückwärts *gegen den Ofen weicht er aus*" (my emphasis, 165). The dog, much like the Bettelweib, stands up (first scene: *aufstehen* / last scene: *sich heben*) and then howls and barks like the Bettelweib moaning and groaning (first scene: *Stöhnen und Ächzen* / last scene: *knurrend und bellend*). Then, as if someone walks toward the dog—comparable to the Marchese walking toward the Bettelweib—the dog moves toward the oven, just like the Bettelweib (first scene: *sich hinter den Ofen verfügen* / last scene: *gegen den Ofen*) and then the dog disappears from the scene similar to the Bettelweib's metamorphosis into invisibility (first scene: *verschied* / last scene: *ausweichen*). The visual nature of this last haunting is emphasized through its designation as "Anblick" (198). The dog, free from human reason and language, brings vision to an otherwise invisible drama of sound. Yet this visualization, this artistic (re)presentation, is a mere substitution and illusion of the Bettelweib's sound, which is itself a (re)presentation of her original fall (*der*

Vorfall). And as such, the dog's visual (re)presentation of an already illusory, invisible *Darstellung* creates a double-sided metaphor that demands the Marchese's own masochistic destruction. This final double *negative Darstellung* creates the fanaticism Kant's figure of *negative Darstellung* is designed to prevent. In Kantian aesthetics, such fanatic vision is "the death of all philosophy" (Helfer 49), and, in Kleist's text, it is the death of the subject.

Ironically, this scene represents the first time a subject attempts to communicate with the Bettelweib's representation. However, the Marchese receives no answer, not even the usual *Geseufz* and *Geröchel* or *Stöhnen* and *Ächzen*, suggesting he is now outside the bounds of linguistic communication. The Marchese shouts "wer da?," yet he receives no answer, no affirmation of his linguistic appeal. His linguistic mode is refused in spite of the dog's visual depiction. The Marchese's exacerbated state (*vom Entsetzen überreizt* [198]) reveals that he is also linguistically implacable and incommunicable, like the Bettelweib. Thus, in his over-excited state he attempts to break down the barriers preventing linguistic compatibility and destroys, diminishes the ninety-degree angularity of his domicile (burning down all four walls), his affirmation of his title and self. Only with the castle is he "der Marchese." Without it he is nothing. Even though it is a scene of total destruction, there are hints of linguistic unification; the signifier (the Bettelweib's audible sound) is joined with a signified (the Marchese's final visual description as bones). Much like Nietzche's idea of metaphoricity, Kleist advocates a complete destruction of the metaphorical fabrication of truth within language by taking metaphors to their exhaustive limits, which is in itself a removal of limits.

Paglia also sees within Romanticism the tendency towards self-destruction as a means of self-definition. In the case of the subject's over-inflated sensible state when confronted with the Sublime, Paglia describes how the subject must diminish itself, often violently, in an attempt to define (limit) itself. She calls it "the erotics of mastectomy" (263)—a surgical reduction of self. "Romanticism, swelling, contracts itself in Decadence. Mutilations and amputations belong to an aesthetics of subtraction, a pathological metaphysic in which the imagination reorients itself to the world by a surgical reduction of self" (263). In her description of Achilles' death in *Penthesilea*, a destruction similar to the Marchese's own self-inflicted destruction of self, Paglia illustrates how Achilles repeatedly and willfully surrenders himself to Penthesilea. Similarly, the Marchese surrenders himself again and again to the dominance of the Bettelweib. And much like Achilles, the Marchese's ultimate surrender is his surrender of his life.

Although the Marchese's self-destruction does not involve the sadomasochistic flavor that *Penthesilea* does, the sexual nature of the final scene is erotically charged and masochistic; it is autoeroticism taken to the extreme:

> Der Marchese, der *den Degen ergriffen*: "Wer da?" ruft, und da ihm niemand antwortet, *gleich einem Rasenden*, nach allen Richtungen die Luft durchhaut. . . .Von Entsetzen überreizt, hatte [er] *eine Kerze genommen*, und dasselbe, überall mit Holz getäfelt wie es war, an allen vier Ecken, müde seines Lebens, angesteckt. (165)

With no one but himself to whom he may direct his lingo-sexual frustration, he turns to himself and grabs his "dagger" and wildly, like a fanatic, stabs it through the air. Analogous to the fiery climax of the scene concluding the text, the Marchese substitutes his "dagger" for a burning candle and destroys the limits of his castle and at the same time kills himself, diminishing his title and self to a linguistic metaphor (*weiße Gebeine*), ironically "carried together" by the "Landleuten": "von den Landleuten *zusammengetragen*" (my emphasis, 198). The literal meaning of metaphor is "to carry over," which is similar to the Marchese's bones "carried together" by the people (*Landleuten*). Figuratively, it appears the Marchese has become a metaphor of a metaphor: he is "carried together" or his essence is perpetuated within the language or lore of a society (*Landleuten*). He has become a textual device within *Das Bettelweib von Locarno*, a text Kleist supposedly modeled after a ghost story socially passed on from one person to another.[32]

Linguistic, gender, and sexual confusion all arise in the final scene and fuse together in the metaphorical union of the Marchese and the Bettelweib. The neutralization of the Bettelweib's gender reflects this confusion. The Marchese becomes the visual negative of the Bettelweib's own negative representation. He comes to forfeit his life, mirroring the Bettelweib's initial forfeiture of place and life. Ironically it is a fire—referring back to the fire of the oven—which consumes the Marchese's life. In the end his ashes and bones come to rest at the locus from which the Bettelweib initially rose. Instead of the phoenix rising from the ashes in a glorious rebirth, the Marchese falls into ashes and death. However, his death is only the visual imprint, like a photo negative, of the Bettelweib's passage into invisibility, into *negative Darstellung*. She is the internal and transcendent, psychological aesthetic idea; he is the sensible remnant, an utterance carried on by society through language. They both fuse together and are juxtaposed to each other—the epitome of Romantic irony—to constitute the entirety of the text. The Marchese is the structure or form, the skeletal visual support; the Bettelweib, the internal, audible content.

In her interpretation of Kleist, Paglia mentions the fact that Kleist is a "self-plagiarist" who frequently reuses, substitutes, and interchanges metaphysical themes, language, and motifs from one text to another. That Kleist was moved and troubled by Kant's philosophy is well established through textual evidence and his correspondence. Thus it should be no surprise to find repeated similarities between Kleist's works and the philosophy and theories propounded in Kant's three critiques. More than once Kleist grapples with Kant's figure of the sublime and *negative Darstellung*. Helfer interprets Kleist's text *Über das Marionettentheater* as a redaction of the sublime,[33] as does Hamacher with *Das Erdbeben in Chile*. And now in *Das Bettelweib von Locarno* Kleist plagiarizes his former redactions under a slightly altered guise.

In its structure, language, and content, *Das Bettelweib von Locarno* symbolizes the sublime. And as a means of (re)presenting Kant's figure of the sublime, Kleist chooses the Kantian representation, *negative Darstellung*. The Bettelweib, as a cipher akin to Kant's figure of *negative Darstellung*, renders Kleist's conceptual redaction of the sublime textually sensible. Thus she functions not only as a representational figure akin to Kant's *negative Darstellung*, but also as a text, which represents itself through a self-reflexive narrative.

Yet Kleist's (re)presentational tool is confronted with its own problematic form, its invisibility. Kleist creates a situation where *negative Darstellung* as a "control mechanism whose function is to keep reason within its borders" (Helfer 45) fails. Kleist achieves such a disruption by presenting an example of *negative Darstellung* which closely mirrors Kant's own figure, but which differs in two distinct manners: Kleist's figure signifies audibly; and causes, rather than guards, against illusory knowledge and fanaticism.

Throughout the text the Bettelweib is described as escaping the human eye. However, a visual image—although illusory—is constructed via an audible *Darstellung*, the Bettelweib's image is caught not by the eyes, but by the ears. The Bettelweib does not exceed the senses; she rather expands the limits of sensibility into the realm of hearing, which Kant neglected to address in his figure of *negative Darstellung*. Yet Kleist shows that such an extension of limits offers no "higher" sense of absolute self or self-definition. An expansion of limits only opens up a larger screen for more fanatic and illusory representations; Kleist's expansion reverts into destruction and contradiction. By destroying and tearing down limits, Kleist's aesthetic theory fuses subjects together into one linguistic meta-subject.

Kleist's aesthetic theory foreshadows and gives literal imagery to Nietzsche's idea of metaphoricity. The Marchese's self-destruction and his destruction of his castle is analogous to Nietzsche's image of tearing and destroying, with new metaphors, the spider web constructed by empty "valueless" metaphors.[34] Through a destruction of former signification (the removal of the Bettelweib's gender and corporeal representation as "Frau," and the removal of the Marchese's symbolic "mark" and gender) two incongruous subjects are reshaped and exchanged under a new matrix of signification and meaning.

This element of "exchange" (*tauschen*) and an element of "deception" (*täuschen*) are incorporated within the Bettelweib's name. The prefix "Bettel" reveals a problematic type of exchange within this character. A beggar receives something of value without reciprocal action. She receives self-definition, a name, without "exchanging" an equally valuable offer. The Marchese forfeits his name, his demarcation. All he gains in the exchange process is a "veiled" metaphorical definition that depends on the Bettelweib's own illusory nature as a (re)presentational tool for the text. *Weib* etymologically means "to veil," and this element of her name emphasizes her artistic and aesthetically deceptive function. Together the two subjects come to metaphorically represent a drama. This drama emphasizes through a double metaphor of *negative Darstellung* its own paradoxical signification, which represents itself through an audible linguistic realm, but defines itself within the written linguistic realm. Kleist's text does not construct a "purer" representation; it merely achieves a super-visual state of action or drama that is sublimely deceptive, sublimely aesthetic.

Chapter II

Die Marquise von O . . . : Truth, Lies, and Representation

Recently I noticed a billboard that had an ironic affinity to the advertisement beginning *Die Marquise von O . . .*. The billboard pictured a baby endowed with a lengthy Pinocchio nose and a caption that read: "Is his mother a liar? Call 1-800-who's dad." The billboard suggests several themes also present in the Marquise's ad: precarious sexual relations, a child's conception out of wedlock, a mother's inability or refusal to name the father of the child, and fathers seeking paternal truth. However, today's billboard, written from a decidedly male viewpoint, relies on the scientific double helix to resolve paternal ambiguity. The Marquise's ad, written from a mother's perspective, relies on the intuitive medium of aesthetics to circumvent truth and offer in its place a fiction of paternal truth.

The text's basic plot recounts the adult life of the Marquise, a virtuous widow and mother of two. Following the death of her husband, she relocates her family back to her father's citadel, where she plans to isolate herself and devote herself to raising her children. However, an unanticipated attack by a Russian army ruins her idyllic plans. During the attack on the citadel she is accosted by a rogue group of soldiers who have less than admirable intentions. Hearing cries for help, a Russian officer, the Graf F . . ., intervenes and rescues the Marquise from the soldiers' grasps, but it seems the Marquise is not entirely well. Overcome by the ordeal, she swoons, falls unconscious, and is then carried by the Graf to a "safer" section of the citadel. What happens next the narrator conceals behind a linguistically unspeakable dash. Yet following the attack the Marquise is pregnant, and the narrator implies the Graf in fact raped the Marquise.

The unwitting conception of a third child shatters the Marquise's vow of celibacy and the air of normalcy she had hoped to gain under the protection of her father's roof. Subsequently, the Marquise's willing or unwilling failure to identify the father of the unborn child results in her banishment from her father's household. Even though several clues implicate the Graf, and the reader easily—perhaps too easily—identifies the Graf as the child's father, the Marquise remains ironically baffled when confronted with questions pertaining to the child's paternal origins. Before her banishment, the Graf visits the Marquise and her family to ask for her hand in marriage, and during her exile the Graf again visits the Marquise to repeat his proposal. Both times the Marquise displays her vehement opposition to his asking, apparently unaware of the Graf's underlying reasons for seeking marriage. Yet when all clues seem to point toward the Graf as the father of her unborn child and just a simple acquiescence to his request for marriage would guarantee her social standing and reestablish her familial relationships, she instead publicly announces her pregnancy through an ad in the local paper. Not only does she announce her scandalous and unwitting pregnancy, but she also states that she will marry the perpetrator if he presents himself on the third of the month at 11:00, regardless of his social standing.

The announcement only further enrages the Marquise's father, who perceives the published notice as brash insolence and cunning deception. However, the Marquise's mother intervenes and through her own conviction that her daughter is innocent, also convinces the father of the Marquise's inculpability. The father agrees to allow the Marquise to return home and the two proceed to celebrate a highly emotional reconciliation—an unmistakably erotic scene that strongly questions the limits of their father-daughter relationship. Whereas the Marquise refuses the Graf's advancements, she willing permits her father's libidinal and lecherous caresses. Moreover, her mother, who voyeuristically views the entire reconciliation with unfettered joy, also appears to condone this incestuous scene.

Finally, the day arrives when the true perpetrator of the Marquise's pregnancy will be revealed. Unexpectedly Leopardo the servant, a minor character in the novella, presents himself at the exact mentioned time and date, and the family momentarily believes he is the father. In fact, the Marquise's mother had earlier lied to the Marquise, stating Leopardo had admitted he was the child's father—a possibility not disputed by the Marquise. However, Leopardo's momentary status and impact as father is short-lived, as he announces the arrival of the Graf. Vexed by the Graf's appearance, the Marquise refuses to marry him. Unfortunately for the Marquise, her father reminds her of her promise to marry whomever should appear, and she reluctantly keeps her word. Eventually, the Marquise's disdain for the Graf wanes and the two celebrate a second wedding, one more joyous than the first. In the end they conceive several children, and the novella concludes in a fairy tale-like atmosphere, with a proverbial happy ending.

This superficial plot, striving to discover the identity of the child's father, allegorically reveals a critique of representation. A superficial search for the "original" true father becomes a subtextual search for a representation that "truthfully" represents a now absent "original," visually and linguistically. However, the tenuous resolution of the text—the Graf's problematic representation as father and the Marquise's resistance and subsequent acquiescence to him—suggests representation is inherently problematic and possibly inauthentic, if not wholly incorrect. Moreover, any notion of "originality" is lost in the text's tautological conclusion that alludes to the production of seemingly endless (re)productions: "Eine ganze Reihe von jungen Russen folgte jetzt noch dem ersten" (143).[1] The description of more, seemingly endless, children following or repeating the "original," metaphorically suggests an inescapable tautology—(re)presentations that produce close copies, but not "originality." Ultimately, the text presents a situation where the "truth" of a given representation (i.e., the Graf as representing the child's "true" father) depends upon a communal (familial) consensus—subjectively determined, yet imposed and postulated as objectively absolute.

Unlike the billboard ad, the status of paternal representation in Kleist's text is not synonymous with genetic absolutes and truth. Paternal truth is a fabrication of male-discourse, a tenuous *idée fixe* upon which the dominant male characters—the Graf and the commandant—depend, in order to reaffirm their epistemological foundation for complete hermeneutic understanding and knowledge. However,

Kleist's title female character, the Marquise, disrupts this foundation by infiltrating male discourse and questioning the fragile construction of knowledge and truth that is based on imperfect representations. Whereas the male characters espouse the importance of and need for paternal truth and express an omniscience of absolute knowledge, the Marquise disturbs the patriarchal order by countering their omniscience with unknowledge and their truth with purposeful deception and fabricated lies.

The billboard lacks such an oppositional female figure to question its sexist discourse. Without a disruptive influence, the ad is able to assert undisputedly a heroic, scientifically justified male epistemology of paternal truth (call 1-800-who's-dad), rescuing truth from the grasps of "deceptive motherhood" (is his mother a liar?). The implicit message of the ad suggests women have a vested interest in concealing paternal history for a variety of reasons, all of which—according to the ad—pose a potential threat to patriarchy's panoptical control over a woman's cervix. The ad creates a pathology of deception designed to exclude and marginalize women outside the male-imposed boundaries of genetic mapping, defining paternal "truth." Here the subliminal impact of the Pinocchio imagery becomes apparent: Geppetto creates a son wholly and entirely by himself, without a woman. DNA becomes the realization of an androcentric myth about autocreation: DNA presents a scientifically justifiable means of minimizing a mother's role in conception, leaving fathers the sole heirs of "their" creation and a genetically justified means for establishing judicially recognized truth, paternal truth.

The ad functions as an epistemological pretext to Kleist's narrative, helping to define the subtextual tension that exists between the Marquise's refusal to identify her child's father and a patriarchy's demand for identification. The ad propagates a myth, where women are reduced to a pathology of deception (mothers are liars), and subliminally replaced by an androcentric myth of auto-production (the baby pictured is Pinocchio, a liar and a product of male auto-production). The Marquise undergoes a similar experience: she is banished by her father due to a patriarchally perceived act of deception (she refuses to name the father of her child); and her father tries to remove her "motherly" status by taking her children (*der Forstmeister* [. . .] *forderte* [. . .] *auf Befehl des Kommandanten die Zurücklassung und Überlieferung der Kinder von ihr* [125]). The Graf also tries to usurp the Marquise's motherhood by imposing a fatherly representation that asserts a patriarchal definition and identification in place of her matriarchal "deception." However, unlike the ad, the Marquise manages to inextricably weave herself back into the graces of patriarchal order under a guise (or fiction) of compliance and submission to the male demands of identification. Even though she never *identifies* (represents) the "true" father, she does enable the artificial production of an image, or idea of father, produced not by herself, but ironically by the reader of her announcement and by the reader of the text itself. The Marquise is directly juxtaposed to the billboard advertisement, in that she redefines the parameters for identifying, (re)presenting the father. And instead of being excluded by a myth of male self-reproduction, she creates through her own feminine volition a fiction of fatherhood, a fiction where representation is deceptive, purposely vague, and conceptually vacuous.

Rhetorically, what the Marquise says constitutes the text's critical redaction of representation: she introduces "nichts" as a metaphor for the answer to repeated questions about paternal origins and truth. The Marquise's key sentence, "Ich will nichts wissen" (129), underscores an oppositional theory of representation and constitutes a pseudo-Kantian example of *negative Darstellung*. Yet the text reveals that behind the unspeakable dashes and the word "nichts" resides not a transcendental truth or a priori knowledge, as in the Kantian sublime, but rather simply "nichts." The Marquise's sentence also asserts an element of free agency in the face of patriarchal domination. The volition represented in the Marquise's emphatic "ich *will* nichts wissen" (emphasis mine) establishes the central juxtaposition between a desire for truth and a transcendence of truth. *Die Marquise von O . . .*, I will argue, is a text about the failure of truthful representation and the emergence of illusive or deceptive representation. The Marquise personifies a Nietzschean aesthetic theory that transcends the transcendental paradigm and with it boundaries of truth, lies, and representation. The first section of my analysis focuses on recent scholarship, and suggests the limitation of such scholarship that by and large accepts the Graf as the child's only true father. The next two sections focus on Kleist's theory of representation, showing how Kant's theory of *negative Darstellung* helped formulate Kleist's own theory of negativity, and how Kleist then develops an aesthetics of negativity out of the word "nichts"—an aesthetics of nonrepresentation. The final section focuses on the Marquise as a proto-Nietzschean artist who embraces and fictionally produces deception as a means of transcending the Idealist search for truth.

Recent Scholarship

The result of the Marquise's nonscientific mode of paternity testing creates a myriad of paternal possibilities. Critics (Kunzel, Vinken and Haverkamp, Pfeiffer, Schmidhäuser, Winnett) traditionally identify the Graf as the father and downplay or completely ignore the significance of other possibilities. Yet the text suggests other potential fathers. Both the Marquise's own father and the servant, Leopardo, find themselves in questionable circumstances, exposing them as just as likely fathers as the Graf. More significant are the metaphysical possibilities of paternal origin and truth. The Marquise's emphatic denial that the Graf is the father of her child and her repeated definition of her child as divine (*dessen Ursprung* [. . .] *göttlicher* [. . .] *als der anderer Menschen* [127]) suggest a metaphysical conception, a metaphysical father. However, the text undoubtedly casts the Graf as the repenting, rueful father who knowingly takes advantage of an unknowing, innocent Marquise. The "irony" of the text seems to juxtapose the reader's seemingly privileged perception against that of the characters and especially the Marquise's faulty perception. Readers quickly and easily recognize the textual clues suggesting the Graf's guilt, while the Marquise and her family appear unable or willing to link the clues together and identify the Graf as the child's "true" father.

Taking the text's suggestion of paternal truth literally, recent critics tend to focus on the lack of critical attention dedicated to the Marquise's rape. Winnett and Kunzel vigorously argue the text trivializes the Marquise's rape through its sympathetic portrayal of the Graf, which subsequently leads to misplaced scholarly attention. The scholarship they attack tends to focuses on the enigmatic nature of the Marquise's steadfast denial of the Graf as her child's father. Dorrit Cohn presents a psychoanalytic critique, identifying the implications of the word *bewußt* throughout the text. Her argument identifies the Marquise's denial of the Graf's fatherly validity as a result of repressed desires she subconsciously recognizes, yet is incapable of consciously admitting. Marguerite De Huszar Allen also focuses on the Marquise's inability to accept the Graf as her child's father as an expression of a psychological "denial" of truth; the Marquise cannot accept that her savior is also her rapist. Luke and Reeves identify the prevalence of chance, ambiguity, and chaos found throughout Kleist's works and interpret these topoi as key hermeneutic characteristics of Kleist's *Weltanschauung*. They explain the Marquise's actions as evidence of her trying to come to terms with and accept the "gebrechliche Einrichtung der Welt."[2] However, the Marquise's rejection of the Graf as suitor and father of her child goes beyond the unstable and unpredictable nature of the world and the conscious repression of subconscious desire. I suggest the Marquise's denial is more valid than readers and critics traditionally accept. As Lillian Fürst argues, the "irony" of the text's narrative is duplicitous; the narrative's explicit framing of the Graf is intended to deceive the reader into believing he or she maintains a privileged perceptive vantage. To understand the ironic disparities between a reader's perception and the Marquise's seeming lack of perception, it is beneficial to read the Marquise's inability to recognize the Graf's culpability ironically, or in other words un-ironically and at face value. The Marquise denies the Graf is the father due to the fact he is *not* the *only* possible father.

Lillian Furst defines the ironic structure in the text as "Double Dealing," that is, the narration presents an ironic presentation of irony. The reader becomes as entwined in the deceptive narrative and irony of the text as the protagonists themselves, and his or her alleged superior vantage proves to be as obscured as the characters' own visual and cognitive capabilities:

> Our confident superiority to the protagonists is impaired as we find ourselves confronting perplexities *with* them. Their predicaments are projected onto us as we begin to discover that we have been dealt not a manageable set of dualisms, but double-dealt, as it were, a refractory knot of philosophical enigmas. The irony of *Die Marquise von O . . .* is therefore an irony of

> duplicity, itself double and duplicitous. Its neat, almost schematic surface of dualities acts as a mask for the epistemological and ontological crises which it explores. Kleist has assumed the guise and the devices traditional to irony, but for his own ulterior purposes, for the covert exposition of problems far beyond the overt matter of his story. The ironic game being played with the reader is a complex and hazardous one. (Furst 93)

Furst identifies the major theme of duplicitous deception as a game played not only on the characters, but on the reader as well. Her investigation concludes Kleist's irony is a "duplicitous double-dealing that distrusts and subverts every position . . . it is suspended in a state of indeterminacy and contradiction" (Furst 94). Yet Furst does not take this statement to its philosophical limits, into "the epistemological and ontological crisis" afflicting Kleist's text. Most importantly, Furst does not call into question the Graf's representation of "true" fatherhood when, at the same time, she argues about the indeterminacy and subversive nature of the irony in the text. Kleist's entire narrative, marred by duplicitous irony, indeed leads to a "state of indeterminacy and contradiction." However, unlike Furst, I would argue the indeterminacy and contradiction undermine the Graf's status as father, the possibility of representing originality, and the concept of truth itself. For if Furst is correct in her analysis, then seeking the "true" father, or truth itself, is marred by the ironic narrative that presents only indeterminate approximations, appearances, and contradictions—i.e., finding "truth," reality, and absolute knowledge is presented as impossible. The Graf cannot be the father, nor can he not be the father. This twofold irony is the trap of negative representation Kleist sets for his readers.

Deceiving the reader with narrative traps is a practice Kleist repeatedly utilizes in his works. In his analysis of *Über das Marionettentheater*, Paul de Man introduces the notion of *Fälle* as "traps" (de Man 290) for the reader. De Man specifically identifies the allegory of dance as an instantiation of a trap of aesthetic education:

> But Fälle, of course, also means in German "trap," the trap which is the ultimate textual model of this and of all texts, the trap of an aesthetic education which inevitably confuses dismemberment of language by the power of the letter with the gracefulness of a dance. This dance, regardless of whether it occurs as mirror, as imitation, as history, as the fencing match of

> interpretation, or as the anamorphic transformations of tropes, is the ultimate trap, as unavoidable as it is deadly. (de Man 290)

The trap of "aesthetic education" de Man finds in *Über das Marionettentheater* is easily applied to *Die Marquise von O . . .*. But in the novella the trap is not a dance, a mirrored reflection, or a fencing match, but rather the narrative clues that seem to implicate the Graf as a representation of "Father." If these narrative clues are traps, then the reader's "aesthetic education" is decisively flawed, and the Graf is most likely not the only potential father. It is, therefore, beneficial to examine the less scrutinized candidates: both the Marquise's father and the servant Leopardo are such candidates.

A close examination of the Marquise's relationship with her father reveals a father-daughter relationship that is less than traditional.[3] The strongest evidence for this is found in a scene portraying the two as "honeymooners" (*wie Brautleute* [39]). The overtly incestuous scene garners prolific critical attention, and critics (Vinken, Haverkamp and Weineck) generally interpret the scene as the visual inverse of the initial, hidden "rape." However, with the exception of Weineck and Krüger-Fürhoff, recent critics deny the scene reveals other potential fathers.[4] Irmela Marei Krüger-Fürhoff, dedicates an entire article to the incestuous scene. She not only views the scene as a key to uncovering the aesthetic limits of theatricality, representation, and dramaturgy, but also entertains the question: "where does a father's love end and incest begin?" (Krüger-Fürhoff 71). Focusing on the text's theme, which fuses together extra-familial sexuality with an exaggerated form of intra-familial devotion, Krüger-Frühoff suggests the Marquise's father is both "father" and "lover"—in every sense of the words. The father is, as she cites, "he—he himself" (77). Later in my analysis I will also explore, in detail, the commandant's paternal potential and examine the aesthetic implication of incest as a figure of aesthetic transcendence, extending the reader's eye beyond the limits of social taboos and into the unspoken, unrepresentable realm of negative representation.

The other potential father is Leopardo. Unlike the overtly sexual reunion with her father, Leopardo's paternal potential is shrouded in ambiguous suggestions. The Marquise's mother jokingly states Leopardo confessed he is the father, and the Marquise neither wholly confirms nor denies this possibility. The Marquise clearly recalls seeing Leopardo leaving her presence as she awoke from a "nap": "Ich sah ihn von meinem Diwan gehen, als ich erwachte!" (135), yet never does she deny the possibility she "slept" with him. Superficially, the Marquise's claim she was sleeping can be taken literally. It is possible she was sleeping and a simple case of coincidence that she sees Leopardo walking away from her as she awakens. Such a reading upholds an innocent view of the Marquise, leaving her completely absolved from any complicit or willful consent to a sexual act. However, her statement does not completely remove Leopardo from the list of potential fathers, as he may indeed have impregnated (i.e., raped) the Marquise in her "sleep." Therefore it is significant to explore Leopardo's potential as father, even though critics largely ignore his potential.

However, I argue the most likely father of the Marquise's child is a metaphysical fabrication—a fictional idea. Even though the Marquise is pregnant, the process of discovering the real physical father, for the reader and characters alike, becomes an aesthetic process that defines the father fictionally. After the Marquise emphatically refutes the Graf's suitability as her child's father, the mother opines, "whom have we been expecting" (109)[5] ("wen erwarten wir denn") (140). The mother's statement reveals more than a simple plurality of potential fathers; her response allows for an almost infinite interchangability of substitute fathers, each equally viable as the next. The Graf, the servant Leopardo, or the Marquise's father, the commandant, are all likely candidates for the child's father; it is just a matter of picking one of them. However, the *equally valid* interchangability of *physical* paternal representation undermines representation's own certainty, its absolute claim to originality. Like representation, which attempts to (re)present and recover an original that is now absent or lost, each *physical* father offers a potential representation and with it an historical heritage signifying originality. However, like representation, each father is an illusion or substitute for the "original" and each historical heritage signifies nothing more than a believable fiction.

The Marquise focuses upon this illusory and fictional artificiality of representation to evade truthful identification and fictionally construct a *metaphysical* idea of "father." The Marquise's ad constitutes a fictional construction of the artificial concept "father." This fictional construction of father results from the process of her writing the ad and subsequent readings of the ad (by characters and readers alike) and the circumstances leading to the production of the ad itself. Structurally, the ad begins the entire text, functioning as the impetus to read the "body" of the text. Thematically, however, the ad is dependent upon the narrative for its own production. A tautological relationship between structure and thematic narrative mirrors the father-child relationship played out in the narrative. The child becomes a cipher for the "body" of the text that supports or fulfills the question raised by the Marquise's ad: "who is the child's father?" Moreover, in my argument I will suggest the Marquise is the symbolic mother and author of the text (child) and that the father is akin to Kant's aesthetic idea, an unrepresentable concept that becomes physically sensible (concrete) through an indirect analogy.[6] In this case, the analogy works negatively through a negative representation. The ad is a representation that evokes a representation of father without representing a father, but instead by representing the absence of a father. That is why the narrator and the Marquise repeatedly use "nichts" in reference to paternal questions throughout the text. It is the aesthetic manifestation of Kleist's own negative theory of representation.

Kleist's Theory of *negative Darstellung*

Kleist's critical approach to representation and its relationship to truth has been repeatedly traced back to his "Kantkrise" letter of March, 1801. Critics traditionally locate the source of Kleist's "Kantkrise" either in Kant's philosophy or in Fichte's Kantian idealism: in particular, the notion that "das Ding-an-sich" is only knowable in a subjective sense, and that objective a priori knowledge is an impossibility.[7] Subsequently, Kleist abandoned his earlier aspirations of "Wahrheit und Bildung" (633), and developed a profound distrust of *Wahrheit* and a feeling of futility toward *Bildung*:

> Der Gedanke, daß wir hienieden von der Wahrheit nichts, gar *nichts*, wissen, daß das, was wir hier Wahrheit nennen, nach dem Tode ganz anders heißt, und daß folglich das Bestreben, sich ein Eigentum zu erwerben, das uns auch

> in das Grab folgt, ganz vergeblich und fruchtlos ist, dieser Gedanke hat mich in dem Heiligtum meiner Seele erschüttert. (my emphasis, 636)

What is identified, called, "*genannt*," i.e., (re)presented, as *Wahrheit* is for Kleist ultimately nothing. In the form of incomplete representation—incomplete names, places, unheard whispers, and unintelligible utterings—"nichts" becomes synonymous with representation, constituting the ultimate referent of Kleistian representation. What comes to replace Kleist's once idealistic aspirations of *Wahrheit* and *Bildung*—his "einziges" and "höchstes Ziel" (634)—becomes an aesthetic theory of "nichts" and a sense of futile repetition that leads not to a heightened sense of *Bildung* or *Wahrheit*, but rather to a state of infinite unknowability. Kleist takes Kant's philosophy and his theory of *negative Darstellung* beyond the regulative role to which Kant limits it. In so doing, he demonstrates that *negative Darstellung* is a deceptive representation or "Schein" that when unveiled reveals not an absolute truth, but rather nothingness. In her interpretation of Kleist's play *Der zerbrochne Krug* Helfer succinctly defines Kleist's rewriting of Kant's figure of *negative Darstellung* as a "figure of negativity": "The Kleistian subject looks over the border, looks around, and sees nothing. This "nothing" is the death knoll not merely of representation, but of *Darstellung* as a transcendental construct" (Helfer 173). In Kleist's texts representation becomes a rhetorical, visual figure in and of itself, incapable of representing an original, and ultimately capable of representing nothing but a deception of truth and a representation of "nothing."

In her study of *Darstellung* Helfer illustrates how the philosophical and syntactical significance of the term is deeply rooted in vision. *Darstellung* implies the act of making a concept visible, a literal placement (*stellen*) before (*dar*) the eyes.[8] Moreover, illusion or deception (*Täuschung*) also plays a central role in the philosophical definition of *Darstellung*. Representation is an exchange or *Tausch* of an image for an object; a representation stands in place of the actual object, which is absent. However, the representation is not the actual "original" object; it is a reproduction that deceives (*täuscht*) the subject's senses as a means to enable the subject to ideate, contemplate, and discuss abstract ideas and concepts that may be physically absent, temporally past, or physically untenable. In early Romantic aesthetic and philosophic theories of representation, Kant's figure of *negative Darstellung* is seen as the representational tool enabling the sensible representation of nonsensible or a priori concepts, specifically aesthetic ideas. For the Romantics deceiving the senses is a means of transcending the limits of sensible knowledge and gaining a momentary glimpse into a priori concepts and truth.

This illusory element inherent in *Darstellung* and Kant's *negative Darstellung* becomes the visual lacuna upon which Kleist fixates when he implements his own theory of negativity. Whereas Kant's figure of *negative Darstellung* carries with it a suppression of vision[9] as a means of guarding his own philosophic presentation against "fanaticism," Kleist invites his readers to look, visually examine, and be visually misled, deceived, and confused by representations incapable of transcending the rift between *Wahrheit* and *Schein*. Representation and the visual are for Kleist nothing but deception, a deception precipitating self-destruction, chaos, confusion, and a dismantling of knowledge and truth.

Kleist frequently addresses this problem of deceptive representation in letters, epigrams, essays, and anecdotes as well as in his novellas and dramas.[10] In the epigram titled *Die Marquise von O . . .* Kleist sardonically exaggerates a case of visual deception: "Schamlose Posse, sie hielt, weiß ich, die Augen bloß zu" (22). Although the epigram is not a preface per se to the narrative, its title suggests an interpretive significance for the novella. In the epigram Kleist stresses the visual problematic thoroughly informing the text: the relationship, if any, between "truth" and vision—visual representation. The epigram, directed to the sensitive reader of the time offended by the sexual theme the novella explores, reveals not only a purposeful act of deception, but also grounds such deception in vision with the phrase "sie hielt . . . die Augen bloß zu." If the epigram does indeed hold an interpretive key to the novella, it would suggest the Marquise is anything but innocent and, if anything, purposely deceptive (*schamlose Posse*). The image of perverted, impure vision—purposely and deceptively closed eyes—undermines not only the ethical and moral sense of innocence within the narrative, but also the representational status of the text itself and its own representational validity, seemingly lost in an allegory of corrupt representation. However, can and should the reader trust the narrator's textual warning? The narrator states, "Sie hielt, *weiß ich,* die Augen bloß zu" (my emphasis, 22). The narrator's statement is essentially a paradox. He dismisses the possibility of absolute, or correct, knowledge, all the while expressing his own "absolute," or correct, knowledge (*ich weiß*). The theme of corrupted vision and corrupted representation taints the validity of the narrator's own assertion. Kleist's epigram turns back on itself and draws into question textual and narrative claims of truth, suggesting through its like-named title that the novella's own narrative is rife with similar narrative corruption.

The narrator's credibility in *Die Marquise von O. . .* is also questioned in the novella's subtitle. The interpretive significance of the subtitle is found in its theme, which mirrors the narrative structure of the novella: the attempt to (re)present a past event. The subtitle acknowledges, more subtly than the epigram, impure vision as the culprit of subsequent corrupt representations; however, the subtitle appears straightforward and forthcoming: "Nach einer wahren Begebenheit, deren Schauplatz vom Norden nach dem Süden verlegt worden" (104). Again the explicit reference to truth (*nach einer wahren Begebenheit*) is ironic. This textual verification, a type of historical witness, undermines the actual mimetic truth of the text and the author's own credibility, just as truth and absolute representation is undermined by the epigram. Such explicit reference to truth suggests truth is not to be found in the text itself, in its mimetic retelling of the *Begebenheit*, but rather through a backward oriented process, a "*nach*," which reveals no singular original or truth, but rather an infinite process of representational regression. Figuratively the word *nach* evokes the English equivalent "based," as in "based on a true incident."[11] However, the word literally implies a backward process, as in "to follow," "to be after, or behind." Literally the word more closely exemplifies the backward process of (re)presentation, which is in de Man's words, an "infinite structure of regress."[12]

On the surface, the backward-oriented structure of the subtitle implicitly mirrors the Jena Romantic motif of representation: there is a (re)casting or (re)flection of an "original" theme (*wahre Begebenheit*) merely moved or "displaced" (*verlegt*) from one location (*Schauplatz*) to another; "Schauplatz" (the scene) stresses vision's role in representation; and "Schauplatz" also signifies a locus (*Schauplatz* as stage) of this visual reflection. However, in this process of "displacement" an error in transport has occurred. The scene has been verlegt. "Verlegen" means to move, and is conceptually equal to the act of (re)presentation. The scene is (re)presented through an exchange of location; however, the prefix "ver" implies a mistake or error.[13] Reading the subtitle this way suggests the (re)presentation was compromised, and that the integrity of the subsequent representation is decisively incorrect. Thus, such avowals of truth (*nach einer wahren Begebenheit*) have been considerably jeopardized and function now as a means to question representation and its assertions of truth, rather than to reaffirm these assertions. Like the epigram, the subtext presents an unmistakable theme of incorrect representation impeded by faulty vision. Here a faulty (re)flection or transference of the visual (*Schauplatz*) questions the "truth" of the text's own (re)presentational status.

In the actual body of the text, this theme of corrupted representation due to faulty vision manifests itself in scenes where characters are literally unconscious and unable to see, identify, or even open their eyes. These scenes represent the visual problem complicating the allegorical figure of representation, and urge the reader to interpret implicit visual or ocular references like unconsciousness, fainting, and sleep as extended metaphors of corrupt and deceptive representation. The most commonly examined episode of unconsciousness is the Marquise's swooning faint and the Graf's alleged rape: "bewußtlos niedersank. Hier — traf er . . . " (106).[14] After reading the epigram's cynicism toward "closed eyes," the Marquise's unconscious fainting appears spurious and possibly purposely deceptive. Moreover, even without the interpretive help of the epigram, the Marquise's unconsciousness represents a suppression of vision, either willful or not. The suppression implies an inability to (re)present. The narrator uses the infamous dash, a deliberate sign of negativity and a literal expression of Kant's figure of *negative Darstellung*, to emphasize the utter lack of effective representation due to vision's reliance upon sensory information. Functioning like an epilogue, this initial scene preemptively taints all other tropes of fainting, unconsciousness, and closed eyes. And like the former, each is followed by incomplete knowledge, confusion, contention, and a purposeful intent to deceive, skewing any possibility of correct and truthful representation.

Two scenes featuring a similar visual impediment directly affecting the effectiveness and veracity of representation occur directly after the Marquise's purported rape. Following the fall of the citadel, the Russian general asks the Graf to identify the Marquise's attackers. Yet the Graf claims he was unable to see, "ihre Gesichter zu *erkennen*" (107, my emphasis). Here, visual impediment is the excuse for incomplete knowledge or *un*identification, and also functions as a deceptive form of rhetoric, hiding the Graf's own participation in the event. Later the messenger brings news of the Graf's "mortal" wounding, having seen him "*mit eignen Augen,* tödlich durch die Brust geschossen" (my emphasis, 108). Ironically, the messenger *misinterprets* through ocular representation the "true" severity of the Graf's wounds, giving rise to the following scene of *mis*identifying the Graf as a ghost when he inexplicably returns to the commandant's home.

The text also employs the metaphor of "Ohnmacht" as a means to widen the scope of vision's impeding role in "effective" representation. The Marquise is stricken with several bouts of "Übelkeiten, Schwindeln und *Ohnmachten*." (109). Awakening from one of these unconscious bouts ("aus einer langen Gedankenlosigkeit *erwachend*") (my emphasis, 109), the Marquise remarks she just had a sensation she was pregnant: ". . . daß sie eben jetzt eine Sensation gehabt hätte, wie damals, als sie mit ihrer zweiten Tochter schwanger war" (109). Her cognitive lapse (*Gedankenlosigkeit*) arises from a lapse of vision (*erwachen*). The correlation between a cognitive lapse and a lapse of vision stresses vision's primary importance in enabling complete representation and subsequently effective knowledge. Like other incidences of incomplete representation and ambiguity, the pregnancy, a cognitive quandary (not if, but by whom), is linked to ocular metaphors.

"Ohnmacht" can also be interpreted as a visual metaphor, signifying purposeful deception. After the Marquise is examined by a midwife, who unambiguously confirms the Marquise's pregnancy, the Marquise falls unconscious: "fiel . . . in *Ohnmacht*" (my emphasis, 124). The scene is surrounded by a context of identifying, naming, and representing, as epitomized by the mother's query: "Willst du den Vater mir nennen?" (124). However, in spite of her mother's request for enlightened knowledge, the Marquise refuses to identify the father. Instead of being forthcoming with her mother, the Marquise devises a deceptive scheme. For indeed the Marquise admits having knowingly conceived, "ich habe wissentlich empfangen" (124), but only wishes to know if an immaculate conception is possible: "Und ob die Möglichkeit einer unwissentlichen Empfängnis sei?" (124). The Marquise's question suggests a desire to hide her pregnancy behind a deceived pretense of immaculate "innocence." Even though the midwife denies the possibility, she does offer a solution: "[sie] gab ihr auch die Mittel an, wie man, in solchen Fällen, dem Leumund der Welt ausweichen könne" (124). The fact the midwife offers her a means to evade the world's condemnation indicates the midwife understands the Marquise's desire to cover-up, conceal, or vanquish not just her pregnancy, but more importantly the public's unfavorable perception and criticism of her and her pregnancy (*dem Leumund der Welt ausweichen*).

Other cases of unconscious-like states, such as sleep, also are surrounded by character's deceitful intentions. For example the Marquise's mother tries to deceive the Marquise into identifying the "true" father of her child by telling the Marquise Leopardo admitted he is the father. With this lie the mother hopes to gain an unambiguous confession from the Marquise, stating who the father is. However, the Marquise's response is highly ambiguous. The mother's plan backfires as the Marquise remembers "ich . . . sah ihn von meinem Diwan gehen, als ich *erwachte*!" (my emphasis, 135). Instead of unconsciousness (*Ohnmacht*), a metaphorical nap signifies a possible deception. One way to interpret the scene is that the Marquise was indeed asleep, and Leopardo took advantage of the Marquise's state, raping her without her knowing. Another is to employ the same metaphorical significance of "Ohnmacht" for metaphors of unrepresented, unseen sex. This would suggest the Marquise was doing much more than sleeping through a hot dreary afternoon. This interpretation is also substantiated by the Marquise's obvious embarrassment: "[sie] legte ihre kleinen Hände vor ihr in Scham erglühendes Gesicht" (135). Ironically, the Marquise's embarrassment is what compels the mother to confess her lie and *blindly* profess the Marquise's innocence. The Marquise's visual awakening from a state of "closed eyes" is juxtaposed to her mother's own inability to visually perceive the Marquise's embarrassment. The mother is essentially blinded by the Marquise's farcical "nap." The Marquise maintains the role of the deceiver and persuader who successfully sways her mother's perception to the Marquise's own advantage: "Wie glücklich bin ich, daß Sie von meiner Unsträflichkeit *überzeugt* sind!" (my emphasis, 136). The Marquise's deception eclipses her mother's own attempt to deceive, and figuratively "pulls the wool over her eyes."

Moreover, Kleist's characters are not only blindfolded, they are also gagged. Kleist experiments with the failure of representation and incomplete knowledge by expanding representation's referential scope beyond mere visual media. Kleist does this in several works. In her analysis of *Der zerbrochne Krug*, Helfer claims Kleist's text at times " . . . raises the question of the relationship between visual and verbal representation" (162). However, Helfer concludes Kleist's fusion of visual and verbal representation does not necessarily end in more effective representation. According to Helfer, this lack of effective representation, regardless of the medium, is what moves Kleist beyond the typical boundaries of "the eighteenth century's debate on aesthetic imitation (*Nachahmungsdebatte*)." Kleist creates texts that "draw attention to the fact that representation may be predicated on false assumptions or error" (Helfer 162). Regardless of the medium, it appears Kleist's theory of representation is preemptively compromised by faulty sensory perception, whether visual, verbal, or aural. In *Die Marquise von O . . .*, Kleist again explores the relationship between visual and verbal representation. And like Helfer, I argue Kleist's theory of verbal representation is skewed by "false assumptions and error."

In the text incomplete verbal representation is epitomized by the infamous dash signifying the Marquise's rape. In addition to this initial dash, several other "dashes" indicate a failure of effective representation, representation that conceals, suggests, and inspires conjecture, but that which ultimately fails to *reveal* a singular, unambiguous truth: "würd ich — . . . diese Wünsche — . . . indem sie dies sagte — " (117); "diesem Russen zum zweiten Mal ergeben! — " (118); "einer unwissentlichen Empfängnis sei? — " (124); "diktiert — " (125); "ein einziges, heimliches, geflüstertes —!" (129); and in the end "auf einen Lasterhaften war ich gefaßt, aber auf einen — — — Teufel!" (141). Like a metaphorical referent to the "original" dash, each dash is semiotically and thematically linked to the "original" dash (the Marquise's rape). Whether the discussion is about marriage, surrender, a pregnancy, the Marquise's expulsion, or a dirty little secret too shameful to utter, each dash is metaphorically bound to the "original" dash. And each metaphorical representation fails to (re)present, much like the "original" dash. Every dash epitomizes Kleist's negative representation in that "nothing" is the ultimate result of the representation.

In addition to the interrupted speech signified by the dashes, there are also several scenes where characters are literally speechless. The Marquise is "speechless" (*sprachlos* [105]) after her ordeal with the soldiers; the Graf . . . F unexpectedly appears after the Marquise and her family thought he was dead which "made them all speechless" (74) (*machte alle sprachlos* [109]); the mother's oxymoronic statement, "a clear conscience and a midwife!" (88) (*ein reines Bewußtsein und eine Hebamme* [122]), is followed by "and speech failed her" (88) (*die Sprache ging ihr aus* [122]); after having read the shocking response to the Marquise's ad, "the Colonel's wife became speechless" (99) (*verging . . . ihr* [der Mutter] *die Sprache* [131-132]); before the Marquise and her father have their "passionate" reconciliation the mother says to the Marquise, "it's just that he can't speak!" (106) (*er kann nur nicht sprechen* [137]). And during the Marquise's reconciliation with her father, neither she nor he can muster the linguistic strength: "Die Tochter sprach nicht, er sprach nicht" (138). As with the dashes, each episode of speechlessness does signify, but specifically what is signified is imperceptible and conceptually infinite in its scope of possibility. Unlike Kant's *negative Darstellung*, Kleist's negative representation does not enable concretization of a singular, a priori concept—a process by which the subject becomes conscious of his faculties of reason and judges himself a moral subject of reason. Rather Kleist's negative representation signifies a concretization of infinite chaos—a judgment that prevents the subject's faculty of reason from discerning the limits between deception and truth.

In other words, Kleist's theory of negative representation exaggerates Kant's figure of *negative Darstellung*. Kleist's theory suppresses vision into invisibility and language into ineffability, leading the subject to fanatical danger, chaotic ambiguity, and self-destruction. These are the very pitfalls against which Kant intended *negative Darstellung* to guard, but to which Kleist's characters repeatedly succumb as their representational prowess fails to elevate their knowledge and aesthetic education beyond sensible, illusory limits.

In *Die Marquise von O . . .* the aesthetic pitfall is the text's method of negative representation. The trap of aesthetic education is that the reader feels an overwhelming hermeneutic task to interpret the truth content and fill in the gaps which the text's ironic representation fails to provide. Moreover, like the dilemma afflicting Kleist, the reader is compelled to distinguish between what is truth (*Wahrheit*) and deception (*Schein*). Yet unlike the bear in *Über das Marionettentheater*, perfectly reading the author's "*Seele darin*," there is no "*Seele*" to be read in *Die Marquise von O . . .*; there is no transcendental "truth," but rather only a deceptive appearance that lures readers and characters alike into its hermeneutic trap.

"Nichts" as an Aesthetic Trope

Rhetorically, "nichts" is the only verbal signifier providing any knowledge and understanding about the Marquise's mysterious pregnancy, but at the same time "nichts" eludes the text's aesthetic traps by expressing nothing specific—no knowledge or sensible understanding. The commandant admits, "daß er *nichts* von der Sache verstehe" (115). The Graf exclaims, "*Nichts, Nichts* . . . es ist *nichts* geschehen" (118). As the Marquise tries to maintain her "vortreffliche" (104) character in spite of the "unspeakable" deed, "nichts" repeatedly appears. Her mother grills her for truthful answers: "Ist es weiter *nichts*, als der Ausspruch des Arztes? Weiter *nichts*, als dein innerliches Gefühl?" (122). The Marquise responds, "*Nichts* weiter, meine Mutter" (122). "*Nichts*, Julietta?" (122) asks the mother suspiciously, and the Marquise answers with the paradoxical and double negative "ich *verschweig* Ihnen *nichts*" (122). When the Marquise's mother tries to trick her into naming the father, the mother fabricates a story of which "*nichts* wahr ist" (135). And three times the Marquise expresses a desire to know "nichts" instead of hearing of or contemplating a possible marriage with the Graf: "Ich will *nichts* wissen" (129); "[die Marquise] wollte von Vermählung *nichts* wissen" (142); and when the commandant asks her why the Graf is so much more repulsive than any other, she answers the question with ". . . *nichts* . . . " (142). Thus, it is not surprising that at the novella's end the Graf is completely " . . . *vernichtet*" (141).[15] Nothing is what the commandant understands; nothing is the Marquise's most inner sense (*Gefühl*); nothing is what she tells her mother; nothing is the truth that constitutes the fodder of the mother's fictional lie; and nothing is the threefold representation of a marriage between the Graf and the Marquise that leaves him representationally destroyed (*vernichtet*). "Nichts" is completely (un)metaphorical or "unbildlich"; it fails to repaint a picture of anything and thereby suggests that its referent—the symbolic origin of the Marquise's "unspeakable" pregnancy—is itself an indecipherable vortex of nothingness. Unlike most tropes which utilize metaphorical imagery, "nichts" transgresses traditional aesthetic limits by presenting without image or signified.

"Nichts" is metonymically linked to the Marquise's child in that each representation of "nichts" influences her child's own representational status (who is the child's father?). Perhaps this is the reason why the Marquise attributes a higher, transcendental divinity to the "Ursprung" of her child exactly because it is, like "nichts," imperceptible and unmetaphorical: "[Das junge Wesen], dessen *Ursprung*, eben weil er *geheimnisvoller* war, auch *göttlicher* zu sein schien, als anderer Menschen . . ." (my emphasis, 126).[16] On a subtextual level, the Marquise's act of equating her child's "Ursprung" with the notion of "geheim" suggests that the "being"—her "innerliches Gefühl"—has no sensible externality to reflect, no signified for its signifier. Superficially, "geheim" means secret, and this meaning corresponds to the general atmosphere surrounding the "unspeakable" nature of the child's origin and the Marquise's desire to conceal the shameful details of the pregnancy. However, "geheim" is originally derived from the root word "Heim" meaning domestic, the antithesis of foreign, "unheimlich."[17] The twofold meaning of "geheim" suggests there is no external, foreign designation that can represent the origin of her child. The child's origins are locked up in the "unspeakable" realm of the Kantian idea—a pure concept with no sensible equal external of its inner conceptualization.

This has a twofold implication. Not only does it cast doubt upon the very existence of origin in a phenomenal sense, but it also appears to negate the Graf, a foreigner, from ever truthfully representing the child's origin. If "geheim" indeed indicates the child's father is located in the domestic sphere, then other potential father candidates originating from the outside would appear to be disqualified as the true father. For example, Leopardo's fatherly status is textually suggested through the Marquise's revelation: "Ich war einst in der Mittagshitze eingeschlummert, und sah ihn von meinem Diwan gehen, als ich erwachte" (135). And both the Marquise and her mother momentarily believe Leopardo is the father, as he is the first to appear at the exact time and day during which the "true" father should arrive: "Die Weiber erblaßten bei diesem Anblick" (140). Yet Leopardo's fatherly status is theoretically disqualified because he is outside the family, a foreigner "aus Tirol" (135). It appears one must look inside the family circle—remain within the confines of "geheim"—for an appropriate representation of father.

Krüger-Fürhoff suggests that the Marquise's father, the commandant, is the father of her child: "The mother herself sexualizes her husband's relationship to the Marquise by introducing both him and the child's imaginary begetter with the same disconnected 'He—he himself'" (Krüger-Fürhoff 77). In addition to the mother's comments, the commandant exhibits jealous characteristics normally associated with a lover, not a father, and these jealous manifestations only further substantiate Krüger-Fürhoff's analysis.

Most likely the seeds of the father's jealousy are planted during the storming of the citadel when the commandant is left with no choice but to surrender simultaneously his citadel and daughter to the Graf's overwhelming military and sexual vigor. The military atmosphere of the attack on the citadel is purposely presented with phallic symbolism and double entendres, emphasizing the twofold implication of the father's surrender: " [der Graf] . . . den Schlauch in der Hand . . . regierte den Wasserstrahl . . . [und] . . . steckte er, die Naturen der Asiaten mit Schaudern erfüllend, in den Arsenälen und wälzte Pulverfässer und gefüllte Bomben heraus" (106). The euphemistic implications of "Schlauch" and "Wasserstrahl," used in conjunction with the verb "stecken," strongly suggest the Graf's aggression is occurring on two levels: sexual as well as military. Most importantly, the Graf's military and sexual potency is juxtaposed to the commandant's own military and sexual "weakness." And finally, the imagery of the commandant's surrender is presented with the same sexual symbolism as his weak defense of his citadel; the commandant lowers his *sword* to the Graf. In the presence of superior virility, the Marquises father has no choice but to surrender his citadel / daughter to another man, and relinquish his patriarchal control. This initial usurpation of his power serves as the impetus for his "lover-like" jealousy.

Ironically, the commandant's first manifestation of jealousy occurs during his second, metaphorical surrender to the Graf. And again the commandant stands in danger of losing his daughter to the Graf's overwhelming virility. However, this time the Graf's militaristic acumen is replaced with a linguistic expediency. The Graf uses language "sedulously" (81) (*geflissentlich* [115]), whereas the commandant stifles language: "[er verstehe] von der Sache nichts und forderte die Familie auf, davon weiter nicht in seiner Gegenwart zu sprechen" (115). Thus, under the Graf's overwhelming, linguistic pressure the commandant has no choice but to surrender "twice already . . . to this Russian" (84) (*diesem Russen schon zum zweitenmal ergeben!* [118]). The Graf's ability to outmaneuver the commandant on any grounds—whether the battlefield, language, or the bed—incites the commandant's jealous rage: "Nun so macht! macht! macht! *rief* der Vater, indem er sich umkehrte" (my emphasis, 118). The commandant's emotional capitulation signifies not only the anger of the defeated, but also, more significantly, the anger of a jealous lover, faced with the real prospect of losing his love to another, younger, more virile man.

The Marquise's actions also cast doubt upon the assumed "platonic" nature of their father-daughter relationship, and suggest that her father's status as "father" is doubly ironic. Rather secretively, the Marquise reveals the strange sensation of pregnancy only when "her father had left the room for a moment" (73) (*der Vater sich, auf einen Augenblick, aus dem Zimmer entfernt hatte* [109]). And the Marquise's and her mother's joking remarks about who the possible father may be are interrupted and curiously end as "the Colonel returned to the room and the conversation was broken off" (74) (*der Obrist kam, das Gespräch ward abgebrochen* [109]). The Marquise's examinations by the doctor and midwife are also kept from her father until, finally, he discovers the pregnancy and orders the Marquise to leave. The secretive gossip she and her mother attempt to hide from her father appear more like the deceptive guilty actions of an unfaithful lover, than a daughter fearful of paternal scorn.

When the commandant does discover the Marquise's pregnancy, his actions resemble those of a jealous lover, not a concerned or even strict father. Rather than direct confrontation, the commandant dictates a letter stating she must leave the house; when the Marquise tries to embrace her father and pleads for his sympathy, like an injured lover, he passively turns his back; and what happens next recalls the sexual imagery of the citadel's defeat. The Marquise falls to his feet embracing his knees, and suddenly a pistol goes off, splitting the ceiling, yet missing its mark. "Sie warf sich ihm, der ihr den Rücken zugekehrt hatte, eben zu Füßen, und umfaßte zitternd seine Kniee, als ein Pistol, das er ergriffen hatte, in dem Augenblick, da er es von der Wand herabriß, losging, und der Schuß schmetternd in die Decke fuhr" (125). Like the previous scenes concealing sexuality behind metaphors of war and violence, here again the pistol and the errant shot suggest more than poor marksmanship. In a manner which recalls the commandant's inferior sexuality when he initially lowered his sword, here again his sexual prowess seems to be less than effective, if not entirely passive, as his cowering to a back wall reveals: "er . . . eilte, während die Marquise zu ihm hineintrat, nach der hintern Wand" (125). Finally, acting like a wounded, rejected lover, the commandant demands the Marquise leave her two children with him. Thus, the soap-opera-like scene concludes with a battle for child custody. Does her father's order suggest he actually has grounds for custody? The father's claim can be interpreted as an indication he believes the Marquise is incapable of raising the children due to her "immoral" behavior, or the father's claim could be more literal. He may actually be the father of the two previous children, a claim suggesting a long incestuous relationship.

The prospect of an incestuous history between the Marquise and her father is strengthened during their reconciliation. The scene is unmistakably sexual, brimming with all the features of "make-up sex." She sits upon his lap with eyes closed, as he lecherously leans over her with puckered lips and lustful eyes and kisses her on the lips. All the while the mother gleefully watches in a voyeuristic trance that mirrors her husband's own gazing eyes:

> Sie [die Mutter] vernahm, da sie mit sanft an die Tür gelegtem Ohr horchte, ein leises, eben verhallendes Gelispel, das, wie es ihr schien, von der Marquise kam; und, wie sie durchs Schlüsselloch bemerkte, saß sie auch auf des Kommandanten Schoß, was er sonst in seinem Leben nicht zugegeben hatte. Drauf endlich öffnete sie die Tür, und sah nun — und das Herz quoll ihr vor Freuden empor: die Tochter still, mit zurückgebeugtem Nacken, die Augen fest geschlossen, in des Vaters Armen liegen; indessen dieser, auf dem Lehnstuhl sitzend, lange, heiße und lechzende Küsse, das große Auge voll glänzender Tränen, auf ihren Mund drückte: gerade wie ein Verliebter! Die Tochter sprach nicht, er sprach nicht; mit über sie gebeugetem Antlitz saß er, wie über das Mädchen seiner ersten Liebe, und legte ihr den Mund zurecht, und küßte sie. (138)

In opposition to the other sexual scenes, signified only by a dash or the repetition of a theme of "unconsciousness," this scene is very explicit. It represents the polar opposite of the other "unspeakable" sexual encounters. It is domestic, "geheim," to the point of being incestuous. The two lovers are enclosed in a room, in opposition to the open court of the Marquise's initial sexual encounter. And even though the sexual encounter is internal, intra-familial (*geheim*), it is not (un)metaphorical or without outside sensual representation. In opposition to the nonvisual imagery of the other scenes, the visual imagery of this scene is punctuated by the mother's voyeuristic gaze, framing the lovers in a picture-like state through the "Schlüsselloch" (138), as well as by the phrase "das große Auge voll" (138).

Krüger-Frühoff interprets this incestuous scene as an aesthetic reproduction of a breach of taboo, a transgression "of the limits of (un)knowability" (Krüger-Fürhoff 82). She also compares the scene to an aesthetic production, claiming it resembles the popular *tableaux vivants* of the late eighteenth and early nineteenth centuries. Through the explicit framing of the scene through the frame of the keyhole, the incestuous scene is indeed aestheticized and represented and thereby suggests the transcendental power of an artistic production in transgressing limits: moral and metaphysical—a transgression potentially capable of reveling a hidden truth. Gerhard Neumann offers a similar analysis of the scene, identifying it as an experiment designed to question, dissolve, and go beyond the limits of social taboos—a process that coaxes out the truth: „daß er in seinem Experiment die Wahrheit gerade aus der Tabuverletzung herauszureizen sucht . . ." (171). However, outside empirical influence is kept at bay, beyond the door, beyond closed eyes, and beyond unconsciousness. The mother's gazing eye invites a reader along to breach this taboo limit of (un)knowability, yet no characters outside the family witness the scene. By the next day (*beim Anbruch des nächsten Tages*), the aesthetic production effectively ceases to exist; and the matter is not spoken of again. Only internally within the "geheimlich" walls of familial lust is representation provided with literal or "truthful" aesthetic imagery. However, outside that internal realm "truthful" representation becomes impotent and is substituted with metaphorical illusion and, ironically, a literalization of negative representation—"nichts." It is an epistemological loophole epitomized by the Marquise's emphatic avowal of negativity: "ich will nichts wissen."

The Marquise's statement is neither a forfeiture of truth nor an argumentative surrender of the literal for the metaphorical, but rather a transcendence of truth and an assertion of free volition expressed through her own aesthetic agency. The Graf, however, challenges the Marquise's attempt to construct a new aesthetic order. During the scene in which the Marquise utters these words, she is revisited by the Graf, a figure synonymous with the external, physical realm and foreign aggression, who attempts to force empirical knowledge and consciousness upon the Marquise. Recalling biblical imagery, the scene rewrites Eve's fall into mortality and consciousness.[18] The Marquise sits in a bower walled off from the outside world. The Graf, much like a snake, "umschlich die Mauer" (128) and "durchstrich die Gänge" (128) toward the unsuspecting Marquise. Like his biblical counterpart, the snake, the Graf's ultimate goal is to force knowledge on the Marquise. For Eve, consciousness and knowledge come with eating the forbidden fruit; for the Marquise, it would come with an aural digestion of the Graf's linguistic explanation: "ein einziges, heimliches Geflüstertes — " (129). However, Kleist has rewritten the scene. The Marquise refuses to hear his explanation, and instead she admonishes the Graf to hear her and her disavowal of knowledge and consciousness: "Sie hören! . . .*Ich will nichts wissen*, versetzte die Marquise" (my emphasis, 129). Here the verb "versetzen" means to interject. Literally, "versetzen" also means to displace or place incorrectly. Thus, the Marquise displaces the Graf's linguistic representation and effectively defers his attack of empirical knowledge and consciousness: the unwanted exogamous union of her child's divine "Ursprung" with his foreign representation of fatherhood.

The phrase displaces, "versetzt," the Graf's linguistic attempt to show, to represent, but more importantly, it inverts the function of representation, which is to promote "cognition." The Graf's claims of omniscience "als ob ich allwissend wäre" (129) is "versetzt" with a notion of unknowledge, "Ich will nichts wissen." The Marquise contemplates the nature of her child's origin and decides due to its nature as "geheimlich" that an outside exogamous representation is incapable of transferring the pure idea of her child's origin into an empirical, sensible form. The Graf is poised to reveal everything, an "alles" that exhausts all logical and known possibilities, and leaves the Marquise with no other option than to surrender to the Graf's imposition of "truth" and omniscient knowledge or to evade the Graf's entire system of logic, knowledge, and all-encompassing truth by espousing a completely opposite theory of representation that reveals "nichts."

In addition to usurping the Graf's omniscience through the representational figure "nichts," the Marquise's statement, "ich *will* nichts wissen," (my emphasis) also inverts the Graf's hegemonic control; her decision not to hear and obey the Graf's "einziges, heimliches geflüstertes —" presents a personal, independent volition or "Wille." Against critics who claim the Marquise is a passive victim of male sexual aggression whose wants and desires remain unknown, I would argue the Marquise is an aggressive, sexually active figure of pure "freewill," who blatantly reveals what she wants through negation.[19] She does not want marriage, she does not want to be lambasted with the Graf's literal representation of fatherhood, and she does not want the consciousness the Graf is poised to offer. To understand the Marquise's emphatic volition of "nichts" as a literal representation of nihilistic apathy is to fall victim to the deception she professes with her statement. Her statement embraces, through negative analogy, everything the Graf's system of knowledge trivializes, ignores, and brushes to the periphery. The "nichts" she willfully asserts is a metaphorical representation of infinite impossibility, enhanced not by rational states of conscious reason and logic, but rather by unconscious states of chaotic fluidity that escape the Graf's rational and conceptual grasps.

This intangible, chaotic fluidity is apparently dominant within the Graf's own subconscious, as his dream of the swan, "Thinka," freely floating upon a *fluid* plane indicates. Metaphorically, the Graf's dream reveals the Marquise's untouchable independence. The Graf's inability to lure the Marquise to himself stresses the Marquise's independence; and in the Graf's dream, the Marquise's "earthly" impunity is emphasized through her submersion into the water, cleansing herself of the Graf's earthly defilement, "Kot":

> Hierauf erzählte er mehrere, durch seine Leidenschaft zur Marquise interessanten, Züge: wie sie beständig, während seiner Krankheit, an seinem Bette gesessen hätte; wie er die Vorstellung von ihr, in der Hitze des Wundfiebers, immer mit der Vorstellung eines Schwans verwechselt hätte, den er, als Knabe, auf seines Onkels Gütern gesehen; daß ihm besonders eine Erinnerung rührend gewesen wäre, da er diesen Schwan einst mit Kot beworfen, worauf dieser still untergetaucht, und rein aus der Flut wieder emporgekommen sei; daß sie immer auf feurigen Fluten umhergeschwommen wäre, und er Thinka gerufen hätte, welches der Name jenes Schwans gewesen, daß er aber nicht im Stande gewesen wäre, sie an sich zu locken, indem sie ihre Freude gehabt hätte, bloß am Rudern und In-die-Brust-sich-werfen. (116)

The Marquise is surrounded by water, burning with erotic sexual lure. The Marquise's submersion into this fluid bath—a visual plane of sexual eroticism beyond which the Graf cannot perceive—allows her to reemerge cleansed of physical excrement. The swan's submergence into the allegorical waters of the subconscious, beyond the Graf's visual capability, reveals the hidden nature behind the Marquise's bouts of unconsciousness. The swan's purposeful submersion, which cleanses her of "outside" identity (Kot) and which pronounces defiance and elusiveness (*nicht im Stande* [. . .] *sie* [. . .] *sich zu locken*), is synonymous with a mental submersion into an aesthetic state of subconsciousness, imperceptible by male discourse. Excrement, a symbolic sexual stain, is the means by which the Graf attempts to defile her image, diminish the Marquise's social validity and prestige, and thus control, possess, her weakened psyche. But the burning, purifying erotic water surrounding the symbolic Marquise, "Thinka," negates the Graf's sexual defilement—his semiotic system of object definition and conceptual possession. And out of this eroticized fluidity, the Marquise emerges with an independent psyche, proud, unblemished, and literally beyond the grasps of the Graf's conceptual limitations: "er [war] aber nicht im Stande gewesen, sie an sich zu locken, indem sie ihre Freude gehabt hätte, bloß am Rudern und In-die-Brust-sich-werfen" (116). She is imperceptible, intangible, and exudes an alluring, independent, and highly nontraditional form of female sexuality.

The Marquise's enigmatic sexuality is further complicated by the name "Thinka." The name appears feminine; however, the swan's (and symbolically, the Marquise's) gender vacillates between the third person references "er" and "sie." Within the Graf's feverish dream, she (Thinka / the Marquise) becomes a confusion of the masculine gender of "der Schwan" and the feminine persona of "Thinka." The androgyny stresses her sexual independence, suggesting she requires no "other" for procreation. The etymological significance of "Thinka" also suggests the Marquise's auto-procreative capabilities. "Auch der Name des Schwans hat symbolische Bedeutung: Thinka ist die Abkürzung von Kathinka, der Koseform des russischen Jekaterina = Katharina = die Reine" (Kircher 119). Not only does the Graf's pure image of the Marquise coincide with her ability to cleanse herself once "mit Kot beworfen," but it also suggests she may indeed conceive a "child" completely within herself, without committing the "original" sin, i.e., the need for external or exogamous "others": she is "pure."

In this context, the seemingly outlandish question the Marquise asked the midwife, "ob diese Erscheinung im Reiche der Natur sei?" (124), appears justified by the subtextual perspective the Graf's dream of "Thinka" provides. In his dream the Graf portrays the Marquise as being, at least metaphorically, a conceptual equal of the Virgin Mary. The midwife exclaims that "dies, außer der heiligen Jungfrau, noch keinem Weibe auf *Erden* zugestoßen wäre" (my emphasis, 124). Yet within the Marquise's anamorphic status as both woman and swan (*Thinka*), *floating* on a fluid plane of aesthetic imagery, the Graf portrays the Marquise as being capable of transcending typical boundaries such as earth (*Erde*) and submerging herself into a supersensible state of conceptual innocence comparable to the virgin innocence of Mary. The Graf's dream offers a different perspective on the Marquise's role as mother and father. The Graf sees himself as essentially removed from the procreative process; in the dream he is unable to posses and control the Marquise, and in reality he stands at the moment of representational judgment as the child's father "wie *vernichtet*" (141). The Marquise's ambi-sexual procreative status is suggested through a metaphorical process, a *Vorstellung*—"wie er die *Vorstellung* von ihr, in der Hitze des Wundfiebers, immer mit der *Vorstellung* eines Schwans verwechselt hätte" (my emphasis, 116). Therefore it only seems natural that her child also maintain a metaphorical status and not a literal one. As I will argue in the following analysis, the literal "body" of the text (the child) is ironically the metaphorical imagery of the text itself; the search for a "father" is a self-reflective investigation of author and narrative authority, continuously drawing itself into question, as do the epigram and the novella's subtitle.

In other words, the pretense of searching for the father of a literal child is an aesthetic trap. The Marquise's advertisement sets up the reader for hopeful interpretive solutions. Yet these interpretive solutions are impeded by the ad, which furthers the representational quandary of paternal truth. Like the Marquise's emphatic disavowal of knowledge and consciousness (*ich will nichts wissen*), the Marquise's ad represents negatively and through negation—"ohne ihr Wissen" (104). Through the ad she creates the illusion that "a" father will reveal himself. But the ad does not offer knowledge, origin, or truth; it offers only an illusion that is substantiated through a hermeneutic process (reading), destined to fail and end in tautological redundancy (*Eine ganze Reihe . . . folgte jetzt noch dem ersten*) and appearance (*Schein*).

The Marquise as Author

Through her ad and the deceptive hermeneutic process her ad effects, the Marquise exemplifies a proto-Nietzschean example of the intuitive artist. In *Über Wahrheit und Lüge im außermoralischen Sinne* Nietzsche proposes that all language, metaphors, and signs are lies. Only by forgetting that metaphors are deceptions can we establish a common sense of truth. When a person ignores the social conventions that create "truth," he or she commits a "lie." According to Nietzsche, this "lie" is only perceived as a lie if the person intends harm through this lie.[20] Metaphorically, the Marquise's lie harms social convention. The central "lie" in *Die Marquise von O . . .* is the Marquise's scandalous announcement in the local paper. The announcement is scandalous not because of its obvious admission—that a widow without her knowledge is impregnated—but because she "publicly" announces her situation; in this way she defies (harms) social convention. Hartmut Kircher also locates the severity of the Marquise's lie in the fact that she openly declares what is usually kept "geheim." "Ein Ärgernis ist kein Ärgernis, solange es geheimgehalten werden kann. Öffentliche Bekanntmachung aber gilt als Tabuverletzung" (Kircher 114).

The taboo the Marquise breaks is precisely what the Graf tries to reinforce with his "allwissend" claims of truth and social respectability, a name (public legitimacy) for the child. Instead, the Marquise devises an aesthetic approach to perpetuate her child's a priori unknowablity by creating an aesthetic text with which the child will become synonymous: "Ein Mittel, bei dem sie, als sie es zuerst dachte, das Strickzeug selbst vor Schrecken aus der Hand fallen ließ. Durch ganze Nächte, in unruhiger Schlaflosigkeit durchwacht, ward es *gedreht und gewendet,* um sich an seine ihr *innerstes* Gefühl verletzende, Natur zu gewöhnen" (my emphasis, 127). The means by which she will uncover the father of her child is the introduction of a text, a fictional fabrication, based not on empirical, truthful reflection, but rather on a subjective aesthetic process, turned violently inward and weaving and turning with her "Strickzeuge" as if from within herself. What she creates is an aesthetic foundation for the discovery of the child's father. She admits the failure of truthful representation by "publicly" stating she is unable to identify the father. Instead she artificially fabricates the conditions for the fictional production of a father. The "lie" she commits is that the father (a cipher for truth) must be aesthetically produced. Thus, she commits the social faux pas of recognizing, instead of forgetting, that the fragile foundation of truth is a fictional illusion, a lie.

With this lie the Marquise's authorial image is now set. It is, then, rather fitting that she is described as knitting hats and socks, deciding the organization of the rooms, which books she would put in which rooms and where her easel should go when she conceives the idea of writing the ad:

> [Sie] saß in der Gartenlaube, und dachte, während sie kleine Mützen, und Strümpfe für kleine Beine strickte, wie sie die Zimmer bequem verteilen würde; auch, welches sie mit Büchern füllen, und in welchem die Staffelei am schicklichsten stehen würde. (126)

The Marquise's image is that of not only an educated artist, capable of knitting and painting, but that of an author. The knitting she does is the *texere* (meaning to weave) of the text itself; the stockings and hats are the text's outer structure; the easel is the imagery; and the organization of her house is the text's overall organization.[21] In writing the advertisement that begins the text, the Marquise establishes the text's theme and presents the essential problem: who is the father of her child. The text, a fictional attempt to construct an answer to the Marquise's advertisement, is the result or product of her advertisement. If the Marquise is in fact the author of the advertisement, and the text is an extension thereof, then the authorial control of the text in general falls into the Marquise's hands. The child she gives birth to is symbolically Kleist's own text; and the Marquise herself is the symbolic author who, with closed eyes, pens the text, a "schamlose Posse" (22).[22]

At this point the Marquise takes on the paradoxical definition of being simultaneously divine goddess and worthless "nichtswürdige" tramp. Following the publication of her ad, the commandant facetiously remarks "Oh! sie ist unschuldig . . . Sie hat es im Schlaf getan . . . die Närrin!" (131). Then, once the response to her ad appears the following day, the commandant repeatedly defines the Marquise as being worthy of nothing, or if anything, worthy of deception:

> O die Schändliche! . . . o die verschmitzte Heuchlerin! Zehnmal die Schamlosigkeit einer Hündin, mit zehnfacher List des Fuchses gepaart, reichen noch an die ihrige nicht! Solch eine Miene! Zwei solch Augen! Ein Cherub hat sie nicht treuer! . . . Ihre nichtswürdige Betrügerei, mit Gewalt will sie durchsetzen . . . Auswendig gelernt ist sie schon, die Fabel, die sie uns beide, sie und er, am Dritten 11 Uhr morgens hier aufbürden wollen. (132)

The commandant's description of the Marquise ironically reaffirms her aesthetic control of the text, which itself represents "nothing" but a fictional approximation or illusion of paternal truth. The "nothing" she professed wanting to know (*Ich will nichts wissen*) actually comes back to define both her and the representational capabilities of her text (*nichtswürdige Betrügerei*). The commandant attacks not only the figure of the Marquise, but also her image as author. Recalling the eye motif from the epigram warning readers not to trust die Marquise—a symbolic author—the commandant cynically attacks the spurious nature of the Marquise and her text with the statement: "Zwei solch Augen! Ein Cherub hat sie nicht treuer!" (132). Yet most importantly this spuriousness is defined as destructively deceptive: "*mit Gewalt* will sie durchsetzen" (my emphasis, 132). The Marquise expresses danger through her volition (*ich will nichts wissen*). Through this volition the Marquise threatens to dismantle the Graf's patriarchal discourse (his *einziges heimliches geflüstertes —*) that is trying to impose the existence of a tangible "truth" and paternal origins. In this insolent and defiant image the Marquise most closely approximates Nietzsche's notion of the destructive intuitive artist.[23] Like Nietzsche's intuitive artist, the Marquise deconstructs truth by lying against social convention with her "contemptible pretence" (*nichtswürdige Betrügerei*). Then she unashamedly proceeds to deceive with "so sweet a face" (*solch eine Miene*) and create a "story" (*eine Fabel*) that she and an implied, anonymous father will "tell [. . .] on the third at eleven in the morning" (100), literally "am Dritten 11 Uhr morgens hier *aufbürden* wollen" (my emphasis, 132). Ironically, but fittingly, her father associates the Marquise's story (*Fabel*) with a process of bearing (*aufbürden*) a child; the text is symbolically born.[24]

In opposition to her father's scorn, the Marquise's own mother attributes a "pure" divinity to the Marquise. In her mother's eyes the Marquise is a goddess or saint much like Mary: "O du reinere als Engel sind," "du Herrliche, Überirdische" (135). Here the mother attributes a divine pureness to her daughter that parallels the divine status of the Marquise's own child (*göttlicher als andere*), which itself represents a "pure" noumenal concept. In both cases the Marquise's dual identification works to define her overall aesthetic function. She is both the "überirdische" goddess of the text, its creator and author, and, "with the cunning of a fox" (*mit zehnfacher List des Fuchses*) the creator of the text's deceptive imagery and illusions of truth.

The Marquise's twofold and deceptive aesthetic agency is further substantiated by her libido, which the narrative conceals through verbal metaphor. She claims childlike innocence, "my conscience is as clear as that of my own children's" (88) (*daß mein Bewußtsein, gleich dem meiner Kinder ist; nicht reiner* [122]). Yet she openly admits to the midwife, "I conceived knowingly" (91) (*ich habe wissentlich empfangen* [24]). Even though it is not certain readers should believe her words, this sudden admission, juxtaposed by vehement denials and claims of innocence, offers an interesting interpretation of her sexual persona. This persona is further substantiated by another seemingly inconsequential narrative comment: before the Graf saves her from the rogue band of "Scharfschützen" she ironically "was just about to sink to the ground" (69) (*unter den schändlichsten Mißhandlungen, zu Boden sinken 'wollte'* [my emphasis, 105]). The English translation does not provide this ironic glimpse into the Marquise's behavior, nor does a superficial reading of the German. However, the phrase "zu Boden sinken *wollte*" literally implies a desire to "sink" to the ground. It is not certain her desire to "sink" to the floor conveys an actual sexual consent or just the desire to avoid the conscious recognition of such a traumatic experience and "sink" into an unconscious state; however, the presence of an indirectly implied willingness at such a moment creates an ambiguous contradiction that begs interpretation. Similarly, by reading the opening scene from a subtextual, euphemistic viewpoint, more evidence of the Marquise's active libido is suggested:

> Bald darauf kehrte er auf den Waffenplatz zurück, gab Befehl, der Flamme, welche wütend um sich zu greifen anfing, Einhalt zu tun, und leistete selbst hierbei Wunder der Anstrengung als man seine Befehle nicht mit dem gehörigen Eifer befolgte. Bald kletterte er, *den Schlauch in der Hand*, mitten unter brennenden Giebeln umher, und *regierte den Wasserstrahl*; bald steckte er, die Naturen der Asiaten mit Schaudern erfüllend, in den Arsenälen, und *wälzte Pulverfässer und gefüllte Bomben heraus.* (my emphasis, 106)

Literally, the Graf saves the citadel from burning to the ground and prevents unexploded ammunition from completely razing the fort. Metaphorically, he dowses the Marquise's own burning sexual inferno, defuses her bottled-up sexual lust. The veiled sexual metaphors are obvious. And the sexual innuendo and metaphoricity help contribute to the Marquise's own affinity to metaphorical signification.

The metaphorical possibility for her child's father is created by the Marquise's ad. By metaphorical, I mean she creates through a story an aestheticized (visual-verbal) (re)presentation. Moreover, her representation is negative: she does not present a father, but rather the absence of father. The only sexual intercourse with potent consequences—intercourse evoking conception (*gesegnete Leibesumstände*)—can take place through tropes, linguistic metaphor, subtextual innuendo, and most importantly physical absence. This metaphorical aesthetic language is notably absent in the descriptions of the three candidates for "father" presented in the text. The father-daughter scene which is preemptively undermined by gazing eyes (*Das große Auge voll*) and her father's verbal impotency (*er kann nur nicht sprechen*), is visual, yet lacks the verbal component to inspire a likewise metaphorical pregnancy; the scene is a literal representation of a sexual act. Also, the verbal absence of the Graf's "einziges geflüstertes —" or his polite, possibly rote French during their initial encounter again expresses a lack of metaphorical (visual) language, further suggesting his unsuitability as the "metaphorical" child's father. "Sexual" scenes with both the Marquise's father and the Graf are informed with either literal or completely absent language—essentially unaesthetic language. And it is primarily this unaesthetic language that strongly suggests their unsuitability as father of the Marquise's child. And even though Leopardo's possible fatherhood is revealed rather metaphorically, through sexual innuendo, and the metaphorical intent to deceive (the basis for Leopardo as a possible paternal candidate is a lie), he is a physical, tangible—sensibly limited—being.

For the Marquise, the concept of father is metaphorical, multifarious, inconclusive, and physically vacant. This is why she meets every attempt to reasonably clear up the enigmatic questions concerning her pregnancy with such stern obstinacy. Not only would an unambiguous, absolute answer effectively rob her of her own freewill, but it would also impose an artificial "truth" where she is unable or unwilling to do so. Thus, when the Graf admits to her that he is "fully convinced of [the Marquise's] innocence" (96) (*von [ihrer] Unschuld völlig überzeugt* [129]), she responds with "what!" (*wie*) and, disgusted, flees. And when her mother surprisingly believes in her innocence despite the Marquise's linguistically ambiguous admission of sleeping with Leopardo, she emphatically replies, "Under such extraordinary circumstances, how was it possible for anyone to trust me?" (104) (*Wer konnte mir, unter so unerhörten Umständen, Vertrauen schenken?* [135–36]). Finally, when her family is willing to accept the Graf and his representation of fatherhood, she experiences a paroxysm of emotion and attempts to "exorcise" her family's senses, which have been possessed by an enlightenment-like desire for tangible "truth," with a dowsing of holy water: "sie griff in ein Gefäß mit Weihwasser, das an der hinteren Tür befestigt war, besprengte, in einem großen Wurf, Vater und Mutter und Bruder damit, und verschwand" (141). The family's senses have been desensitized to illusion. The mother tellingly makes this point by asserting in reference to the Graf: "wen sonst, wir *Sinnberaubten* als ihn" (my emphasis, 140). Their senses have been robbed and displaced by a patriarchal assertion of "truth," the Graf. Their senses, now dulled, no longer attempt to discover the illusive nature of the Graf's self-proclaimed "truth" and fatherhood. The family's senses accept him and his image as what he proclaims to be: the child's father, the truth. The Marquise abhors this state of sensual sedation as effectively portrayed in her spraying of her family members with holy water. It is a symbolic last-ditch attempt to restore her family's senses to a state of aesthetics.

Nothing stresses the text's fictional status better than the metaphorical statements made concerning the Marquise's inexplicable sensations of pregnancy: "Frau von G . . . sagte, [die Marquise] würde vielleicht den Phantasus gebären, und lachte. Morpheus wenigstens, verstzte die Marquise, oder einer der Träume aus seinem Gefolge, würde sein Vater sein; und scherzte gleichfalls" (109). Ironically, another name for the Marquise's child is never presented. I would argue the metaphorical name Phantasus is the most appropriate because the child's physical significance is located metaphorically. In the end there are no direct physical descriptions of the child; his sensible representation is as vacuous as his father's, and, like his father, readers complete his incomplete, absent representation. Moreover, literal paternal definition is absent; the child is never referred to as "sein Sohn" or "sein Knabe." The child's patriarchal origin remains as ambiguous as it was in the story's beginning. Therefore, the fictitious myth of "Morpheus" and "Phantasus" becomes as valid a paternal origin as the Graf, Leopardo, or her father. Erika Swales draws a similar conclusion: "Thus the Marquise comes close to the truth when she jokingly suggests that the god of sleep and dreams must be the father of her child" (145).

"Phantasus" in Roman mythology is actually an inanimate object, a literary concept originating within Ovid's mythological literature about Mount Olympus. Thus, "Phantasus," as an inanimate and literary concept, is a rather appropriate name for her "child," for it fails to provide any tangible essence outside the aesthetic realm of illusion. This suggests that the child the Marquise bore is a son whose essence is arguably fictitious. The "Ursprung" of this text, the symbolic father, is equally fictitious. "Morpheus" (the Roman god of dreams and illusion who appears with human form), like "Phantasus," does not exist phenomenally; he is a literary concept.[25] The Marquise's frequent spells of unconsciousness, sleep, and day-dreamlike stares that follow several scenes dealing with a discussion of the "unspeakable"—sex—complete Morpheus' own signification of dreams and illusion. Their metaphorical union presents the mythical opportunity for the metaphysical conception of the Marquise's aesthetic idea, her text.

The other mythical reference that substantiates the metaphorical nature of the Marquise's child occurs immediately after the doctor concludes the Marquise is indeed pregnant. The Marquise is described "wie von Donner gerührt" (120). The description has a dual implication. Literally, the description reveals the Marquise's mental state. At the same time, "von Donner gerührt" functions as an intertextual signpost that refers to Zeus or Jove and his leitmotif of thunder and the lighting bolt. Metaphorically or subtextually, the sexual implication is that the Marquise has been "touched" by Zeus' lighting.

Like Hercules in *Amphitryon*—another example of Zeus' meddling affairs with mortals[26]—the Marquise's "göttliches" child is a product of a mythological conception, be it Zeus or Morpheus. And the midwife's comment that "the gay corsair who had come ashore in the dark would come to light in due course" (90) (sich der muntere Korsar, der zur Nachzeit gelandet, schon finden würde [124]), only confirms the metaphysical and mythical conception about which the Marquise and her mother joke. In Ovid's Metamorphoses, Morpheus does in fact arrive with wings, not unlike the winged corsair the midwife prophesizes.[27] Morpheus, a literary figure from Ovid's Metamorphoses, and "Donner," a literary metaphor, unite within the Marquise's persona and together establish the metaphorical and fictional origin of the Marquise's "göttliches" child. Within this mythological context, the Marquise reflects the necessary elements for aesthetic creation. She comes to symbolize a dual image of both mother and father, and she possesses the creative powers of each within herself. Even her name reflects the mythical and metaphorical duality within her—a name revealing a feminized form of Jove in the name "Juliette."[28] Like the Graf's aesthetic representation (*Vorstellung*) of the swan as a metaphor of the Marquise, the Marquise's sexual gender incorporates male and female signification, and expresses an androgynous independence, self-procreative aesthetic agency.

The Marquise epitomizes Nietzsche's intuitive subject, the artist who creates (deceives) not according to reason, but rather according to an embracing of illusion as a means of eluding the idealist, perpetual search for truth and absolute representation. Nietzsche states, " . . . art treats illusion as illusion; therefore it does not wish to deceive; it is true. . . .Art speaks the truth quite generally in the form of lies" (Nietzsche 96). The truth of Marquise's text is that it is a shameless farce, a lie—a piece of prose deceptively dressed in the metaphors of representation and the expectation of revelation. Yet the text purposely fails to reveal and satisfy the expectation of "truthful" representation. In the end the Marquise reinforces the deceptive nature of the text by stating the Graf "würde ihr damals nicht wie ein Teufel erschienen sein, wenn er ihr nicht, bei seiner ersten Erscheinung, wie ein Engel vorgekommen wäre" (143). The Graf's dichotomous appearance as both devil and angel does not establish a concrete basis of difference, meaning, and textual hermeneutics, as one might expect, but rather ironically resolves into a synthesis of "Erscheinung"—appearance. The angelic and diabolic become synonymous in their mutual negation, and dissolve the limits between truth and lies in a shroud of shameless deception. In the end it appears that any outside foreign representation of her child's origin is as valid an exchange (*Tausch*) of deception (*Täuschung*) as any other; in other words there is no singular "true" representation of father. Ironically, like his foreign currency he lays upon the child's crib, "20,000 Rubel" (143), the Graf's representation of fatherhood is an invalid form of currency in the Marquise's Italy. In the least it is a form of currency requiring an "exchange" (*Tausch*), suggesting a process of representation, a *Täuschung*, is required to achieve "validity." The statement: "Eine ganze Reihe von jungen Russen folgte jetzt noch dem ersten" (143), although hinting superficially toward more young children, suggests with the ambiguous "nach dem ersten" that one Russian is as good as the next in representing the Marquise's metaphorical, priceless child. For ultimately they all fail to convey true representational value. "True" representation becomes lost in an infinite state of hermeneutic regression. And all that can concretely be ascertained, gained, or portrayed through this infinite representation of regress is the amorphous, and metaphorically-charged, deceptive verbal utterance "*nichts*."

The Marquise's theory of representation constitutes a paradigmatic opposition to the transcendental theory of representation. Her theory struggles to elude societal demands for truth, syllogistic logic, and lifeless scientific proof. Today DNA is the scientific absolute that metaphorically and literally replaces a mother's word with a new semiotics of the double helix—a fruition of Socratic logic and its desire for complete unambiguous understanding. Yet in Kleist's text the Marquise's "extra-moral" artistic freedom, although bound and fettered by society's linguistic chains and the "Wort" (142) she must maintain, continues to deceive and produce "eine ganze Reihe von jungen Russen" (143) whose infinite regressive representations purposely fail to encapsulate the true essence of the Marquise's child, *Die Marquise von O . . .*.

Chapter III

Das Käthchen von Heilbronn: Artificial Appropriations of Gender

Having endured both the unfavorable reception resulting from Goethe's performance of *Der zerbrochne Krug* and Goethe's criticism of *Amphitryon* and *Penthesilea*, Kleist may have wanted to construct his next play, *Das Käthchen von Heilbronn*, in a manner more appealing to the public and to his contemporary critics, most significantly Goethe. The play was popular and in that sense a success. Kleist's contemporaries such as E.T.A. Hoffmann and Brentano lauded the play, and E.T.A. Hoffman went so far as to say Kleist redefined for him the forms of Romanticism through a poetics of somnambulism.[1] However, Goethe remained less than impressed and supposedly threw a copy of the text into a fire, calling the text a miraculous mixture of sense and nonsense and damned artificial.[2] Moreover, despite its public popularity, several newspaper reviews also criticized the play for its banal language, its incomplete character development, and for being too superficial.[3]

Such criticism concerning the thematic and linguistic structure of *Das Käthchen von Heilbronn* misinterprets the parodic intent informing the play. The notion Kleist produced the play exclusively for public approval is rather unlikely. Kleist did not graciously accept criticism, but he was not unaccustomed to it, nor was it in his nature to bow to public taste or popular literary trends. Kleist did indeed wish to establish himself as a successful writer, recognized by the public and by Goethe; however, he perceived his relationship with the literary establishment in terms of a competition.[4] Kleist wrote *Das Käthchen von*

Heilbronn in the spirit of such competition, superficially adhering to a simplistic model of Romanticism as a means to discredit, mock, and challenge the aesthetic program of those writers recognized by critical acclaim and popular taste.

In a manner which parodically exaggerates the male-oriented aesthetic running throughout much of Romanticism, the storyline of *Das Käthchen von Heilbronn* relates how a simple adolescent girl, Käthchen, meets her divinely determined knight in shining armor, the Graf vom Strahl, devotes herself and her life to him, and finally marries him, elevating her social standing. The thematic tension of the text is constructed around a dream both Käthchen and the Graf share. The Graf dreams about a divine female, the daughter of the emperor who is destined to be his bride, and Käthchen dreams about her future groom and how they will be married the following Easter. However, the Graf and Käthchen are unable to recall the significance of their dreams in a wakened state and confusion sets in. Käthchen meets her groom and, without knowing why, inexplicably falls to his feet and exhibits a dog-like devotion to him. At first Käthchen's blind devotion is misunderstood and repelled; she is, after all, the daughter of a blacksmith, not of the emperor as the Graf's dream foretold, and is from too low a social standing for the Graf to marry. The Graf then meets Kunigunde, who is a descendent of a long line of Saxon kings, and her pedigree convinces the Graf she is the woman identified in his dream. Determined to win the Graf's property and his hand in marriage, Kunigunde repeatedly tries to kill Käthchen. Eventually, however, Käthchen's identity as the emperor's daughter is revealed, and Kunigunde's suitability for marriage is drawn into question. In a patriarchal manner openly portraying women as commodities of male possession, control of Käthchen passes from her surrogate father, Theobald, to the Emperor, and finally to the Graf, as the emperor commands: "nehmt sie . . . zur Kirche" (531), thus concluding the play.

The possibility Kleist's play can be read as an example of protofeminist aesthetic theory initially appears far-fetched. However, what appears misogynist is actually a parody of representations of women in Romantic aesthetic theory. The focus of my reading will show how Kleist's aesthetic theory strives to subvert Romanticism's essentialist and artificial appropriation of the female image. By concentrating on both Käthchen's and Kunigunde's thematic and structural functions within the play, I will argue Kleist's portrayal of women constitutes a misunderstood parodic aesthetic that calls into question the patriarchal discourse of Romanticism and what I perceive as androcentric theories of aesthetic production excluding women. Finally, I will show how Kleist's own parodic critique of Romanticism can be read as a proto-feminist aesthetic that presents a process of feminine dissolution and absence, rather than a proactive presence, as one might expect.

The first section of my analysis reviews recent criticism, and outlines the predominant inclination to establish a "positive" interpretation of Käthchen, and even of Kunigunde, as a starting point for a feminist reading. The second section interprets Käthchen and Kunigunde as amalgams of idealist representations of women. These two characters embody an aesthetic akin to both Kant's theories of *negative Darstellung* and the idea, and the Romantics' image of woman as a Fichtean "Other" from which male subjects derive their self-definition. Ultimately both female figures fail to present a viable female "presence." Rather than representing otherness, each female character parodically represents a reflection of male imagery, physically and conceptually. In conclusion, I suggest the Hegelian "Master-Slave dialectic" invites the possibility for a feminist reading in a text overladen with feminine subordination and male dominance: the "dissolution" of the "feminine" creates a negative space from which the parodic aesthetic subverts the text's own discourse.

Recent Scholarship

That *Das Käthchen von Heilbronn* can be interpreted as a parody of Romanticism is not new to Kleist scholarship. From the time of its appearance in Kleist's own literary journal, *Phöbus*, to today's most recent scholarship, the play's parodic tone and import have been identified and its effectiveness debated and measured.[5] However, reading the play's representation of women as a parody of Romanticism's essentialist ideal concept and image of femininity has remained unexplored. Rather, much of Kleist scholarship accepts

Käthchen's presentation as a subordinate servant to her master at face value, and dismisses Kunigunde's image as caricature as unimportant. Even though most critics recognize Kunigunde's exaggerated artificiality, these same critics too easily accept Käthchen's subservient behavior without entertaining the possibility Käthchen's exaggerated subservience and devotion may itself be a parody.

Most male critics praise Käthchen's Rousseauean devotion to the Graf as a manifestation of absolute loyalty and as evidence of unmediated instinctual truth, ignoring the blatant sexist position the text establishes. A Kleist contemporary, von Bülow, interprets the portrayal of the heroine, Käthchen, as the epitome of Kleist's concept of "loyal" love: "Nach dem Bruche [mit Julie Kunze] begann er das Käthchen von Heilbronn zu dichten, und ward dazu gewissermaßen von dem schmerzlichen Bedürfnisse angetrieben, seiner ungetreuen Geliebten beispielsweise an seiner Heldin zu zeigen, wie man lieben müsse" (qtd. in *Lebensspuren* 240–1). Interpreting Kleist's play as an autobiographical allegory of Kleist's troubled relationships with women, Bülow does not assign any aesthetic importance to Käthchen's devotion. Bülow's uncritical interpretation of Käthchen's willing subservience cannot be taken out of the gendered social context of early 19th-century Europe, where Rousseauean definitions and expectations of gender were still popular. However, Käthchen's interpretation as a signifier of some "truth"—or the perception she represents "truthfully"—still permeates Kleist scholarship today.

More recently, Gerd Ueding has interpreted Kleist's play as a *Traumwelt* opposing Romanticism's telos of truth.[6] Analyzing both Käthchen and Kunigunde as poetological instantiations of Kleist's own aesthetic theories, Ueding interprets Kunigunde as a symbol of aesthetic deception whose illusory nature is polarized by Käthchen's "true" form: "Kunigunde steht am Ende da als das personifizierte Bild des zersetzten Scheins, und ihr gegenüber treten die unverletzten, zum Zielbild ihrer selbst gelangten Traumfiguren: Käthchen [. . .]" (181). Ueding's analysis offers an interesting interpretation of a transcendental *Bilderwelt*, resisting truth and true representation within Kleist's play, but he contradicts his own argument by suggesting Käthchen's character personifies "true" aesthetic illusion (185). Ueding attempts to delineate between artificial aesthetic *Schein* and true aesthetic *Schein,* an argument that indirectly asserts a prelapsarian representational pureness to Käthchen's image. In this manner, Ueding's analysis reaffirms the traditional male interpretation of Käthchen as the archetypical "feminine" ideal. Moreover, Ueding does not extend his analysis into the logical gendered implications of his own analysis. For if the *female* characters Käthchen and Kunigunde symbolize a contradictory response to a canonical Romantic aesthetic through their symbolic imagery, as Ueding suggests, then Kunigunde and Käthchen, as *female* representations of an antithetical aesthetic perforce call into question the status of the "feminine" within the Romantics' aesthetic program. Instead, Käthchen emerges in Ueding's analysis as a figure of absolute "truth," reaffirming the Romantic image of femininity and the definition of gender the text actually strives to satirize.

Stephens takes exception with other male critics' interpretations of Käthchen as a pre-Fall figure of innocence and truth. Whereas Ueding's analysis is concerned with the metaphysical implications of the imagery associated with Käthchen and Kunigunde, Stephens claims metaphysical interpretations fail to explain the real, nonmetaphysical abuse Käthchen endures under a dominant patriarchy: "It is in no sense the world of dream, but the simple fact of Käthchen's suffering, which no amount of extravagant imagery can disguise" (133). Stephens' analysis exposes important considerations concerning Käthchen and Kunigunde that help define metaphysical assumptions about the representational function of each character, without overlooking the very real physical abuse each endures. For example, Stephens defines Käthchen's representation as an embodiment of "the text's preferred version of the feminine," and conversely identifies "something distinctly 'masculine' . . . about Kunigunde's actions, if not her image in others' eyes" (148). Stephens' analysis is correct in its assumption about Käthchen and Kunigunde as projections of mere male fantasy, but Stephens downplays the importance of parody in the overall understanding of Käthchen's character: "[Käthchen's] passivity and incomprehension [. . .] may be read as a parody of such delineations of the middle-class female stereotype [. . .]. However, the amount of sympathy Käthchen arouses through her suffering in the court scene tends to work against any awareness of parody becoming dominant" (150). Stephens identifies Käthchen's parodic "passivity" as evoking sympathy, an emotion he believes annuls parodic intent. However, Käthchen's parodic "passivity" is not a plea for sympathy, but rather a mode of criticism. Stephens succeeds in explicating many important issues concerning Käthchen's and Kunigunde's relationships to a violent, dominant patriarchy. Yet his misappropriation of parody forces his conclusion to assume a polemical view which does not alter the traditional interpretation of Käthchen as a "celebration of patriarchal authority" (Stephens 148).

Most female critics analyze the overtly patriarchal discourse of the text, but do not assign any parodic significance to either Kunigunde's obviously artificial or Käthchen's overtly sexist representation. Instead, with a few exceptions, women commentators illustrate how Käthchen still manages to salvage an honorable "feminine" independence and definable otherness through isolated acts of devotion, bravery, and independence within the overtly patriarchal structure of the text.

Brown uncovers several "positive" attributes in Käthchen. For example, she praises Käthchen's actions during the fire scene, where Käthchen charges into a burning, crumbling castle at Kunigunde's behest, and notes she is "the only person who is willing to take action" (434). Brown overlooks the fact that Käthchen's "bravery" is an exaggerated subservience and obedience, not independence: Käthchen follows Kunigunde's orders. Moreover, while Brown accords "feminine" importance to Käthchen, she casually dismisses Kunigunde's function as mere comical relief and unimportant: "All is extreme with her [Kunigunde] [. . .]. In short, the general impression borders on comic caricature [. . .]. Nothing about Kunigunde's behaviour suggests that she belongs to the same gallery of heroic females as Penthesilea" (343). Brown concedes Kunigunde may cast a "parodistic impression" (343), but her analysis leaves one wondering why she does not afford Kunigunde's "parodistic impression" the critical importance typically associated with satire and parody.

Mommsen does not consider the possibility of parody and instead interprets Käthchen and Kunigunde as allegorical manifestations of Kleist's embittered relationships with Goethe and with Kleist's rival Zacharias Werner. She defines Kunigunde as a representation of Werner's Romantic aesthetic—artificial and false—and interprets Käthchen as a pure representation of a true aesthetic form. The Graf's decision to eventually marry Käthchen rather than Kunigunde—i.e., to choose the correct, true aesthetic—symbolizes for Mommsen Kleist's goal of eventually obtaining Goethe's favor and overcoming Werner and his "artificial" aesthetic. Mommsen's research offers important interpretive insights into Kleist's paradoxical attitude toward Goethe, but her reading of Käthchen as a representation of a "true aesthetic" is problematic. Mommsen's literal adaptation of Kleist's historical relationships as an interpretive exegesis of the text's female characters presents Käthchen as the epitome of truth and object of masculine desire. In her literal interpretation, Mommsen's argument accepts the superficial sexist discourse of the text and perpetuates the long line of criticism uncritically accepting the text's sexist position.

In her study *Spirited Women Heroes* Julie Prandi sets out to identify the social discourse determining Käthchen's textual representation and the subsequent critical reception of the character. Her thorough analysis of typical definitions of women in the Enlightenment and *Goethezeit* presents a good introduction to the gender problematic at work in Kleist's play. Prandi outlines the development of male-imposed projections of femininity and concludes that the male conception of "normal" behavior for women in philosophical and moralistic treatises establishes a set of common normative feminine "virtues." It is these virtues, Prandi argues, that Kleist reflects in Käthchen and that criticism in turn reflects. However, Prandi also tries to invert the sexist portrayal of Käthchen by locating decidedly "pro-feminine" and "positive" attributes in Käthchen's character. In the end, Prandi's analysis comes to a contradictory conclusion: Käthchen prefigures nothing more than pure male fantasy: "She [Käthchen] appears more a dream woman designed by Strahl than a self-determining subject" (41). This conclusion contradicts Prandi's own argument, which tries to establish Käthchen as an independent "self-determining subject." However, Prandi does begin to confront the basis of the text's parodic import: Käthchen is a reflection of male desire, couched, however, in a parodic discourse.

In contrast to the "traditional characterization of the title figure as one of those archetypes of the *ewig Weibliche*,"[7] Cullens and von Mücke interpret Käthchen as an inconsequential pawn of the "patriarchal cosmos" (483), and forgo any attempt to discover specifically "positive feminine" attributes in her behavior. Instead they afford a more "feminist" significance to Kunigunde and her manufactured construction, claiming she personifies an early expression of the female "vamp" who is empowered with an anti-patriarchal program designed to undermine the male characters' power structure—specifically language. Their Lacanian reading offers a new and convincing approach to the play. And like Prandi's, their analysis asserts the foundation of Käthchen's characterization is a patriarchy's representation of desire. However, their analysis concludes this patriarchal discourse is left unchallenged, whereas it is drawn into question in *Penthesilea*. Cullens and von Mücke read *Das Käthchen von Heilbronn* as a failed example of a feminist challenge to patriarchal discourse, but parody does not assume any critical importance in their argument.

Another Romantic text representing what critics have perceived as a failed feminist aesthetic is Dorothea Veit-Schlegel's novel *Florentin*. The novel has long been criticized for its lack of a distinctly "feminine" voice, and for its simplistic adherence to Romantic themes. However, Helfer constructs a feminist reading by analyzing the absence, rather than the presence, of woman's voice in *Florentin*. Helfer argues the mistake critics traditionally make in analyzing *Florentin* and the reason for their harsh reception of the novel is their insistence on discovering positive images of femininity within a novel written by a woman. In a formulation that draws on Iragaray, Helfer maintains, "[. . .] 'woman' cannot be defined positively in Veit-Schlegel's essentialist feminist critique, because 'woman' herself is a product of the very discourse she proposes to subvert" (157). Veit-Schlegel subverts the dominant discourse using a "parodic masculine discourse" (146). This discourse mimics the Romantic theme of male self-definition, central to Romantic aesthetic theory, by presenting a non-novel in response to Friedrich Schlegel's own novel about self-definition, *Lucinde*. Veit-Schlegel's aesthetic parodies the Romantic aesthetic: an autoerotic instantiation of male narcissism that uses women as images onto which the male subject tries to project himself to appropriate a sense of femininity, and subsequently to achieve aesthetically the feminine procreative essence Romantic authors perceived "naturally" inherent in women:

> In Romantic theory the Fichtean self-positing subject defines itself via poesy as poesy. The woman as childbearer, however, is the true source of Romantic poesy. This creates a profound identity crisis for the man: the self-positing male subject cannot define himself fully except by somehow becoming a "woman" so that he, too, can "give birth" to Romantic poesy, and hence to himself as a self-positing subject. (Helfer 151)

Instead of constructing a truly "feminine" aesthetic, the male subject creates a homoerotic aesthetic, excluding positive female characters. *Florentin* does not end with a perfected self-definition, but rather with a continuous deferral of self-definition. Hence, Helfer states *Florentin's* own aesthetic theory creates a theory of absence, rather than of presence: not knowing how to overcome the problem of creating a space for the true feminine within a masculine discourse, Veit-Schlegel presented what she knew a feminist discourse would *not* entail, and approached the problem of creating a "feminine" voice through a parodic discourse providing deferral and absence, not completion or presence.

I argue *Das Käthchen von Heilbronn* functions in much the same manner. Although Kleist was male, this does not preclude him from confronting the same problem of creating a decidedly "other" feminine voice. The Romantics' simplistic appropriation of the "female" as a means of achieving self-definition was extremely problematic for Kleist; he repeatedly confronted this theme in all his works from *Die Familie Schroffenstein* to *Der Findling*, in which a violent failure of the Fichtean "other" as a means of self-definition results in a destruction of the subject.[8] In an attempt to overcome the mainstream male aesthetic of Romanticism, a highly androcentric and at times homoerotic theory of self-definition, Kleist uses a parodic aesthetic mimicking Romanticism, much like the parodic discourse in *Florentin*. Thus, in *Käthchen*, as in *Florentin*, there are no positive images of "femininity," nor any women to speak of; there are only male images of "females" as reflections of a male aesthetic. Although Kleist's play repeatedly has been identified as a parody, its aesthetic representation of women traditionally has remained outside the scope of parodic possibility. By reading the female characters as examples of a parodic masculine aesthetic, I will show how Kleist constructs a means for a femininst critique of the male-determined aesthetic theories of Romanticism. Kleist does not create an overt challenge to the limits of patriarchy as he does in *Penthesilea,* but undercuts the traditional image of "femininity" as represented and employed in Romantic aesthetic theories by mimicking this discourse parodically.

Käthchen and Kunigunde as Ciphers of Romantic Aesthetic Theory

In *Kritik der Urteilskraft* Kant confronts the problem of providing a sensible representation of pure concepts, or ideas. Kant's solution is the representational figure *negative Darstellung*. It is called *negative* precisely because the representation represents that which cannot be represented—i.e., the representation is in a sense a lie. What *negative* Darstellung does permit with this lie, however, is the concretization of pure concepts, allowing one to transcend the limits of the senses and explore the limits of one's imagination. *Negative Darstellung* deceives the senses into accepting the representation as a tangible expression of ideas. Kant downplayed the significance of *negative Darstellung* and even stressed its inherently deceptive function. However, the Romantics rewrote the theory to accommodate it within their definition of *Poesie*—an aesthetic figure extending the limits of a subject's sensibility into the realm of ideas. In what became known as *Bildungsromane* and in other literary genres, the Romantics employed their reinterpretation of Kant's theory as a means for defining the subject. The male subject undergoes a process of aesthetic development, culminating in his own self-definition, as his aesthetic education allows him to transcend sensible limits and define himself through *Poesie.*

Like many of his Romantic contemporaries, Kleist was profoundly affected by Kant's philosophy. For Kleist, Kant's influence precipitated the infamous *Kantkrise*—a crisis developing out of Kant's denial of objective knowledge. Thus, unlike his Romantic contemporaries, Kleist did not view *negative Darstellung* as a means of obtaining absolute truth. Rather, Kleist presents in his works situations and incidents where faulty representation, inadequate language (either metaphorical or literal), and erroneous self-reflection culminate in the destruction of subjects and a dismantling of perceived truths. Kleist mimics the themes, language, and rhetoric central to the Idealist philosophy arising from Kant's theory of *negative Darstellung*. However, his mimicry is intended to critique Idealism, not to embrace it.

In *Das Käthchen von Heilbronn* Kleist engages Idealist topoi of aesthetic reflection, self-definition, and the problematic distinction between *Wahrheit* and *Schein*. Kleist employs a parodic representation of Idealist philosophy to draw into question Romantic aesthetic theories. In Romanticism women represent the true source of *Poesie* and frequently function as the aesthetic Fichtean "other" onto whom the male subject projects his own reflection to gain self-definition. Kleist mimics this practice by creating a parodic aesthetic that displays exaggerated female figures representing Romantic theory whom male characters strive to posses and control. Käthchen and Kunigunde represent "woman" in a manner akin to the representational mechanisms of Kant's notion of the pure concept or idea and *negative Darstellung*. Käthchen functions subtextually as a cipher for the a priori idea, and Kunigunde functions as the sensible, a posteriori representation, *negative Darstellung*. Together they form an aesthetic totality, reflecting the masculine idealized image of woman as an aesthetic figure of Romantic *Poesie*.

Käthchen's paradoxical function as an a priori idea is manifested in the opening scene, where a secret court, the *Vehmgericht*, convenes to hear the complaint brought against the Graf vom Strahl. Käthchen's father, Theobald, accuses the Graf of using black magic and consorting with Satan to seduce Käthchen and turn her into his loyal servant. Theobald's statement to the court creates an image of Käthchen befitting a god or angel—anything but a *mortal* physical being.[9] More importantly, during Theobald's testimony Käthchen is physically absent, a seemingly minor detail emphasizing her metaphysical essence as the idea. In Käthchen's absence, Theobald compares her to a heavenly being, an angel: "Ein Wesen von zarterer, frommerer und lieberer Art / Müßt ihr euch nicht denken, und kämt ihr, auf Flügeln der / *Einbildung, zu den lieben, kleinen Engeln*, die, mit hellen / Augen, aus den Wolken, unter Gottes Händen und Füßen / Hervorgucken" (my emphasis, 433). Theobald stresses Käthchen's divine status with the phrase "zu den lieben, kleinen Engeln," and defines her within the context of aesthetic imagination, "auf Flügeln der Einbildung." Theobald then further emphasizes Käthchen's metaphysical status by comparing her to a child of god: "als ob der Himmel von Schwaben sie erzeugt, und von seinem Kuß geschwängert, die Stadt, die unter ihm liegt, sie geboren hätte" (433). Later Theobald describes Käthchen as an unpossessable being, an object of male desire, yet physically untouchable: "die Ritter, die durch die Stadt zogen, weinten, daß sie *kein Fräulein* war; ach, und wäre sie eines gewesen, das Morgenland wäre aufgebrochen, und hätte Perlen und Edelgesteine, von Mohren getragen, zu ihren Füßen gelegt" (my emphasis, 433). Even though the literal implication of Theobald's description refers to Käthchen's social status, too low for knights to marry, her status as *kein Fräulein* nonetheless emphasizes a physical intangibility. Even if Käthchen were a (physical) "lady," Theobald still casts her as a godlike image: she would be an icon, a living goddess idolized with pearls and precious stones set at her feet (*Perlen und Edelgesteine, von Mohren getragen, zu ihren Füßen gelegt*). Finally, Theobald exclaims Käthchen has grown tired of the physical world's appeal: "die Welt, der liebliche Schauplatz des Lebens, reizt [Käthchen] nicht mehr" (479). Käthchen is not only a figure incompatible with the physical world, but a figure whose affinity with the supersensible supersedes her longing for a physical life.

This affinity to the supersensible becomes a defining characteristic for Käthchen. Following his description of Käthchen as a divine being, Theobald characterizes Käthchen's actions, which place her in the realm of supersensible gods and immortals. Theobald explains how Käthchen throws herself from a thirty-foot-high window in an act of apparent immortality: "Und da wir an das Fenster treten: schmeißt sich das Mädchen, in dem Augenblick, da er [der Graf vom Strahl] den Streithengst besteigt, dreißig Fuß hoch, mit aufgehobenen Händen, auf das Pflaster der Straße nieder: gleich einer Verlorenen, die ihrer fünf Sinne beraubt ist!" (436). Not only does she survive the fall, but her lack of physical reality is mirrored in her lack of sensibility: "[sie ist] ihrer fünf Sinne beraubt." Following this initial act of apparent "senselessness," Käthchen's metaphysical nature is repeatedly reflected in her lack of sensibility. Graf Otto questions why she threw herself "*sinnlos* auf die Straße" (my emphasis, 443); the Graf vom Strahl calls her a "Närrin, die verwünschte, *sinnverwirrte*" (my emphasis, 443); and Eleonore later asks Käthchen "bist du [Käthchen] bei *Sinnen*" (my emphasis, 514). Like pure concepts and ideas, Käthchen lacks a concrete relationship with the senses. This lack repeatedly eludes reason and prohibits complete comprehension of her a priori essence.

Käthchen herself demonstrates her problematic relationship with the senses when she physically enters the courtroom, yet is unable to express herself sensibly. She does not speak intelligibly, nor hear or see correctly, nor is she able to clearly explain her mysterious behavior. Despite the judges' pleas that Käthchen explain herself, speak understandably, she remains incomprehensible, intangible (*unbegreiflich*) to the judges' faculties of reason and understanding. Despiter her physical presence, she paradoxically remains a noumenal figure outside the faculty of their sensible judgment and resists sensible definition at every turn:

> GRAF OTTO. Hier Jungfrau, wenns beliebt; hier ist die Schranke!
> HANS. Hier sitzen deine Richter!
> KÄTHCHEN. *sieht sich um.*
> Ihr versucht mich.
> WENZEL. Hier tritt heran! Hier sollst du Rede stehn.
> KÄTHCHEN. *stellt sich neben den Grafen vom Strahl, und sieht die Richter an.*
> GRAF OTTO. Nun?
> WENZEL. Wirds?
> HANS. Wirst du gefällig dich bemühn?
> GRAF OTTO. Wirst dem Gebot dich deiner Richter fügen?
> KÄTHCHEN. *für sich.* Sie rufen mich.
> WENZEL. Nun, Ja!
> HANS. Was sagte sie?
> GRAF OTTO *befremdet.*
> Ihr Herrn, was fehlt dem sonderbaren Wesen?
> *Sie sehen sich an.*
> KÄTHCHEN. *für sich.* Vermummt von Kopf zu Füßen sitzen sie,
> Wie das Gericht, am jüngsten Tage, da! (441)

At first Käthchen appears confused, and mistakenly turns to the Graf, misidentifying him as her judge. Yet her confusion quickly contaminates the cognitive reasoning of judges, who attempt to come to some kind of enlightenment "truth," understanding, and ultimate knowledge concerning the enigmatic Käthchen and her decision to leave her father and follow the Graf. The court setting not only conjures up the biblical image of the Judgment Day with Käthchen's statement "wie das Gericht, am jüngsten Tage," but also functions as a metaphor for the Kantian process of submitting all knowledge to a tribunal.

Yet here knowledge is not gained, but rather hindered by Käthchen, a metaphor for the unrepresentable pure concept. The judges' repeated questions remain unanswered, if not outright ignored, and are juxtaposed by Käthchen's statements and her general lack of questioning or concern for knowledge. She is the one others attempt to understand, the one who represents an incomprehensible otherness beyond the judges' sensible grasps (a *sonderbare[s] Wesen*). Whereas the judges, representatives of enlightenment understanding, require information, Käthchen holds back information. When the Graf is given control over the questioning and finally manages to elicit some semblance of information from Käthchen, she can offer only vacuous explanations that elude concrete signification. The main question the court and the Graf demand Käthchen clarify is what caused her to leave her father and follow the Graf: "Was ists, mit einem Wort, mir rund gesagt, / Das dich aus deines Vaters Hause trieb? / Was fesselt dich an meine Schritte an? (444). Yet all Käthchen can answer in response to this central enigma, which defines her character and her actions is: "ich weiß es nicht" (444). After the Graf fails to get Käthchen to reveal some indication of her mysterious behavior, the questions eventually stray away from analyzing her blind devotion to the Graf. And what Käthchen does reveal not only does not resolve the mystery, but also surprises and confuses Käthchen's judges and the Graf:

> DER GRAF VOM STRAHL. Was will ich wissen?
> KÄTHCHEN. Was du willst wissen?
> DER GRAF VOM STRAHL. Heraus damit! was stockst du?
> Ich nahm, und hezte dich, und küßte dich,
> Und schlug den Arm dir —?
> KÄTHCHEN. Nein, mein hoher Herr.
> DER GRAF VOM STRAHL.
> Was sonst?
> KÄTHCHEN. Du stießest mich mit Füßen von dir.
> DER GRAF VOM STRAHL.
> Mit Füßen? nein! Das tu ich keinem Hund.

> Warum? Weshalb? Was hattst du mir getan?
> KÄTHCHEN. Weil ich dem Vater, der voll Huld und Güte,
> Gekommen war, mit Pferden, mich zu holen,
> Den Rücken, voller Schrecken, wendete,
> Und mit der Bitte, mich vor ihm zu schützen,
> Im Staub vor dir bewußtlos nieder sank.
> DER GRAF VOM STRAHL.
> Da hätt ich dich mit Füßen weggestoßen?
> KÄTHCHEN. Ja, mein verehrter Herr.
> DER GRAF VOM STRAHL. Ei, Possen, was!
> Das war nur Schelmerei, des Vaters wegen.
> Du bliebst doch nach wie vor im Schloß zu Strahl.
> KÄTHCHEN. Nein, mein verehrter Herr.
> DER GRAF VOM STRAHL. Nicht? Wo auch sonst? (449–50)

Instead of answering the question that began this inquisition, Käthchen manages to avoid an answer, forcing the Graf to pursue other questions irrelevant to the question about Käthchen's devotion. The paradoxical result is a confused Graf, who finds himself being led to conclusions and revelations he does not remember or understand. In other words, Käthchen, functioning as a cipher for a pure concept, forces the Graf to accept a conclusion that shares no relation to the question or investigation with which he began; his final line of questioning, although freeing him,[10] brings him no closer to conceptually grasping Käthchen's ineffable, a priori existence. In fact, his questions force him to contemplate not Käthchen's actions, essence, or meaning, but rather himself. His investigation of Käthchen comes back to reflect himself.

As a result of the Graf's egocentric questioning, Käthchen physically disappears. After the Graf's failed investigation of Käthchen's enigmatic behavior, Käthchen promises to obey the Graf and then suddenly faints. It is as if her promise to obey the Graf's wishes actually occludes her own physical presence: "KÄTHCHEN. Was willst du? Sprich. / DER GRAF VOM STRAHL. Verfolg mich nicht. Geh nach Heilbronn zurück. — Willst du das tun? / KÄTHCHEN. Ich hab es dir *versprochen. Sie fällt in Ohnmacht*" (my emphasis, 452). Käthchen's promise, *Versprechen,* contradicts her otherwise incompatible relationship with language, the ineffable essence the Graf attributes to her in his monologue in the first scene of the second act. However, Käthchen's linguistic promise is an error, a mis-reflection of the Graf's own desire. The Graf's desire that Käthchen return to Heilbronn is presented rhetorically as if it were her desire as well (*willst du das tun*?). Duden defines *Versprechen* as a promise; its etymology (*versprechen*) conveys a misrepresentation other than what one had hoped to convey. Käthchen's message does not convey her wish; it is merely the Graf's own words mis-conveyed through her mouth. She utters a promise, a linguistic representation of the Graf's desire—his will—and she literally faints; mentally she disappears. Textually Käthchen's fainting corresponds to her disappearance from the scene. It is as if her physical body has disappeared along with her mental faculties. No stage directions indicate what happens to the body, nor do any characters refer to her for the remainder of the scene. Textually, physically, and mentally Käthchen is dissolved by a mis-conveyed linguistic promise.

During the first act, Käthchen's image as an a priori concept is complicated by the fact she is being represented. She is physically present during much of the act, and others give Käthchen a sensible veneer through their own perceptions and descriptions as they attempt to represent her linguistically. However, this veneer is more a mirror than an outline of Käthchen's own essence. Each linguistic representation of Käthchen not only reflects those who attempt to define her, but her own language reflects an other's language, as illustrated with *versprechen*. Even though others may try to capture, name, and define Käthchen linguistically—as Theobald, the judges, and the Graf all attempt—her a priori status repeatedly thwarts complete linguistic definition.

This is why the Graf later finds himself lamenting the fact he *cannot* linguistically posses Käthchen and, with her, a "pure" aesthetic. Käthchen's essence is beyond his linguistic grasps: "wie nenn ich dich?" (454). Like her prepubescent name, *das* Käthchen, she is literally an *infans*—a child without language. Because the Graf cannot define Käthchen linguistically and posit (*setzt*) her within language (*Satz,* a tangible object or *Begriff*), he is unable to use her as a reflective means for his own self-definition as a subject. Therefore, the Graf searches for a new art, comprised of every language on earth that could transform Käthchen's linguistically prepubescent dream essence into a possessable physical being, a woman: "Du Schönere, als ich singen kann, ich will *eine eigene Kunst erfinden,* und dich weinen [. . .].

Doch wenn ich jemals ein *Weib* finde, Käthchen, *dir gleich*: so will ich die Länder durchreisen, und die Sprachen der Welt lernen, und Gott preisen in jeder Zunge, die geredet wird" (my emphasis, 454–5). The Graf desires a similar (*gleich*) substitution, a fusion of art and woman, to complete Käthchen's aesthetic transformation into the physical. What the Graf wishes to find is an aesthetic, sensible representation of Käthchen's a priori supersensible conceptuality, a *negative Darstellung*—he wants *Poesie*. And in opposition to Käthchen's childlike (*infans*) ineffability, the sensible (if not sensual) substitution for and transcendence of Käthchen's dream-like essence is the mature physical *Weib*, Kunigunde.

The overtly physical Kunigunde is as different or "ungleich" from Käthchen as the definitions of the metaphysical and the physical. Kunigunde represents Käthchen's polemical opposite in every way. Whereas Käthchen belongs to the supersensible realm of dreams and ideas, Kunigunde despises dreams, calls them "Geschwätz"(470), and represents pure physicality and sensible aesthetic reproduction. She is compared to a painting or image, "dies wesenlose Bild" (461); a mosaic creation, "eine mosaische Arbeit" (520). Whereas little mention is made about Käthchen's outward aesthetic appearance, reference to Kunigunde's physical appearance appears repeatedly: "ihr kleines verwünschtes Gesicht" (457), "ihre falschen Zähne" (458), and "[. . .] Wangen hatt [sie] als wie unsre Lore" (463). Moreover, Käthchen rarely, if ever, appears worried about her outward appearance or displays a desire to beautify herself. In stark contrast, Kunigunde repeatedly gazes into mirrors: "sie [betrachtet] sich im Spiegel" (472); "sie [Kunigunde] stellte sich vor dem Spiegel" (483); and she often is busy putting on makeup, "sie setzt sich vor einer Toilette nieder" (469); "sie [Kunigunde] läßt sich . . . die Haare . . . zurecht legen" (469); and, finally, "Rosalie, bei der Toilette des Fräuleins beschäftigt" (521). The repeated emphasis on Kunigunde's outward appearance, an exaggerated superficiality, defines her representational status as an aesthetic construction, literally an artistic creation.

As an aesthetic reproduction, Kunigunde shares a relationship with language—written and spoken—that is impossible for Käthchen as an *infans*. This linguistic difference is introduced in the way each character first appears in the text. Käthchen appears with her eyes bound, stressing the visual problematic paramount in representing a priori concepts: "Käthchen mit *verbundenen Augen*, geführt von zwei Häschern" (my emphasis, 441). Yet Kunigunde's mouth is gagged, as if to lessen the effect of her linguistic persuasion: "FREIBURG. . . . Schauermann! hier ist ein *Knebel* losgegangen" (my emphasis, 460). Having been captured, bound and gagged, Kunigunde's loose gag incites Freiburg's sudden fear, signifying the danger Kunigunde is capable of evoking through language. And it appears Freiburg's fears are well founded. For it is through language that Kunigunde eventually manages to escape, and stimulates the argument between Freiburg and the Graf, resulting in Freiburg's near-fatal wound: "Und [Kunigunde] wimmert' und druckt' mir die Händ und blinzelte, und *sprach so vernehmlich,* wie ein kluger Hund: mach mich los, lieb Bübel, mach mich los! *daß ichs mit Augen hört und mit den Fingern verstand*" (my emphasis, 463). Unlike Käthchen, whose linguistic utterances result in confusion and ambiguity, Kunigunde's language, though hindered by her bound, imprisoned state, is completely clear and concise, *vernehmlich.* Moreover, Kunigunde's entire presence "speaks." The Köhlerjunge understands Kunigunde's language with almost every sense, his eyes, ears, and fingers.

Throughout the second act where Kunigunde replaces Käthchen as the object of the Graf's affections, Kunigunde's relationship to language thoroughly defines her character. Before the Graf physically meets Kunigunde, he receives a message that the Rheingraf has declared war on the Graf and his family in Kunigunde's name:

> FLAMMBERG. Der Rheingraf fordert, *im Namen* Fräulein Kunigundens von Thurneck, den Wiederkauf Eurer Herrschaft
> Stauffen; jener drei Städtlein und siebzehn Dörfer und Vorwerker,
> Eurem Vorfahren Otto, von Peter, dem ihrigen,
> unter *der besagten Klausel,* käuflich abgetreten; grade so, wie dies der
> Burggraf von Freiburg, und, in früheren Zeiten
> schon ihre Vettern, in *ihrem Namen* getan haben. (my emphasis, 456)

Whereas Käthchen is unnamable (*warum kann ich dich nicht mein nennen*), Kunigunde's "name" is the impetus for action, war, and contractual disputes; it is her defining feature, inciting men to carry out her requests. Already this passage hints at the real power in Kunigunde's affinity to language. Kunigunde uses documents, letters, and contracts as the medium of her representation. Here *die besagte Klausel,* a written document or pre-text, is substituted for Kunigunde's actual physical presence, and prepares readers for her introduction into the play's narrative. Later, while Kunigunde is busy putting on makeup, she anxiously asks her servant where her legal documents are, as if they hold as much self-defining importance as the mirror she gazes into: "KUNIGUNDE. *Nachdem sie sich im Spiegel betrachtet. . .* .Hast du mir alles dort zurecht gelegt, was ich dem Grafen zugedacht, Rosalie? *Urkunden, Briefe, Zeugnisse*?" (my emphasis, 472). The words *Zeugniss* and *Urkunde* both suggest a process of representing; indeed, *Urkunde* is related to the word *Erkenntnis,* meaning to recognize.[11] Therefore the documents appear to do much more than just function as a type of leitmotif for Kunigunde's character. Her documents actually "recognize" and constitute her subjectivity; they are a self-reflexive means for her self-definition. Kunigunde literally posits herself in language and is conversely posited by language, recognized by language. She becomes a cipher for language, a *Satz.*

In her mutually recognizing relationship with language, Kunigunde repeatedly draws her own self-certainty into question by her "desire" to "supercede" her limiting linguistic definition. Soon after she gathers her documents with Rosalie, she ironically uses them to forfeit her previous claims to the Graf's property: "die Dokumente sinds, den Streit betreffend, um eure Herrschaft Stauffen, die Papiere auf die ich meinen Anspruch gründete" (475). After both the Graf and his mother are unwilling to allow Kunigunde to forfeit her claim, Kunigunde tears up the documents, seemingly annulling all written proof of her claim: "Hier diese rasche Brust entscheidet so! *Sie zerreißt die Papiere und läßt sie fallen*" (476). Most importantly, it appears Kunigunde annuls not only her claim to the Graf's property, but also to herself, as she destroys the papers—the defining trait of her subjectivity. However, her dramatic decision is more than just contradictory; it is purposely deceptive.

Kunigunde appears to be functioning in accordance with the Romantic notion of aesthetic discourse, which is self-critical and deceptive. Schlegel's essay *Über die Unverständlichkeit* epitomizes the importance of deception, confusion and subsequent incomprehensibility to the Romantic program. By being seemingly contradictory and incomprehensible, Kunigunde's destruction of the documents enacts this Romantic deception. Two episodes foreshadow Kunigunde's deceptive destruction of the documents. The first takes place in the ninth scene of the second act, where Kunigunde's appearance is directly compared to Romantic clothing, a suit. The description of the suit as being partially completed or fragmentary recalls the unending nature of Romantic Poesie, and within such a context the suit functions as a metaphor for Romantic discourse: "Kunigunde, in einem *halb vollendeten, romantischen Anzuge* [. . .]" (my emphasis, 469). The text directly associates Kunigunde with Romantic imagery, imagery one simply dons and removes with the ease of a jacket. Importantly, her Romantic adornment is fragmentary (*halb vollendet*), and is hence comparable to Schlegel's definition of Romantic *Poesie*: "Die romantische Dichtart ist noch im Werden; ja das ist ihr eigentliches Wesen, daß sie ewig nur werden, nie *vollendet* sein kann" (my emphasis, F. Schlegel 183). In Romantic theory, this fragmentary aesthetic promotes confusion and deception. This confusion, deception, and fragmentation insures a continuous development by avoiding closure. The Romantics perceived each reading and interpretation as a means to try to create a continuation of the text as an ever-evolving, living aesthetic. Kunigunde becomes this fragmentary, living aesthetic.

The second episode represents Kunigunde's deceptive intent more directly than her "Romantic" appearance. Right before Kunigunde dramatically destroys the documents in front of the Graf, she and Rosalie discuss Kunigunde's intent to deceive and trap a bird. Significantly, in this conversation references to the Graf become confused with references to the bird:

> ROSALIE. Gewiß! Da ist die Spur. Was wars? Ein Zeisig?
> KUNIGUNDE. Ein Finkenhähnchen wars, das ich vergebens
> Den ganzen Morgen schon *herangelockt*.
> ROSALIE. Seht nur dies Federchen. Das ließ *er* stecken!
> KUNIGUNDE gedankenvoll.
> Gib mir doch —
> ROSALIE. Was, mein Fräulein? *die Papiere*?
> KUNIGUNDE lacht und schlägt sie.
> Schelmin! — Die Hirse will ich, die dort steht.
> Rosalie lacht, und geht und holt die Hirse
> (my emphasis, 472–3)

The literal object of Kunigunde's intended deception is a finch; however, Kunigunde and Rosalie metaphorically exchange the finch with the Graf within their discussion. The "*er*" Rosalie refers to is conspicuously ambiguous, and implies both the Graf, subtextually, and the finch, superficially, as objects of Kunigunde's deception. Rosalie's reply reveals this exchange when she mistakenly believes Kunigunde requests the documents (*die Papiere*?) and not the millet meant for the bird's deception. Although Kunigunde meant for Rosalie to give her the millet, Rosalie, with justification, mistakenly believes the deceptive trap is found within the papers. Like the millet, the papers signify Kunigunde's attempt to deceive, trap and completely negate the Graf and his written linguistic claims to the property, which defines his self-certainty. Thus, it is clear Kunigunde's use of written language functions both as a coercive power, inciting men to battle in her name, and as a deceptive tool with potentially deadly consequences.

Throughout the second act, Kunigunde shares a close relationship with spoken language, written language, and deceptive language. She is compared to a Romantic text; she functions contradictorily and deceptively as a Romantic text; and she is self-reflexive, recognizing herself in language and simultaneously being recognized by language. Kunigunde's hermeneutic importance in the text is her symbolic representation of Romantic language.

Kunigunde also shares a close relationship with philosophy. Her deceptive demeanor and serious playfulness with language—with possibly deadly consequences—suggests she is a cipher not just for any language or any sensible representation, but a cipher for *negative Darstellung*, a sensible representation of supersensible a priori ideas:

> *Negative Darstellung* forces the subject to think the supersensible—the idea—without actually producing an objective presentation of this idea. Thus, it presents nothing except the process—the striving or effort (*die Bestrebung*)—of *Darstellung* itself. It is self-presentation or *Selbstdarstellung* in the Romantic sense of the word, and it is no coincidence that the notion of "negativity" becomes constitutive for Idealism and Romanticism. (Helfer 45)

Kunigunde substitutes Käthchen's supersensible essence—an idea—with her own sensible representation; her linguistic struggle to usurp the Graf signifies her metaphorical striving to insert herself into the Graf's discourse of ownership, possession, and self-definition; and finally Kunigunde does force subjects to think. Freiburg compares Kunigunde to a philosophical topic of discussion and contemplation: "Ei, da will ich über sie philosophieren. Da will ich euch einen *metaphysischen Satz* über sie geben, wie Platon, und *meinen Satz* nachher erläutern, wie der lustige Diogenes getan" (my emphasis, 461). Freiburg's contemplation ultimately assures Kunigunde's insertion into the linguistic system as he defines her by means of a *Satz*. Language, here an entire philosophical tenet (*Satz*), is the medium through which Kunigunde is represented and, ironically, represents. She appears to be functioning much like Fichte's notion of the empirical "not-I," which an a priori "I" posits in order to define itself. Fichte's philosophy is grounded linguistically, where he uses the verb setzen to define the subject's process of self-positing: the result of which is a *Satz*.[12] Like Fichte's model, Kunigunde is represented by language (Freiburg's *Satz*), and she, in turn, represents or reflects Freiburg through a linguistic medium. This localized interplay between language and representation foreshadows the subtextual relationship between Käthchen and Kunigunde as a dynamic process of linguistic representation.

In the third act, the structural center of the play, Kunigunde and Käthchen share the stage for the first time, suggesting their joint appearance has thematic and structural, as well as aesthetic and philosophical significance. I have argued Käthchen functions like a pure concept, a Kantian idea. I have also stated Kunigunde symbolizes the physical, sensible reproduction of such a priori ideas as a figure akin to Kant's figure of *negative Darstellung*. Kunigunde represents a poetic figure deceptively powerful in opposition to Käthchen's metaphysical passivity. Their eventual unification on stage in the third scene subtextually presents a concretizing of the pure concept into a sensible representation. Or linguistically, the juxtaposition of Käthchen and Kunigunde united on stage creates a type of semiotic reflexivity, a linguistic unification of form and content. Käthchen's ineffable representation as the a priori ideal female image is signified through Kunigunde's a posteriori aesthetic appearance. In other words, Kunigunde becomes the signifier and Käthchen the signified, and together they form a sign, a textual system.

However, their unity in the third act is hardly collaborative and appears based more on mistakes or arbitrary circumstance than on purpose or will. Even though Käthchen assumes the subservient role as slave to her linguistic master, Kunigunde, Käthchen redirects the message of signification so drastically that she undermines Kunigunde's linguistic control. This linguistic interplay between Käthchen and Kunigunde begins with the inferno engulfing Kunigunde's entire castle. As the castle burns and is about to crumble, Kunigunde realizes she has left an important piece of information in the castle—a case containing the Graf's picture—and pleads for someone to retrieve it. Acting on Kunigunde's desire, Käthchen storms into the castle to retrieve the case and picture. However, Käthchen's action reflects the opposite of Kunigunde's original desire, her original signification:

> KUNIGUNDE *schwach.*
> Das Bild, das Ihr mir jüngst geschenkt, Graf Friedrich!
> Das Bild mit dem Futtral!
> DER GRAF VOM STRAHL. Was solls? Wo ists?
> KUNIGUNDE. Im Feu'r! Weh mir! Helft! Rettet! Es verbrennt.
> DER GRAF VOM STRAHL.
> Laßt, laßt! Habt Ihr mich selbst nicht, Teuerste?
> KUNIGUNDE.
> *Das Bild mit dem Futtral,* Herr Graf vom Strahl!
> Das Bild mit dem Futtral!
> KÄTHCHEN *tritt vor.* Wo liegts, wo stehts?
> *Sie gibt Schild und Lanze an Flammberg.*
> KUNIGUNDE.
> *Im Schreibtisch*! Hier, mein Goldkind, ist der *Schlüssel.*
> (my emphasis, 493)

In accordance with Kunigunde's affinity to aesthetic representation, she appears distraught about losing the Graf's picture, his image. Although the Graf explains to Kunigunde she has him himself, the real thing, Kunigunde appears more concerned about a reproduction of the Graf's image, his representation. Moreover, it is not just the image that concerns Kunigunde, but the case that contains the image; in other words it is the frame, the limits of his representation that is the cause of her concern. The case symbolizes language through the Graf's name, literally inscribed on the case: "DER GRAF VOM STRAHL. Nun, beim gerechten Gott, das muß ich sagen — ! — Ihr wolltet das Futtral? / KUNIGUNDE. Ja und nichts anders! *Ihr hattet Euren Namen drauf geschrieben*; Es war mir wert, ich hatts ihr eingeprägt" (my emphasis, 499). And where else but in her writing desk, a locus signifying her linguistic affinity to the written word, does she keep the

Graf's image and its linguistic frame? Arguably, this scene is the key (*Schlüssel*) to understanding Kunigunde's fixation with the Graf's written name, his linguistic representation. The Graf's name is an integral component of Kunigunde's production of language. Ironically, Käthchen fails to recover the case, and instead recovers only the picture—the signified of the case's linguistic representation. Käthchen's failure metaphorically dissects the Graf's signifier (*das Futteral* with the Graf's name inscribed on it) from his signified (*das Bild*) and ultimately fractures the linguistic totality of the Graf's subjectivity in the third act.

That the Graf's subjectivity is drawn into question in the third act is appropriate because the third act structurally reflects the aesthetic production of the text itself. The third act is the structural center of the play, and it thematically engages the theme suggested by the text's alternate title, *die Feuerprobe*. Metaphorically, the text's theme of fire destroys and levels polarities, and posits a Hegelian-like resolution, *Aufhebung*, of thesis (Käthchen) and antithesis (Kunigunde), forming a new synthesis, the text. And at the center of this fusion lies the Graf, both as a conceptual image (his picture) and as a linguistic representation of that concept (the case and the documents). In other words, the third scene presents a subtextual construction of the Graf as a linguistic text. In the text's mimicry of Romanticism the third act reflects the goal of Romantic *Poesie*: the subject defining himself through writing himself in *Poesie*. In his famous definition of *Poesie* in Athenaeum Fragment 116, Schlegel claims in the act of writing, an author writes himself, defines himself: "[. . .] Doch gibt es noch keine Form, die so dazu gemacht wäre, den Geist des Autors vollständig auszudrücken: so daß manche Künstler, die nur auch einen Roman schreiben wollten, von ungefähr sich selbst dargestellt haben" (Schlegel 182). Here a similar process of self-definition takes place. As in Romantic texts, women are the creative forces for this process of textual construction. Käthchen carries the Graf's image from a burning inferno, in effect preserving his, and the text's, imagery. Kunigunde is concerned with transforming his image into language, and, to do so, she imposes linguistic limits with the *Futteral* and more directly with the limits of the written legal word—property deeds. However, the Graf's self-definition appears compromised by fragmentation: during the fire his image (*Bild*) is divorced from its textual signifier (his name upon the *Futteral*). Thus, the anticipated hermeneutic key (*Schlüssel* [493]) to understanding the "central" importance of the text in the text's "central" act has been destroyed by Käthchen's and Kunigunde's inability to jointly create a complete aesthetic definition of the male subject. The key components of the text's own aesthetic, Kunigunde and Käthchen, fail to effectively represent, drawing the text's representational validity into question.

Käthchen and Kunigunde as Failed Representations of Femininity

The reason Käthchen and Kunigunde fail to construct an effective representation for the Graf's self- definition lies in the fact they are artificial representations of femininity. Each functions as an exaggerated aberration of masculine projections of ideal femininity. Käthchen represents the conceptual masculine ideal of the "ewig Weibliche,"[13] and Kunigunde is the physical manifestation of this ideal. What follows will illustrate how each female character contributes to undermining the definition of the male subject due to their inherent artificiality. Because each represents not a viable *feminine* "other," but rather a distorted inversion of a masculine projection, the Graf fails to obtain self-definition.

Representational validity is foremost undermined by Kunigunde's physical form, which is deceptive, artificial, unnatural, and fractured:

> FREIBURG. So will ich es dir sagen. Sie ist eine mosaische Arbeit, aus allen drei Reichen der Natur *zusammengesetzt*. Ihre Zähne gehören einem Mädchen aus München, ihre Haare sind aus Frankreich *verschrieben*, ihrer Wangen Gesundheit kommt aus den Bergwerken in Ungarn, und den Wuchs, den ihr an ihr bewundert, hat sie einem Hemde zu danken, das ihr der Schmied, aus schwedischem Eisen, *verfertigt* hat. – Hast du *verstanden*? (my emphasis, 520)

Kunigunde's image is a conglomeration of pieces, none of which is inherently her own. She is wholly manufactured—"zusammengesetzt" and "verfertigt" out of foreign incongruities—a complete homogenization of physical attributes, stemming from three realms of nature and four European countries. Importantly, Kunigunde is, for the second time, compared to a syntactic construction: she is *zusammengesetzt*. Previously, Freiburg defined Kunigunde as a *Satz*, a linguistic sentence and, more abstractly, a philosophical tenet. Essentially, Kunigunde's affinity to language is analogous to Fichte's linguistic subject, who posits (*setzt*) itself in language as a *Satz*. Through a similar linguistic *setzen*, Kunigunde's subject is again defined as language and a text. Yet Kunigunde's linguistic and textual veracity is questioned due to an implied fragmentary physique (*zusammengesetzt*). This fragmentary nature results in a linguistic error: *verschrieben*. In German the prefix "ver" is highly ambiguous and can often be interpreted as implying a mistake: "[Ver] drückt in Bildung mit Verben aus, dass eine Person etw. falsch, verkerhrt macht."[14] Therefore, "*Ver*fertigen" not only means constructed, but also implies an error may have occurred in Kunigunde's physical constitution, unveiling a potential flaw in her physical veracity. Moreover, her status as a viable linguistic medium is incurably flawed due to the fact she is "verschrieben."[15] Superficially, "verschreiben" means to order, yet it also means to make an error in writing; metaphorically she has been mis-written. Furthermore, because *verstanden* immediately follows *verschrieben* and *verfertigen*, the notion of "understanding" is also compromised. The alliteration of the three "ver-" prefixes creates an acoustical kinship that is carried into a semantic relationship: all three verbs, by referring to the three realms of nature from which Kunigunde is structured, graduate from a constructive error to a linguistic error, which finally culminates in cognitive confusion. Thus the question "hast du verstanden?" is intended to be taken ironically. As a linguistic text, Kunigunde is flawed, confused, and confusing.

Kunigunde's mis-written image criticizes many salient features central to early Romantic aesthetic theory. The most obvious of these is the Romantic notion of "Symphilosophie." Kunigunde's multifarious constitution, *eine mosaische Arbeit*, overly exaggerates the eclectic nature of Romantic *Symphilosophie*, which is comprised of various authors, genres, and an infinite number of interpretations. Moreover, Kunigunde's manufactured totality, which draws aesthetic influence from "three realms of nature," emphasizes her fragmented state. This aspect of Kunigunde's aesthetic reflects Athenaeum fragment 206, which argues fragments are simultaneously incomplete, independent, and fragmentary, yet also form a closed totality: "Ein Fragment muß *gleich einem kleinen Kunstwerke* von der umgebenden Welt ganz abgesondert und in sich selbst vollendet sein wie ein Igel" (my emphasis, Schlegel 197). Like the hedgehog in Schlegel's definition of the fragment, Kunigunde's "mosaic" construction is simultaneously fragmentary and appears as a totality. Additionally, Kunigunde is defined as an artwork (*dies wesenlose Bild* [461], *eine mosaische Arbeit* [520]), much like Schlegel's fragment (*gleich einem kleinen Kunstwerke*).

Elsewhere, Kunigunde's fixation with mirrors exaggerates the self-reflexive theories of Romanticism in which every text contains its own autocritical theory.[16] This theory of self-criticism is also played out through Kunigunde's parodic description as being dressed in "einem halb vollendenten romantischen Anzug" (468). The "halb vollendet" again presents an exaggerated critique of Romanticism's predilection for fragments and alludes to the Romantics' use of *Unendlichkeit* as a means to avoid closure. However, the sharpest critique is found within the "Anzug" itself. This article of clothing—one which is literally pulled on and over the skin like a mask (*Anzug* is derived from the verb *anziehen*, which means to pull on)—suggests her aesthetic appearance is likewise "pulled on." This implies Kunigunde's representation is trite and easily donned or removed. Like her makeup, hair, teeth, physique, and cheeks, Kunigunde represents a superficial, almost rouge-like, application of Romantic clichés.

Like her fragmented and artificial physique that calls into question Romantic aesthetic theories through parodic exaggeration, Kunigunde's gender also critiques the Romantic female image as a vehicle for male self-definition. Her gender is arguably as artificial as her aesthetic physique, which presents a conspicuous problem for the Graf's self-definition:

> In Romantic theory the Fichtean self-positing subject defines itself via poesy *as* poesy. The woman as childbearer, however, is the true source of Romantic poesy. This creates a profound identity crisis for the man: the self-positing male subject cannot define himself fully except by somehow becoming a "woman" so that he, too, can "give birth" to Romantic poesy, and hence to himself as a self-positing subject. (Helfer 151)

Kleist's text mimics this theme of the Romantic self-reflecting subject. Although his self-definition via a woman is not as explicit as Julius' self-definition via Lucinde in Schlegel's *Lucinde* or Heinrich's self-definition via Mathilde in Novalis' *Heinrich von Ofterdingen*, the Graf also requires a female counterpart for his self-definition, for his life. Without the prospect of a "suitable" female (*das fähig wäre, ihn zu lieben* [469]), the Graf falls deathly ill. Yet when he glimpses this perfect woman through the delirium of his illness, he quickly recovers: "Geh, Mutter geh, und laß nun in allen Kirchen für mich beten: denn nun wünsch ich zu leben" (471). Moreover, his ideal woman leads to a heightened aesthetic awareness. He becomes a storyteller, a poet of sorts: "Ach, und erzählte, und fand kein Ende zu erzählen" (471). Kunigunde is, it seems, the reflective substitute of this ideal woman the Graf saw in his fevered hallucinations: "Und nun meinst du, diese Kaisertochter sei ich?" (471). However, her status as a female is quickly drawn into question, effectively deferring the Graf's self-definition.

In Romantic theory, the male poet's self-defining "other" is predominantly a woman. To effect a successful self-definition, the male subject paradoxically strives to remove the "feminine" from the "other." Ultimately, the subject stares narcissistically at a male, at himself, and his self-definition becomes completely androcentric. This paradigm for self-definition is complicated by Kunigunde's questionable gender. Her gender is anything but fixed and is symbolized most pointedly by an exterior garb (*romantischer Anzug*), ironically a piece of clothing one can easily don and remove. In fact, all of Kunigunde's defining feminine traits are *exterior* props: her makeup, hair, teeth, and most importantly her clothing. The fact that none of these items are inherently her own, and that they *can* be removed, emphasizes her function as a parody of Romantic theories of self-definition. She is overly prepared to be "stripped" of her feminine "otherness." Her "otherness" is nothing more than her "Romantic" (*romantisch*) clothing, a simple exterior garb, draped over a concealed masculinity. When male subjects remove this trait of "otherness" in Kunigunde they are confronted with typically nonfeminine attributes; they are confronted with a male.

Two key scenes featuring Kunigunde in a naked or "ungeschminkt" (521) condition cast serious doubt upon her female sexuality. The first is the grotto scene, in which Käthchen mistakenly sees Kunigunde bathing: "Und nun, da mich das Bad erquickt, tret ich in jene größre Mitte scherzend ein, und denke du, du seists, die darin rauscht: und eben von dem Rand ins Becken steigend, Erblickt mein Aug -" (513). What Käthchen sees remains unmentioned in true Kleistean fashion; what frightened Käthchen can be assumed to be Kunigunde's naked appearance. Moreover, Käthchen's concern is not so much for herself, but rather for the Graf, suggesting that Kunigunde's abnormality will have dire consequences for the Graf and his impending marriage to Kunigunde: "Du mußt sogleich zum Grafen, Leonore, und von der ganzen Sach ihn unterrichten . . . .Durch mich kann er, durch mich, *enttäuscht* nicht werden" (my emphasis, 513) Käthchen is unable to reveal or literally "undeceive" the Graf and his image of Kunigunde. If Kunigunde's naked image constitutes an "Enttäuschung," then her artificial feminine adornment is logically a deception (*Täuschung*), leaving one to speculate she is not feminine. As Kunigunde emerges from the grotto, Käthchen yells: "*Es* kommt!" (my emphasis, 514), suggesting Kunigunde's physical gender is anything but feminine. Later the Graf himself catches a glimpse of Kunigunde undressed and without makeup. Before Kunigunde's servant Rosalie is able to lock the door, the Graf storms in, sees Kunigunde and asks "as if struck by lighting": "Wer war die unbekannte Dame . . . die, wie der Turm von Pisa, hier vorbeiging?"(521). Not only is Kunigunde unrecognizable to the Graf when undressed (*wer war die unbekannte Dame?*), but more importantly he compares her naked state to the leaning tower of Pisa (*wie der Turm von Pisa*). The description certainly conveys severe physical deformity, an architectural blunder trying to compensate for poor footing, an unstable "*natural*" foundation. Euphemistically, the Graf's statement could also be a direct reference to Kunigunde's genitalia. Employing the imagery evoked by the Freudian cliché, "sometimes a cigar is just a cigar," one might invert the cliché to read: "sometimes a tower is much more than just a tower." At the most, Kunigunde is nothing more than a male dressed in "feminine" attributes; s/he is a transsexual dressed up in the aesthetic of the carnavalesque. At the least, Kunigunde's gender is not readily ascertainable without her typical feminine adornment (*romantischen Anzug, gewöhnlichen Glanz*).

Freiburg reveals another aspect of Kunigunde's questionable sexuality when he states the Graf would turn into his own stone image when confronted with Kunigunde's "naked" appearance: "wenn ihre

Reize auf den Stühlen liege, . . . so könne er [der Graf] seine eigne Bildsäule werden und sich . . . aufstellen lassen" (520). When a male sees Kunigunde without her usual "feminine" adornment, he literally turns into his own stone image, an aesthetic representation of himself. The description not only indicates Kunigunde's Medusa-like ugliness without makeup, but also constitutes a self-critical parody of the male-oriented aesthetic in Romanticism that "relies on the male projecting himself onto the female."[17] Kunigunde, the female image the Graf uses to reflect himself, reflects not a true feminized aesthetic, but rather an autoerotic reflection of himself.

Perhaps this is why the Graf repeatedly finds himself in sexually ambiguous situations. His self-defining aesthetic[18] appears either as a self-effeminizing, autoerotic process or as a self-definition through homoerotic unions. In two important scenes the Graf's self-definition takes place within a context of writing, clearly portraying his self-definition as an aesthetic process synonymous with the production of a text. Significantly, in each case his gender and sexuality are drawn into question by homoerotic imagery and a queer subtext that thoroughly informs the very aesthetic process symbolizing his self-definition. For example, when the Graf arrives at his castle and attempts to lower Kunigunde from his horse,[19] he inadvertently cuts his hand, leaving an open wound—a crude metaphor of female sexuality:

> KUNIGUNDE [. . .] *Sie wendet sich zum Grafen.*
> Wie stehts mit Eurer linken Hand, Graf Friedrich?
> DER GRAF VOM STRAHL.
> Mit meiner Hand? mein Fräulein! Diese Frage,
> Ist empfindlicher als ihre Wunde!
> Der Sattel wars, sonst nichts, an dem ich mich
> Unachtsam stieß, Euch hier vom Pferde hebend.
> GRÄFIN. Ward sie verwundt? — Davon weiß ich nichts.
> KUNIGUNDE. Es fand sich, als wir dieses Schloß erreichten,
> Daß ihr, in hellen Tropfen, Blut entfloß. (473–4)

Metaphorically, the Graf's horse is a locus of phallic symbolism.[20] The "lifting" of Kunigunde from his horse suggests more took place than simply cutting his hand on the saddle. And it is clearly the Graf who is penetrated, and not Kunigunde. This penetration of the Graf causes his hand (a displaced metaphor for appropriating feminine voice in writing) to bleed, flow with fluidity. The wound metaphorically indicates the Graf's attempt to define himself through an aesthetic text is an exercise in self-effeminization. A similar textual "wound" occurs earlier when Theobald recounts the day he met the Graf: "Meister, schau her, spricht er [der Graf]: dem Pfalzgrafen, der eure Wälle niederreißen will, zieh ich entgegen; die Lust, ihn zu treffen, sprengt mir die Schienen; *nimm Eisen und Draht* . . . und heft sie mir wieder zusammen" (my emphasis, 435). When the Graf's armor bursts in his heightened lust to engage the Pfalzgraf in an erotically charged battle (*die Lust, ihn zu treffen, sprengt mir die Schienen*), Theobald, Käthchen's father, straightens his armor and seals the tear, imagery again consistent with the effeminate wound in the Graf's hand. The metaphorical importance of *Eisen und Draht* suggests the popular topos of sewing and thread as a metaphor for writing and the production of aesthetic texts,[21] indicating the Graf's tear is a textual tear, a textual effeminization of the Graf's aesthetic self-definition. Theobald's attempt to "straighten" (*einrenkt*) the Graf's metaphorical tear, suggests an attempt to realign his sexuality toward the masculine.

In his heterosexual relationship with Käthchen, whose textual image suggests a representation of "pure" femininity, the Graf's sexuality does momentarily appear resolved, and it seems a successful self-definition is imminent. In two key scenes Käthchen functions as an alternative to the Graf's predilection for same-sex self-definition. The first occurs when the Graf requests that a boy retrieve his "weapons" for him and Käthchen appears, much to his chagrin:

> DER GRAF VOM STRAHL. Mein Schwert! Mein Schild! meine Lanze. [. . .]
> KÄTHCHEN. *mit Schwert, Schild und Lanze.* Hier!
> DER GRAF VOM STRAHL *indem er das Schwert nimmt und es sich umgürtet.* Was willst du?
> KÄTHCHEN. *Ich bringe dir die Waffen.*
> DER GRAF VOM STRAHL. *Dich rief ich nicht*!
> KÄTHCHEN. Gottschalk rettet.
> DER GRAF VOM STRAHL. *Warum schickt er den Buben nicht*? — Du dringst dich schon wieder auf? (my emphasis, 491–2)

As is often the case with Kleist, *Waffen* imply more than just weapons; they have sexual connotations. Here, weapons, or the lack thereof, suggests Graf's masculinity is lacking, and he requires someone, an "other" to provide him with a self-defining certainty of his sexual orientation. Importantly, it is a boy whom the Graf seeks to provide him with "sword" and "lance." It is not a female, least of all Käthchen (*dich rief ich nicht*!), he perceives as being able to provide him with such sexual self-definition. The Graf does not desire Käthchen as his mutually recognizing "other"; rather the Graf prefers a male, *einen Buben*, to fulfill his self-reflexive self-definition. This introduction of Käthchen into the language of "weapons," sex, and homoeroticism interrupts the homoerotic reflexivity that has up until now consisted of ambiguously suggested transsexuals, men, and boys (*Buben*). Käthchen provides the Graf with his "weapons" and metaphorically restores his "manhood."

The second example of Käthchen's ability to restore the Graf's wayward sexuality occurs when Theobald arrives at the Graf's castle to take Käthchen home: "GRAF VOM STRAHL. [Ich] tröste ihn [Theobald] und führ, um ihm das Mädchen zu übergeben, in den Stall hinunter, wo sie [Käthchen] steht, und mir *eine Waffe von Rost säubert*" (my emphasis, 439). The Graf's "weapons" are "rusted," possibly from lack of use. The idea that Käthchen polishes away the blade's rust suggests she not only fornicates with the Graf, but that heterosexual commerce is responsible for restoring the blade's condition. Käthchen, as a sexually active woman, is presented as possessing the ability to heal—as her name, *Heilbronn*, suggests—and restore the Graf's sword, "straighten" his sexuality.

Superficially, Käthchen reflects a restorative "purity" that is contrasted to Kunigunde's "perverse" artificiality. For this reason, Käthchen repeatedly inspires critics like Ueding, Brown, and Mommsen to interpret Käthchen as a positive influence for the Graf's development, his *Bildung*. Certainly the text provides evidence to substantiate this reading: for example, when Käthchen discovers Kunigunde's naked "unnaturalness," the text presents Käthchen as a "pure" representation while unmasking Kunigunde as artificial and perverted:

> ROSALIE. Vergebt! — Fräulein Kunigunde ist in der Grotte.
> ELEONORE. Fräulein Kunigunde? — Wer gab euch den *Schlüssel*?
> ROSALIE. Den Schlüssel? — Die Grotte war offen.
> ELENORE. Habt ihr das Käthchen nicht darin gefunden?
> ROSALIE. Nein, mein Fräulein. *Keinen Menschen.*

ELEONORE. Ei, das Käthchen, so wahr ich lebe, ist drin!
ROSALIE. In der Grotte? Unmöglich!
ELEONORE. Wahrhaftig! In der Nebenkammern eine, die dunkel
und versteckt sind. — Sie war vorangegangen.
[. . .] — O Herr meines Lebens; da ist
sie schon! [. . .]
KÄTHCHEN. *zitternd*. Eleonore!
ELEONORE. Ei, Käthchen! Bist du schon im Bad gewesen?
Schaut, *wie das Mädchen funkelt, wie es glänzet!*
Dem Schwane gleich, der in die Brust geworfen,
Aus des Kristallsees blauen Fluten steigt!
(my emphasis, 511–12)

As her father, Theobald, described her in the first act, Käthchen again appears to belong to the supersensible realm of *invisible*, metaphysical concepts, for Rosalie says she saw no person, *keinen Menschen*. However, Käthchen was there, not readily perceived by empirical senses, but rather there as a preceding, "vorangehende," a priori concept. Käthchen's absolute quality as a "pure" a priori concept does, however, develop a sensible representation, equally as pure and absolute as her a priori status. Eleonore notices Käthchen emerging from the grotto and compares her with a swan, "dem Schwane gleich," emerging as if from a baptismal test of aesthetic purity. Käthchen emerges, reflecting "funkelnd und glänzend." She appears representationally "pure."

Käthchen's beaming reflection is reminiscent of the popular motif of representational purity in Romantic texts. Specifically, in Novalis' *Heinrich von Ofterdingen*, there is a similar test of representational purity with water. A male scribe submits a sheet of his writing to a divine-like woman, Sophie, who dips the writing into the water. When the writing is pure or true, it emerges, *glänzend*, just as Käthchen emerges from the grotto. In Novalis' text, fluid also constitutes a mirror that reflects truthfully, enabling the absolute definition of a subject.[22] And within Kleist's own works, water and the image of a swan as a representation of purity have been used before. In *Die Marquise von O . . .* the female title figure's persona is interchanged with the persona of a white swan. This swan gracefully glides around the waters, "*in-die-Brust-sich-werfen*," much as Käthchen emerges *in die Brust geworfen*. Moreover, her name, Thinka—much like Käthchen—is a diminutive of Katharina—meaning "die Reine." By evoking these intertexual images, the play seems to set up Käthchen as a representation of a pure aesthetic. However, in *Die Marquise von O . . .* the swan's aesthetic beauty, which is also intangible,[23] is a deceptive aesthetic, striving to subvert a masculine discourse. And much like the swan, Thinka, Käthchen's image as a pure representation is an illusion.

Ironically, a key (*Schlüssel*) introduces the hermeneutic importance of the scene, suggesting something of great interpretive value should follow. Yet the key also encourages readers not to accept Käthchen's "purity" as uncompromised, as hermetically sealed. The key deceptively creates the expectation for a wealth of interpretive value. Yet there is no need for such a key because the grotto is already open: "die Grotto war offen" (511). The key is a sham. In spite of all the interpretive anticipation this scene potentially offers, it appears there is no need for interpretive keys, or that the interpretation is, in fact, paradoxical. In the least, this scene is comprimised by a textual break-in. Moreover, Käthchen is responsible for leaving the door open; she set the hermeneutic "trap door."

The reason for Käthchen's failure as a signifier of pure femininity is that she represents a male's ideal image of femininity, rather than her own. The key to understanding Käthchen's inability to reflect a truly "feminine" image is first demonstrated in the third act, when she admits that she is destroyed, *vernichtet*, by her father (a patriarchal figure) who cuttingly places his words, backwardly reflected or inverted, *kreuzweise*, into her breast: " . . . du [Theobald] vernichtest mich! Du legst mir deine Worte kreuzweis, wie Messer, in die Brust!" (480). Later, when the Graf gains patriarchal possession, Käthchen comes to represent nothing more than the Graf's own image, his idealistic fantasy. Just as Kunigunde reflects a concealed masculine physiology beneath "feminine" adornment, so too does Käthchen reflect a masculine psychology behind her "feminine" imagery. The Graf admits: "Wenn ich mich umsehe, erblick ich zwei Dinge: meinen Schatten und sie" (437). Both his shadow and Käthchen's image are fused together within himself as he literally looks around himself, (*mich umsehe*). During the *Feuerprobe* scene Käthchen appropriately carries the Graf's picture, his image, as she becomes a mere medium for his reflection: "Käthchen tritt rasch, mit einer Papierrolle, durch ein großes Portal, das stehen geblieben ist" (497). Together Käthchen and the Graf's picture (*Papierrolle*) stand framed in the opening of a gate, emphasizing their mutual reflection. As Käthchen reveals her dream to the Graf, he recalls looking into Käthchen's face as a reflection of his own: " . . . als ich jetzt, dein Kinn erhob, ins *Antlitz* dir zu schauen . . . da kam die unselige Mariane . . ." (my emphasis, 509). "Antlitz" means face, but etymologically denotes an "Entgegenblickende"[24] or a reflector, a mirror. Käthchen's "Antlitz" reflects an image of himself. And in a manner consistent with Romantic reflexivity, the Graf considers himself "doubled" after discovering Käthchen's dream is exactly like his: "Nun steht mir bei, ihr Götter: ich bin *doppelt*! Ein Geist bin ich und wandele zur Nacht!" (my emphasis, 509). Käthchen and her dream represent a direct (re)presentation of the Graf and his dream. And it is not she who is doubled, but rather the Graf, indicating Käthchen reflects his image: she becomes he. Thus, the notion Käthchen represents an ability to realign the Graf's sexuality and restore his masculinity through her own essence, which the text superficially posits as "pure," is undermined by the fact Käthchen does not reflect a distinctly different "Not-I" from the Graf's I. It appears sex with Käthchen, as the previous "rusted" blade scene suggests, is nothing more than a metaphorical masturbatory act of autoerotic self-indulgence.

Understanding how Käthchen functions not as a separate physical "other," but rather as a mirror image of the Graf himself, helps clarify why the Graf's other attempts to sexually unite with Käthchen also fail. At the beginning of the play, right after the court proceedings with the *Vehmgericht*; the Graf imagines Käthchen in an overtly sexual light, comparing her to an oiled-down bride fit for a Persian king: "Du, deren junge *Seele*, als sie heut nackt vor mir stand, von wollüstiger Schönheit gänzlich *triefte*, wie die mit *Ölen* gesalbte Braut eines Perserkönigs, wenn sie, auf alle Teppiche *niederregnend*, in sein Gemach geführt wird!" (my emphasis, 454). Clearly Käthchen resides within his imaginative fantasy as the Graf identifies her as a "Seele," a physically absent being. She is not a "real" physical being, but rather an idea, his ideal image of femininity. The metaphorical language is also erotically charged with fluid imagery (*gänzlich triefte, mit Ölen gesalbte Braut, and auf alle Teppiche niederregnend*). This imagery symbolizes the mutual transfer of fluids between partners during sex. More importantly, the imagery informs Käthchen with a highly romanticized image of the Romantic female and her affinity to fluidity—a metaphor for her aesthetic language.[25] Moreover, it is language, *Poesie*, the Graf wishes to gain from his union with Käthchen or her like substitute: "Doch wenn ich jemals ein Weib finde, Käthchen, dir gleich: so will ich die Länder durchreisen, und die Sprachen der Welt lernen, und Gott preisen in jeder Zunge, die geredet wird" (455).[26] The Graf associates Käthchen's fluid imagery with a Romantic-like aesthetic potential for truthful self-definition, a definition he mistakenly anticipates Käthchen can provide. However, she does not provide aesthetic potential nor a means for self-definition. Käthchen ironically reflects images from the Graf's own patriarchal lineage. At the scene's conclusion, the Graf gazes at a graphic history of male reflection, and he substitutes Käthchen's image with pictures of his forefathers, framing himself in an androcentric hall of patriarchal self-reflexivity:

> Sie fließen dem Käthchen von Heilbronn! — — — Warum verlaßt eure goldnen Rahmen, ihr Bilder meiner geharnischten Väter, die meinen Rüstsaal bevölkern, und tretet, in unruhiger Versammlung, hier um mich herum, eure ehrwürdigen Locken schüttelnd? Nein, nein, nein! Zum Weibe, wenn ich sie gleich liebe, begehr ich sie nicht; *eurem stolzen Reigen will ich mich anschließen*. (my emphasis, 454).

The first sentence is divided by a typographical specular reflection: the three dashes (— — —) function like a framed mirror, where Käthchen's reflection abruptly gives way to masculine imagery. Literally, the *geharnischten Väter* step out of the frame the three dashes symbolize; they step out of Käthchen's mirror image. Instead of a feminine "other," a graphic history of patriarchy constitutes the Graf's subjectivity. Moreover, the Graf strives to join this graphic representation of patriarchy, and seemingly intertwines the seductive idea of Käthchen with his patriarchal past: "eurem stolzen Reigen will ich mich anschließen" (454).[27] Again, Käthchen remains nothing more than a masculine image, an a priori idea of femininity that the Graf fails to transform into reality.

The Graf's last attempt to unite with Käthchen is couched as an aesthetic production. In other words, the Graf tries to aestheticize Käthchen's a priori idea into a sensible *Darstellung*, a sensual woman. To do this the Graf constructs a mini-play, an aesthetic text, in which Käthchen must play a fictional role: "Nun sann ich mir ein Fest aus, süßes Mädchen, / Zu welchem du die Göttin *spielen* sollst. / [. . .] Gern möcht ich daß du alle Fraun im Schloß, / Selbst noch die Kunigunde *überstrahlst* —" (529). The Graf wants Käthchen's imaginary aesthetic to surpass Kunigunde's real physical presence: "selbst noch die Kunigunde [zu] überstrahl[en]" (529). He wants his supersensible idea, his ideal feminine image (*die Göttin*), to be realized in a manner not only beyond metaphysical limits, but also beyond the physical artificiality represented by Kunigunde's deceptive *Darstellung*: he desires a "true" nondeceptive sensible representation. He wants a "true" *Darstellung* of a *Darstellung*, much like Novalis' fluid mirror that reflects truly. Through this aesthetic fiction, the Graf envisions consummating a marriage to a divine-like Käthchen and completing his self-definition as god.

Significantly, it is at this point where "das Käthchen" becomes "die Katharina," (meaning "the pure"): a (sexually) mature and linguistically feminine (*die* Katharina) woman. Käthchen's transcendence appears complete. However, just when the Graf is about to possess Käthchen, name her his and symbolically enter into a self-reflexive supersensible union that surpasses Kunigunde's physical artificiality, Käthchen sinks: "sie sinkt" (531). Käthchen's ability to provide the Graf with a feminized aesthetic, a linguistic competence to "speak the languages of the world," and an aesthetic means for his truthful self-definition, fails. For it appears Käthchen is self-consumed by a Romantic topos, the metaphor of fluid language. As her linguistic name, *Heilbronn*, suggests, Käthchen appears to be the ultimate fluid "source" for Romantic Poesie and self-definition. However, Käthchen's image, exaggerated by parody, extends beyond its limits, beyond metaphor, and into a literal definition where her linguistic import literally drowns her self. In the end, the Graf is left with nothing but a pool of metaphorical water in which he reflects himself narcissistically.

Kleist calls Käthchen the "Kehrseite der Penthesilea, ihr andrer Pol, ein Wesen, das ebenso mächtig ist durch gänzliche Hingebung, als jene durch Handeln" (797), and he presents the possibility of "power" in an act of submission, "Hingebung." Whereas proactive aggressiveness is palpable in Penthesilea, the less apparent "power" of *Das Käthchen von Heilbronn* resides not in autonomy or dominance, but rather in a negative representation of acquiescence, a total absorption of imposed male imagery retreating completely within itself. Penthesilea literally devours Achilles, signifying her cannibalistic ingestion of the other in order to internalize its power, redirect its strength, and subvert those traditions, definitions, and customs that define and reestablish the cultural infrastructure of Achilles' paternalistic structure. Yet, rather than devouring patriarchy in a simply essentialist inversion of power structures, Käthchen's "Hingebung" can be read as a Hegelian-like act of self-dissolution, self-destruction, and self-negation. She acquiesces to male-oriented objectification and readily defines herself as "slave" not only to the Graf, her thematic master, but subtextually to Kunigunde, whose excessive verbiage and physical image as an exaggerated artistic fabrication become the symbolic structure for the text's linguistic limits. The metaphysical figure "Käthchen" is a slave to language, to linguistic signification. Yet through her self-imposed servitude, she ironically "supersedes" (*überstrahlt*) the patriarchal figure, the Graf vom *Strahl* and Kunigunde in that she, not the Graf nor Kunigunde, gains representative subjectivity by defining the text, *Das Käthchen von Heilbronn*.

Throughout the play both "female" figures are informed by male projections. Kunigunde becomes a physical *Mischung* of gender; Käthchen's ability to transcend the gender traps inherent in Kunigunde's physical aesthetic fails as well. Through this gender problematic, the play succeeds in drawing into question the integrity of traditionally-drawn lines of gender, and criticizes the essentialist theories of aesthetic production in Romanticism. In the end Käthchen's silent fall, "sie sinkt," metaphorically describes the actual aesthetic potential of the text, *Das Käthchen von Heilbronn*, as sinking—not transcending—its own aesthetic and gendered limitations. Through this metaphorical sinking, Kleist's play as an imitation of Romanticism sinks itself, as well as the male-oriented theories of Romanticism.

Chapter IV

Penthesilea: Inscribing the Body with Self-Definition

Would Kleist's *Penthesilea* be a hit syndicated drama for the USA Network? *Xena, Sheena, Buffy the Vampire Slayer,* and *Cleopatra* all represent the latest pop-culture explosion of warrior women. The twenty-first century seems ready, even anxious, to allocate more space within mass media for the aggressive, self-assertive woman. What would have been offensive to the *Leave-It-To-Beaver* audience of television's budding generation of baby boomers, and moral heresy in 1808, has today become commonplace, accepted, and possibly even encouraged. Does this mean the end of the "glass ceiling"? Could this be an expression of unprecedented gender equality being achieved in western pop culture? *Xena's* producer, Steve Rosberg, claims his number one hit series is "groundbreaking in redefining the female action hero."[1] Has Western culture truly progressed away from the Rousseauean-influenced culture of the early nineteenth century that turned its head in disgust from Kleist's *Penthesilea,* deriding the play and its aggressive woman warrior as "unnatural"[2] and "repulsive"? [3] If today's warrior women are more than soft-porn projections of a displaced masculine fantasy of the exotic, then maybe noble suppositions like Rosberg's are valid. However, I have my doubts.

Nonetheless, I cannot help but think Kleist's *Penthesilea* would have evoked a decidedly different reception today than it did in 1808. This does not mean *Penthesilea* is an aesthetic feminist manifesto unable to be appreciated until today. Rather, I would suggest today's sensibilities for representations of violence—whether issuing from women or men—are slightly more calloused. Today it seems a sword-wielding archeress with an unrelenting carnivorous appetite for flesh represents little more controversy than Ted Nugent's ultimate female fantasy. What is undeniable is *Penthesilea* appeals to a twenty-first-century audience and critic. The appeal is symptomatic of the text's ability to evoke a wide spectrum of emotional dichotomies, readily assimilated into multiple interpretive analyses. Whereas a MLA bibliography search for *Der zerbrochne Krug* results in forty-two records; *Der Prinz Friedrich von Homburg* thirty-five records; *Amphitryon* twenty-six records; *Die Hermannschlacht* twenty-five records; *Das Käthchen von Heilbronn* twelve records; *Die Familie Schroffenstein* ten records; and *Die Familie Ghonorez* two records; *Penthesilea* results in eighty-eight records. That is more than twice *Der zerbrochne Krug's* forty-two. Clearly, *Penthesilea* evokes more critical attention than Kleist's other plays, and I would argue this is due to the play's inexhaustible content, which resists definitive hermeneutic understanding.

Contemporary critics frequently focus on Kleist's personal comments about *Penthesilea* and *Das Käthchen von Heilbronn* as a basis for interpreting both plays as a single, interrelated text.[4] Two statements in particular have been taken to be programmatic descriptions of the aesthetic theories enacted in both texts. The first is Kleist's suggestion his two plays belong together like the plus and negative in algebra: "sie gehören ja wie das + und - der Algebra zusammen" (818).[5] The second is his description of *Das Käthchen von Heilbronn* as an inversion of *Penthesilea,* her polar opposite: "Jetzt bin ich nur neugierig, was Sie zu dem Käthchen von Heilbronn sagen werden, denn das ist die Kehrseite der Penthesilea, ihr andrer Pol, ein Wesen, das ebenso mächtig ist durch gänzliche Hingebung, als jene durch Handeln" (797). To take Kleist's word at face value and interpret both texts together, as if their relationship reveals some algebraic equation for Kleistean hermeneutics, is indeed tempting. However, it is not wise to trust the word of an author known for sardonic irony and self-scrutinizing parodies.[6] Jost Hermand argues Kleist's personal opinions about the play provide little interpretive value and provide, at best, ambiguous interpretations: "Doch diese Zeugnisse sind spärlich und obendrein so kryptisch, daß sich aus ihnen die wahre Schreibintention dieses Stücks nicht wirklich erschließen läßt" (34). Certainly, Kleist's personal statements provide avenues for insightful interpretations, but these clues should not limit the methodology for interpretation, demanding a simultaneous examination of both texts.[7] My analysis of *Penthesilea* extends beyond the relationship between *Penthesilea* and *Das Käthchen von Heilbronn* and examines *Penthesilea* as an individual text struggling to secure its own space within the masculine discourse of classical aesthetics.

The play that utterly appalled Goethe and other critics around 1808 and continues to baffle, shock, and inspire scholars today rewrites the classical tale of Achilles and the Amazon warrior Penthesilea. Like Homer's *Iliad,* which consists of twenty-four books, Kleist's play takes place at breakneck pace with twenty-four scenes.[8] Even though the structure of Kleist's play is reminiscent of Homer's *Iliad,* the plot is reversed: Penthesilea kills Achilles. The play seems designed to purposely invert every tradition central to western civilization, mythology, culture, and especially aesthetics—an aesthetics modeled after classical antiquity. The mode of this cultural inversion is represented by Penthesilea, who symbolizes an antipatriarchal discourse, intent on usurping the foundations of western knowledge. The manner in which she achieves this cultural and epistemological disruption is through her refusal to comply to a dialectic of simple oppositions. She presents a "third" concept that is neither thesis, antithesis, nor synthesis.

Her incompatibility within the conceptual structure of western knowledge is immediately stressed in the play's beginning. The play starts *in medias res* as Penthesilea and her Amazons have interrupted the battle between the Greeks and the Trojans. Forced to combat this new "third" element, the Greeks turn their attention away from Ilium and towards the Amazons. The battle takes place off stage, yet is reported teichoscopically. During their first battle with the Amazons, Achilles only narrowly escapes capture by Penthesilea and her Amazon warriors through his cunning intellect: he skillfully maneuvers his chariot in an arc, luring Penthesilea to run her chariot in a faster, straighter path. As Achilles had hoped, Penthesilea overshoots him in her fevered attempt to catch him, and crashes violently. After Achilles safely returns to the Greek camp, Odysseus, Diomedes, and

Antilochus beg him to forget the battle with the Amazons and renew his efforts to overcome the Trojans. However, they are unable to dissuade Achilles from his heightened lust to subjugate Penthesilea. Likewise, Penthesilea's Amazon counsel, Prothoe, is unable to subdue her and her battle lust, and in the next battle, Achilles and Penthesilea resume the tireless struggle to subjugate each other. Achilles knocks Penthesilea to the ground and almost succeeds in carrying her away, but, Prothoe, Penthesilea's closest confidante, rescues her from Achilles' arms. Again a decisive victory remains unachieved, even though Achilles has grievously wounded Penthesilea.

Having gained the upper hand in his latest battle, Achilles and the Greeks storm the Amazon camp. Surprisingly, Achilles approaches the Amazon defenses without armor. The Amazons are unable to shoot Achilles due to Penthesilea's own decree that no Amazon shall touch or harm Achilles except herself. Under the umbrella of Penthesilea's protection, Achilles successfully infiltrates the Amazon camp unopposed. Unable and possibly unwilling to run, Penthesilea chooses not to retreat and instead stays behind with a handful of loyal Amazons, including Prothoe. As Achilles approaches, and his victory appears imminent, Penthesilea faints. Prothoe fears Achilles' victory will push Penthesilea into madness once she awakens. She therefore convinces Achilles to lie, to deceive Penthesilea into believing she is the victor and he her captive. The ruse works. Believing she did in fact capture Achilles, Penthesilea proudly reveals the Amazon customs and rules for seeking out worthy warriors for propagating their population, and informs Achilles of her plan to return to Themiscyra and Diana's temple, where they shall consummate their love at the festival of roses. However, the deception lasts only a moment, for soon the Amazons return to recapture the camp and rescue Penthesilea. Penthesilea quickly learns her capture of Achilles was only an illusion, and she becomes incensed. Now all she needs is an invitation to indulge her rage, and that is exactly what she gets.

Achilles sends a messenger to Penthesilea requesting her to meet him face to face on the battlefield. Believing Penthesilea can only choose a man who surrenders to her in battle, Achilles devises a plan to surrender in order to become a worthy lover for her. However, his feigned humility is only part of his scheme to drag Penthesilea back to

Greece after a month-long orgy at the festival of roses. Achilles comes alone and unarmed, thinking she will gladly accept his humble surrender. However, Penthesilea misreads Achilles' invitation for battle. Fully enraged and feeling betrayed, she prepares for a battle to the death, complete with dogs, elephants, and sickled chariots. Outnumbered, Achilles soon finds himself in a helpless situation. He desperately calls for his friends' aid, but he is beyond help. Discovering Achilles hiding behind a tree, Penthesilea forcefully draws her bow and looses an arrow into Achilles' throat. He crashes to the ground, mortally wounded. Still beset with a voracious rage, Penthesilea and her dogs pounce on Achilles, cannibalizing and ripping his flesh to pieces. Afterwards, Penthesilea falls into a state of delirium. She eventually awakens, and recognizes the extent of her deed. She laments her inability to harness the power of her hasty lip (*Ich bin der raschen Lippe nicht Herr* [234]) and to discern the difference between the acoustically similar *Bisse* and *Küsse*. Penthesilea states she only meant to kiss Achilles. Overcome with guilt and sorrow, Penthesilea forges from the depths of her deepest sorrow a dagger of grief and plunges it into her breast, killing herself. Both heroes die a macabre death.

In every way, *Penthesilea* seems destined to resolve in extremes. From metaphors of raging torrents, hurricane winds, immense precipices and abysses, to the literal killing of the dead (*wer mir den Toten tötete, frag ich* [423]), *Penthesilea* presents a Dionysian vision of theater that anticipates Nietztsche's *Geburt der Tragödie aus dem Geiste der Musik* by 64 years. Kleist's text also presents a theory of self-definition akin to Hegel's "master-slave dialectic." Penthesilea's and Achilles' relentless desire to inscribe self-definition upon the "other" results in their mutual death. *Penthesilea* performs a theory of self-definition that extends beyond the philosophical limitations of transcendental Idealism, resulting in a text Kleist's contemporaries found completely unpalatable to their Idealist sensibilities and incompatible with their theories of self-definition.

My reading of *Penthesilea* analyzes this extreme definition of the subject. Specifically, I will focus on the paradoxical problem of engendering the female subject within masculine discourse. I argue the text's discourse is riddled with the linguistic confusion of metaphor and the literal. Penthesilea as subject reflects this linguistic confusion as the text's masculine discourse attempts to define and understand her disruptive interference. On the one side, Penthesilea's physical body becomes the parchment for masculine discourse, which inscribes its dominance on her through literal physical scars, cuts, and wounds. On the other side, Achilles' attempt to literally inscribe and define Penthesilea's physical being through physical confrontations ironically effects a metaphorical definition of Penthesilea. Through their confrontation, Penthesilea achieves linguistic and authorial control of the text. She becomes a disruptive metaphorical presence that usurps the patriarchal order of reason, history, and myth, and removes the philosophical boundary or "distance"[9] between literal and metaphorical (aesthetic) language. Her presence threatens to undo the aesthetic and philosophical figure of *Darstellung* itself. She becomes a literal agent of total physical destruction, and, in Hegelian terms, completely negates her defining "other" (Achilles). She leaves herself no reflecting "other" to provide a *Darstellung*, a self-definition. Ironically, she is indeed defined. Only her self-definition is incomplete and fractured. Penthesilea creates a space between antipatriarchal and patriarchal discourses. In this space an interplay of competing dichotomies creates an ironic, deconstructive mode of language that perpetually defers absolute textual closure and epistemological stability.

I begin my analysis by tracing Kleist's reception among his peers and with critics today. The intent of my summary of Kleist criticism is to indicate how Kleist's initial negative reception reflects his desire to incense the establishment and to call their theories into question, a thesis many critics (Mommsen, Agee, Lange, Jacobs, Paglia) advance today. My own interpretation is in part developed vis-à-vis a critical overview of this 20th-century literature. Whereas most critics focus on Penthesilea as an active figure, destroying Achilles' self-definition, I suggest Penthesilea is as much a passive figure as she is an aggressive figure: she endures a patriarchy's inscription of identity as much as she inscribes an identity on herself and Achilles. The second half of the chapter looks at Penthesilea's engenderment as a subject of patriarchal discourse. Even though Achilles and Penthesilea struggle for self-definition through their confrontations, in my opinion only Penthesilea—not Achilles—achieves self-definition. The reason for this successful self-definition is Penthesilea's paradoxical relationship with language: she is both an agent of language and a pawn or subject of language. Ultimately, Penthesilea is recognized by the text's language as a living metaphor, whereas Achilles textually disappears.

Penthesilea's Reception and Criticism

Penthesilea's initial reception was largely negative. When the text appeared publicly for the first time—as a fragment in Kleist's journal *Phöbus* in January, 1808, and as a complete text in Cotta's edition in Fall, 1808—several reviews condemned it as inartistic. The most acerbic criticism of Kleist's text and its artistic quality came from an article in the *Nordische Miszellen*: "Nach der Theorie der alten Ästhetiker erregt das Trauerspiel Furcht und Mitleid; an deren Stelle treten hier Entsetzen, Abscheu und Ekel" (*Lebensspuren* 252). Kleist is attacked for his failure to observe the "traditional" conventions of tragic theater, as well as for his crass treatment of the German language: "Die Sprache, unsere schöne Sprache, ist auf das Schnödeste gemißhandelt; unverdauerliche Härten, geschraubte Inversionen haben sie ganz unkenntlich gemacht" (*Lebensspuren* 253). Ironically, the position from which this critic launches his attack is precisely the position that Kleist targets and subverts: the literary establishment's propensity for clinging to traditions and canonical aesthetic judgments. The "twisted inversions" and "indigestible harshness" are intentional: Kleist wanted to make the literary establishment uncomfortable, if not give them a literal case of indigestion.

These early reviews of the play indicate Kleist did not exactly fit in with the literary establishment of his day. However, not all reviews were completely negative. The critics' mixed reviews reflect a confused reaction to Kleist's counter-aesthetic. Varnhagen and Körner largely praise the play, although both critics also mention a sense of misunderstanding and repulsion. Varnhagen himself documents his mixed reaction: "Stellen aus Kleists "Penthesilea" hab' ich beigelegt: ein Meisterwerk, gegen das ich früher (ich kannte aber auch nur ein Fragment) ganz verblendet war" (*Lebensspuren* 250). And Körner's positive impression is diminished by his statement that some parts of the play repulsed him: "Der Gleichartigkeit wegen lege ich die Penthesilea bei. Ich habe sie mit großem Interesse gelesen und mich an der poetischen Kunst gefreut, so sehr auch manches darin auf mich einen *widrigen* Eindruck macht" (my emphasis, *Lebensspuren* 250). In *Miszellen für die Neueste Weltkunde,* Kleist receives praise as a "developing Shakespeare": "Aber die Funken eines vielverheißenden Geistes leuchten überall auch in dieser Übung [*Penthesilea*]. Er kommt mir wie ein werdener Shakespeare vor" (*Lebensspuren* 254). However, this critic states the text's characterization of Penthesilea offends taste and art: "Er [Kleist] beleidigt den Geschmack und empört das Zartgefühl, wo er nur Entsetzen hervorbringen wollte. Das Ekelhafte ist niemals Objekt der schönen Kunst" (*Lebensspuren* 254). Johann Kaspar Manso identifies Kleist's harsh style as being incompatible with the Romantic notion of *Poesie*: "Insbesondere sind die dramatischen Arbeiten von Kleist . . . doch im ganzen höchst abenteuerlich. So etwas kann unsere Poesie unmöglich brauchen" (*Lebensspuren* 256). In fact, one critic suggested Kleist remains outside the Romantics' aesthetic campaign: "[. . .] Vielleicht zählt ihn [Kleist] das schreiende Heer der Romantik nicht zu ihren Kreuzzugsfahnen [. . .]" (*Lebensspuren* 253). If Kleist was an outsider to Romanticism, then he was surely an outsider to Classicism and repugnant to its major proponent, Goethe. Kleist's unorthodox style was too dismissive of traditional definitions of aesthetics, and of the entire notion of "good taste" (Chaouli 125) to allot him a space within either literary trend.

Without question, the literary establishment was defined by Goethe. Goethe's approbation brought writers literary prestige and favor. Kleist desperately sought Goethe's approval, but he never received it.[10] Adam Müller, Kleist's literary partner in *Phöbus,* identified Goethe as the one true judge for Kleist: "Kleist, tief bewegt durch Ihren [Goethe's] Tadel, will durch seine beiden Trauerspiele Penthesilea und Robert Guiskard *den einzigen Richter* gewinnen, auf dessen Urteil es ihm ankömmt" (my emphasis, *Lebensspuren* 169). Unfortunately for Kleist, Goethe's reception was consistently unfavorable. Goethe's initial reaction to *Penthesilea* was clearly negative, but relayed somewhat cordially: "Mit der Penthesilea kann ich mich noch nicht befreunden. Sie ist aus einem so wunderbaren Geschlecht und bewegt sich in einer so fremden Region, daß ich mir Zeit nehmen muß, mich in beide zu finden" (*Lebensspuren* 192). On second reading, Goethe drastically changed his tone and in no uncertain terms condemned the play as repulsive: "Beim Lesen seiner "Penthesilea" bin ich neulich gar übel weggekommen" (*Lebensspuren* 251).

Perhaps offending Goethe was Kleist's intent. After receiving less than admirable praise from Goethe for his earlier plays, *Der zerbrochne Krug* and *Amphitryon*, Kleist very possibly constructed *Penthesilea* to purposely anger critics, especially Goethe. In his translation of *Penthesilea*, Joel Agee suggests Kleist wrote the play not as an appeal, but rather as an attack on Goethe and his aesthetics: "But the greatest affront was the new play. It took up a number of themes that were dear to Goethe and turned them in a direction he could only find loathsome" (xix). Katharina Mommsen also reads *Penthesilea* within the context of Kleist's often combative relationship with Goethe. Unlike Agee, Mommsen argues Penthesilea is paradoxically both an attack on and an appeal to Goethe's own sense of poetic genius, a genius Kleist truly admired. Mommsen substantiates her argument by interpreting Penthesilea as an allegorical representation of Kleist's relationship with Goethe. By assigning Achilles and Penthesilea the roles of Goethe and Kleist respectively, she constructs a compelling biographical interpretation of the text:

> Mehr als im Fall des *Amphitryon* ist denn auch bei der *Penthesilea* Kleists Goetheerlebnis von der Forschung beachtet worden. Bedeutende Kleistkenner [Heinrich und Meyer-Benfey] haben das Verhältnis Penthesileas zu Achill grundsätzlich als Gleichnis von Kleists innerer Einstellung zu Goethe betrachtet. Die Konstellation der Hauptgestalten läßt diesen Bezug auf Goethe deutlicher erkennen als im *Amphitryon*. (41)

According to Mommsen, the play represents Kleist's attempt to gain Goethe's approval and, at the same time, surpass his literary "Ruhm." This dichotomy of love and hate is transposed onto Penthesilea's conflict with Achilles, a lover she can only win by defeating:

> Für Penthesilea gipfelt das ganze Leben und Streben in diesem einen Kampf, wie ja für Kleist das Ziel, Goethe für sich zu gewinnen, von totaler und existentieller Bedeutung war. Als wie schicksalhaft Kleist die Notwendigkeit empfand, daß er um Goethe zu werben habe, wobei dies Werben zugleich die Form des Kampfes, des Wettkampfes annehmen mußte, wird deutlich, wenn Penthesilea ihre Situation mit diesen Worten zusammenfaßt: "Ists meine Schuld, daß ich im Feld der Schlacht um sein Gefühl mich kämpfend muß bewerben?" (43)

To strengthen her biographical argument, Mommsen draws intertextual parallels between *Penthesilea* and Goethe's *Die natürliche Tochter*. Mommsen identifies several of Penthesilea's attributes that closely resemble Goethe's protagonist Eugenie, focusing specifically on each protagonist's riding ability to make her comparison:

> Ein wichter Zug an der Heldin des Goetheschen Stücks—auch im dramatischen Zusammenhang von Bedeutung—ist ihre virtuose Kunst des Reitens. Bereits in der Exposition bezeichnet Goethe seine Eugenie deshalb als 'Amazonen-Tochter,' womit übereinstimmt, daß auch Penthesilea 'Amazone' ist. Als Reiterin ist Eugenie—wie Penthesilea—von besonderer Wildheit, Verwegenheit. (45)

As a mirror image of Eugenie, Mommsen proposes, Penthesilea represents a manifestation of Kleist's competitive spirit with Goethe. Aesthetically, Kleist matches his protagonist's performance against Goethe's; subtextually, Kleist measures his own poetic prowess against Goethe's. Yet Mommsen implies Kleist saw his competition with Goethe as destined to fail. Ultimately, *Die natürliche Tochter* ends in an expression of moderation, whereas *Penthesilea* ends in excess and the failure of moderation. The glory of Penthesilea's victory is overshadowed by the excessively gruesome nature of her triumph and her own suicide. Penthesilea defeats Achilles, yet never gets the opportunity to bask in the ensuing fame from this victory. Instead, Achilles' death is, ironically, her death as well.

This double-edged victory presents an interpretive dilemma for gender analyses. What remains at question is whether or not Penthesilea represents a truly alternative feminist discourse. In her article "Kleists "Penthesilea": Geschlechterparadigmen. Die Frau als Projektionsfigur männlicher Identität—oder doch nicht?," Sigrid Lange confronts the perplexing question of gender and Penthesilea's subjectivity. According to Lange, *Penthesilea* attacks the sacrosanct topoi of classical aesthetics by drawing into question Classicism's mythical projection of woman as the paradigmatic redeemer for men and their imperfections. In the *Goethezeit*, images of such women—"das Ewigweibliche"—perform the function of awakening a sense of humanity in men. Were these women not to redeem men, and lead them to the classical telos of "reine Menschlichkeit" with their "erlösenden Fähigkeit des Weiblichen" (Lange 707), they would fall into depravity and self-destruction. According to Lange, Iphigenie epitomizes this mythical figure of the "Ewigweibliche": "Sie [Iphigenie] konstituiert ein Paradigma, das am Ende des 18. Jahrhunders die poetologische Arbeit an der Differenz zur Antike im Erspielen eines geschichtlichen Weltbildes leistet" (Lange 707). Like Mommsen, Lange views Kleist's attack on the aesthetics of Classicism and its projection of a mythical femininity as an attack on Goethe. Agee makes this argument as well: "Iphigenie modestly, gently pleads the rights of womanhood, which does not share in the glory of men's deeds but knows a wisdom drawn from patience and bereavement; Penthesilea proclaims an Amazon virtue that would have terrified the guests in a Berlin drawing room, and broken their china as well" (xix). According to Agee and Lange, Kleist does not merely call into question projections of femininity like Iphigenia with his Penthesilea; he dismantles the core of such projections: "Penthesilea [zerstört] mit gebotener Rigorosität die Hoffnung auf die erlösende Macht des Weiblichen" (707). Penthesilea destroys the mythical projection of patriarchy's ideal feminine figure.

Penthesilea dismantles Idealist imagery not as a simple anti-Iphigenia, a total negation, but rather as a complex figure of competing dichotomies. Penthesilea is indeed negative in her essence, but negative in the sense that she is neither an outright negation of nor a proponent for patriarchy. This is the point Lange stresses in her interpretation. Penthesilea invades the space[11] of patriarchal discourse as an inconceivable "third" element. As such, she threatens the tenuous security of the Idealist ontological structure by refusing to conform to the logos of "either / or" opposition and differentiation:

> Dennoch wäre es falsch, in der Parallele zu seinem Kommentar zur Zeitgeschichte Kleists Amazonenstaat als einfache Negation des Patriarchats zu verstehen. Vielmehr präsentiert er sich bereits zu Beginn als ein "Drittes" gegenüber den verfeindeten Heeren der Griechen und Trojaner, das sich auf eine Parteinahme ebensowenig festlegen läßt wie die Amazone auf das traditionelle Bild der Frau als das "Andere" zum Mann. Das "Dritte", dialektisch-synthetische Position in der klassischen triadischen Denkfigure These-Antithese-Synthese, ist bei Kleist weder Negation noch Position, sondern im buchstäblichen Sinn keines von beidem. (709)

Penthesilea is untenable as a concept in patriarchal discourse precisely because she does not conform to the male logos of simple "I" versus "Not-I" differentiation. As Lange stresses, Penthesilea is the literalization of the Hegelian notion of "synthesis," which entails negated elements of both the "thesis" and the "antithesis." She is neither thesis nor antithesis, and she contains no element of either (*keines von beidem*).

Penthesilea's "keines von beidem" relationship with the epistemological structure of masculine discourse creates a major crisis of knowledge for the Athenians' patriarchal culture. The Greeks are unable to understand anything outside the paradigm of "force" and "resistance": "So viel ich weiß, gibt es in der Natur / Kraft bloß und ihren Widerstand, nichts Drittes" (326). However, there is a disruptive *Drittes*, Penthesilea. And her dichotomous constitution confuses the Greeks' most basic understanding of two primary elements, fire and water:

> Was Glut des Feuers löscht, löst Wasser siedend
> Zu Dampf nicht auf und umgekehrt. Doch hier
> Zeigt ein ergrimmter Feind von beiden sich,
> Bei dessen Eintritt nicht das Feuer weiß,
> Obs mit dem Wasser rieseln soll, das Wasser,
> Obs mit dem Feuer himmelan soll lecken. (326)

Penthesilea is neither fire nor water, rather she is an enemy to both. As an unknown "Drittes" element, she causes fire to adopt a misplaced metaphor of water (*obs mit dem Wasser rieseln soll* [326]), and water a misplaced metaphor of fire (*obs mit dem Feuer himmelan soll lecken* [326]). The Greek logos of the organic world and its linguistic means of understanding that world is turned upside down.

For Jacobs and Paglia, Penthesilea represents a decidedly different embodiment of feminine self-definition. Jacobs focuses on Penthesilea's function as a "third" element. Penthesilea is completely separate from any type of simple logic of opposition: "Penthesilea brings about no simple realignment reestablishing the structure of opposition. She is the third term, the 'Drittes,' which violates the natural law declaring power and its resistance as the only conceivable forces" (92). Paglia introduces a similar reading, and she interprets Penthesilea's desire to "drag the sun by its golden flames down to herself" (*Bei seinen goldnen Flammenhaaren zög ich / Zu mir hernieder ihn* [368]) as Penthesilea's ability to symbolically dismantle hierarchical structures: "She [Penthesilea] longs to root up sky and planets, to drag down the sun 'by his flaming golden hair,' to pile mountain on mountain. Dionysian vision is disordering and anti-hierarchical" (263). This hierarchical structure is an expression of patriarchy's system of logic and order. In her dismantling of such hierarchies Penthesilea represents a mode of feminine voice, strikingly modern for its time: "Kleist's romantic family romance produced the defiant Amazon manifesto of *Penthesilea,* which rings with modernity. Women have rarely spoken so boldly for themselves as Kleist speaks for them here" (265). Paglia's reading suggests Penthesilea presents an alternative, feminine discourse.

For Jacobs, the Greeks, not Penthesilea, rely on language for rational cognition. She identifies masculine discourse, Odysseus' language, as the vehicle for reason and logic: "the Greeks speak in the name of reason or wisdom and credit language to be its vehicle" (94). Conversely, Jacobs defines Penthesilea as an "anti-word," a presence who disrupts the logic of Greek language: "How could those who live and speak the "word for word" understand the language of the anti-word? For this is the role that Penthesilea plays, at least for a while" (95). Odysseus, and the Greeks in general, represent an epistemology structured on the "word for word" logic of masculine language. Penthesilea's "anti-word" draws its primacy into question. Indirectly, Jacobs seems to be making an argument similar to Paglia's: Penthesilea represents a theory of feminine voice unrecognized and uncontainable by masculine discourse. However, maintaining this aesthetic theory for the definition of the female subject is problematic. Any representation of an alternative theory of female self-definition is inherently linked to masculine discourse, and can easily fall back into a phallogocentric logic of binary opposition.

Cullens and von Mücke also focus on such a push-and-pull dynamic by identifying an important theme within the play's structure: falling and recovering. Their analysis offers a broad interpretation of Penthesilea's many "recoveries from falling" (Cullens and von Mücke 465) as an expression of her disobedience to rules in general—specifically, the rules of physics and gravity: "And Penthesilea is, from the beginning, admired for her quick recoveries from falling. For instance, in the description of her climbing the steep precipice in pursuit of Achilles she seems to be able to defy the laws of gravity" (465). I agree with their analysis, but I would take their argument one step further and place it within the context of Kantian aesthetics, which shaped Idealism's theories of representation and self-definition. I suggest Penthesilea's ability to defy gravity metaphorically engages the philosophical debate surrounding reflection and representation, major tenets of transcendental Idealism.

Kant's theory of the sublime was central to Idealist theories of representation and the definition of the subject. Kleist frequently uses the motif of a "fall" in his texts to explore the sublime and the limits of representation.[12] He employs an interesting inversion of this topos in *Über das Marionettentheater*: the marionettes' ability to be antigrav. Helfer interprets the marionettes as an analogy to Kant's figure of the sublime, where their movement is defined as *erhoben,* a word which is related to *das Erhabene* (the sublime). *Penthesilea* also resembles a Kantian framework of the sublime. Penthesilea's repeated falls and recoveries are similar to the marionettes' ability to be *antigrav.* Whenever she falls, she repeatedly rises, only to fall again. Like the marionettes and their momentary contact with the stage, which keeps their movement perpetual, i.e., *antigrav,* Penthesilea's crashes also cause her to rebound in repeated animation. Moreover, like the marionettes, Penthesilea is directly referred to as a sublime figure: "In jedem schönren Sinn, *erhabne* Königin!" (my emphasis, 378). Kant argues a feeling of the sublime evokes a momentary arrest of life forces.[13] According to Kant, an experience with the sublime inherently involves staking one's life. Undoubtedly, *Penthesilea* is a text where staking one's life is common. However, there is a difference. Kant's theory of the sublime ends in the subject's self-definition as a moral subject of reason. Most importantly, the subject survives. In *Penthesilea* irrational action (*Wahnsinn*) reigns and subjects die.

In his article "Devouring Metaphor: Disgust and Taste in Kleist's *Penthesilea,*" Chaouli reads *Penthesilea* as a redaction of Kantian aesthetics. He argues that metaphors of eating and cannibalism not only call into question the status of aesthetic taste and the basis for Kant's aesthetic judgment, but also actually threaten the figure of representation: "At stake is not merely an expansion of the boundaries of the aesthetic by shocking audiences with the "feverish twitchings" and "wildness" to which our reviewer objects, but rather the very existence of the boundary separating the beautiful from the disgusting, thus threatening the collapse of Kantian aesthetics" (126). Chaouli suggests Kleist employs metaphors of eating precisely because "taste" is so intimately associated with the subject and the subject's senses. Unlike sight or hearing, which provide more subjective distance, taste actually involves the subject becoming one with the object. According to Chaouli, this threatens to undo the figure of representation, which is dependent upon aesthetic distance. He then uses this theory of diminishing aesthetic distance, the end of representation, to explain the confusion of metaphorical and literal boundaries. Once representation is consumed, the boundary between metaphor and reality becomes increasingly unintelligible, until the literal appears to eclipse the metaphorical. However, Chaouli stresses representation is never completely extinguished; the metaphorical returns to define Penthesilea who, at first, threatens to destroy reflection, metaphor, and ultimately representation: "Precisely when Achilles is to die, when, according to the logic we have delineated, the process of metaphorization is to come to an end, the presumed agent of his destruction does not use Achilles's name (i.e., the only signifier with only one signified), but uses instead a metaphor (stag)" (Chaouli 133).

Representation's return just when it is about to extinguish itself, brings the text's conclusion into a tautology. Chaouli identifies this tautological structure as a discourse of *stürzen* and *stützen*:

> That collapsing and supporting, *stürzen* and *stützen*, should be so close, indeed, that the stability of the arch should depend on the simultaneous fall of its elements, is a motif that is employed not just in the passages dealing with the founding of the state, but all over *Penthesilea*. (Chaouli 136)

Importantly, Chaouli identifies this paradox as being constitutive of Penthesilea's subjectivity. He identifies Prothoe's comparison of Penthesilea with an arch (*Bogensturz*) as the locus of Penthesilea's self-definition: "Most explicitly, the image of the arch is evoked by Prothoe as a simile for the constitution of the subject" (136). Penthesilea, like an arch, stands—or is caught—in an infinite state of falling. Her self-definition is produced by a paradox: her internal collapse or dissolution becomes the means for her support and self-definition. *Penthesilea* ends in a tautology, a rhetorical figure resisting closure and epistemological stability.

Although I largely agree with Chaouli's argument, I also believe his interpretation could be expanded. He reads Penthesilea's cutting and marking of Achilles' body without considering the implications of

Achilles' and the text's own discourse ripping, cutting, and inscribing Penthesilea's body. Penthesilea is as much inscribed by Achilles and his discourse as she uses words to inscribe him with her desire, which mutates into rage. By ignoring the implications of the text's inscription upon Penthesilea, Chaouli's argument assumes a dangerously chauvinist position, an empathy with the Greek perspective. What follows will illustrate how Penthesilea not only inscribes Achilles with language in an attempt to define herself, but also how a masculine discourse inscribes Penthesilea's body with a masculinized self-definition, and how she eludes a totalizing masculine self-definition by assuming the paradoxical role of textual character and textual author.

Penthesilea's Inscription by Masculine Discourse

The play's beginning places the reader into Odysseus' language, forcing the reader to see through his masculine gaze and discourse. His narration emphasizes the fact the text begins as a patriarchal projection, struggling to interpret and read Penthesilea's chaotic and confusing intentions. Odysseus' first speech also outlines the basic plot of the play and foreshadows the play's violent end:

> ODYSSEUS. Der Griechen und der Amazonen Heer,
> Wie zwei erboste Wölfe sich umkämpfen:
> Beim Jupiter! sie *wissen nicht warum*?
> Wenn Mars entrüstet, oder Delius,
> Den Stecken nicht *ergreift*, der Wolkenrüttler
> Mit Donnerkeilen nicht dazwischen wettert:
> Tot sinken die Verbißnen heut noch nieder,
> *Des einen Zahn im Schlund des anderen.* —
> Schafft einen Helm mit Wasser! (my emphasis, 323)

Almost preemptively, Odysseus secures a patriarchal conclusion to the text by summarizing its end in the opening lines. Along with setting up the plot, Odysseus also introduces the gender conflict informing the entire play (*der Griechen und der Amazonen Heer, / Wie zwei erboste Wölfe sich umkämpfen*). The competing discourses are in a literal life-or-death struggle for dominance. And it is predicted that if the gods choose not to interfere, both shall fall with their teeth stuck in the other's throat. However, Odysseus' hope for divine intervention, a metaphor for a literary *deus ex machina* (*Wenn Mars entrüstet, oder Delius, / Den Stecken nicht ergreift, der Wolkenrüttler / Mit Donnerkeilen nicht dazwischen wettert* [323]), is shattered. There is no divine intervention, and both do fall to their deaths. Significantly, the details are a little disordered; even though she does tear him apart with her teeth, it is Penthesilea's arrow that is stuck in Achilles' throat, not her teeth: "[sie] jagt den den Pfeil ihm durch den Hals" (413). Rather than a perfect reflection of the text's beginning, the text's ending presents a confusion of details, a distortion.

However, the ending's confusion of Odysseus' predicted outcome is not entirely unexpected. Confusion is one of the themes mentioned in Odysseus' opening lines: "sie wissen nicht warum" (323). The play begins with a crisis of knowledge. Odysseus' patriarchal discourse is defined by an epistemological crisis threatening to dismantle the foundations of its methodological means for representing truth and knowledge. Penthesilea is the cause of this crisis of knowledge. Eluding masculine identification and understanding, Penthesilea threatens the Greeks' intellectual stability and their representational mode of understanding.

To combat this confusion, the Greeks, with Achilles at the forefront, attempt to define, limit, bind, and inscribe an identity upon Penthesilea's subjectivity. Not only do the Greeks attempt this process of inscription metaphorically, i.e., Penthesilea as a concept, but also literally, physically. As a concept, Penthesilea and her discourse are incomprehensible. Antilochus states that the news of Penthesilea's declaration of war (*Aus Köchern mir die Antwort übersenden*! [325]) was incomprehensible to every Greek: "So, Wort für Wort, der Bote, den du sandtest; / Doch keiner in dem ganzen Griechenlager, / Der ihn *begriff*" (my emphasis, 325). The Greeks are clearly in a state of confusion after receiving news of Penthesilea's words. This confusion occurs on a physical and a metaphysical level. *Begreifen* means "to understand," but the word is also related to *Begriff*, meaning "concept," as well as to *greifen* "to grab."[14] Penthesilea is not only metaphorically incomprehensible (*unbegreiflich*), but she is also physically elusive (*ungreiflich*). Therefore, a physical inscription becomes the means for metaphorically assigning meaning and knowledge to Penthesilea's otherwise inexplicable presence, and physically subjugating and discharging her disruptive presence.

The confusion and chaos defining the play's opening is symptomatic of Penthesilea's persona, a persona that exemplifies Dionysian elements. She is either compared to formless chaos (a *nichts* [336]) or to nature's most violent elements. The Greeks define her as a gale (*Sturmwind* [324]), a torrential force of water (*Waldstroms wütendem Erguß* [326]), a bolt of lightening (*Wetterstrahl* [330]), a thunderstorm (*wie Gewitterwolken* [334]) a waterfall (*Wassersturz* [330]), and a flood (*Fluchtgewog* and *Überschwemmung* [330]). She also is compared with organic life, plants and animals: she is planted (*an ihrer Jungfraun Spitze aufgepflanzt* [324]), and has a symbiotic relationship with trees (*um einer Orme Höh* [332] and *in jener Eiche Schatten* [337]). The Greeks describe her as an animal, an unnamed "wildness" (*dies Wild* [329]), a deer (*das Geweih des Hirsches* [329]), a raging hyena (*seht die Hyäne, die blind-wütende*! [332]), or as one of the furies (*die rasende Megär* [334]). She also appears as a giant (*wie ein Riese in der Morgensonne* [335]), eclipsing the sun's light. Finally, she is defined as unrepresentable chaos, a mass imperceptible to the human eye:

> DER MYRMIDONIER. Stürzt, die Königin!
> Und eine Jungfrau *blindhin* über sie —
> [............................]
> DER MYRMIDONIER. Stürzen, Hauptmann,
> Wie in der *Feueresse eingeschmelzt*,
> Zum Haufen, Roß und Reuterinnen, zusammen!
> DER HAUPTMANN. Daß sie zu Asche würden!
> DER DOLOPER. Staub ringsum,
> Vom Glanz der Rüstungen durchzuckt und Waffen:
> *Das Aug erkennt nichts mehr*, wie *scharf* es sieht.
> Ein Knäuel, ein *verworrener*, von Jungfraun,
> *Durchwebt von Rossen* bund: das *Chaos* war,
> Das erst', aus dem die Welt sprang, deutlicher.
> (my emphasis, 336)

The mass of Amazons melts together (*eingeschmelzt*) into a fluid mass of unintelligibility. Individuality, separation, and order are nonexistent. Together they comprise an image of the Dionysian—the loss of the individual in orgiastic formlessness.

The descriptions of Penthesilea and her Amazon warriors are also reminiscent of the Kantian sublime. The metaphors the Greeks use to define Penthesilea are analogous to those objects in nature which Kant identifies as being responsible for awakening the sense of the sublime in the subject: "Kühne überhangende gleichsam drohende Felsen, am Himmel sich auftürmende *Donnerwolken, mit Blitzen und Krachen* einherziehend, Vulkane in ihrer ganzen zerstörenden Gewalt, *Orkane* mit ihrer zurückgelassenen Verwüstung, der grenzenlose Ozean, in *Empörung* gesetzt, ein *hoher Wasserfall eines mächtigen Flusses* u. dgl [. . .]." (my emphasis, Kant 160).[15] Likewise, Penthesilea is compared to thunderstorms (*Gewitterwolken* [my emphasis, 334] and *Gewitterstürm* [my emphasis, 338]), to hurricane-like winds (*wie Sturmwind* [my emphasis, 324]), and to flooding water and torrent streams (*Waldstroms wütendem Erguß* [326], *Wassersturz, Fluchtgewog,* and *Überschwemmung* [my emphasis, 330]). Moreover, the Dionysian chaos the Amazons represent in their chariot pileup is also akin to the Kantian sublime: "Das Schöne der Natur betrifft die Form des Gegenstandes, die in der Begrenzung besteht; das Erhabene ist dagegen auch an einem *formlosen* Gegenstande zu finden [. . .]." (my emphasis, Kant 136). In Kantian aesthetics, the key to experiencing a feeling of the sublime is *negative Darstellung,* a sensible representation of formlessness.[16] Penthesilea and her mass of Amazons lack this representation. Subsequently, the Greeks are locked in a visual and representational lacuna.

The Greeks' representational lacuna is emphasized by a theme of blindness, a lack of vision. Three times Penthesilea and her Amazons are associated with blindness: "die blind-wütende," "eine Jungfrau blindhin über sie," and "das Aug erkennt nichts mehr" (336). Blindness or a lack of vision appears to constitute the Greeks' understanding of Penthesilea. Subtextually, the inability of the Greek eye to "recognize" (*erkennt*) anything places the scene into the context of Kantian *Darstellung* and cognition.[17] In Idealist theories of *Darstellung,* the eye is the key sense which enables cognition or *Erkenntnis.*[18] This is precisely the Greeks' problem. There is a visual lapse and, consequently, a lack of representation. To remedy this problem, the Greeks will try to veil Penthesilea with artistic representation. Significantly, the means for creating such artistic illusion, the eye, is compared to a tool for cutting: "wie *scharf* es sieht" (my emphasis, 336). The fact that seeing, an act necessary for representation, is defined as a process of cutting creates a physically violent context surrounding representation. This violent motif defines the text's mode of representation for the remainder of the play: to represent means to cut, to inscribe.

Inscribing the Amazons, specifically Penthesilea, becomes Achilles' goal. To understand and make sense of Penthesilea, the Greeks must create a sensible representation that transcends her otherwise "invisible" state, impeding their cognition. The lust that drives Achilles to confront Penthesilea repeatedly is ultimately his epistemological need to define and understand her through visible wounds: "Nicht ehr zu meinen Freunden will ich lenken, / Ich schwörs, und Pergamos nicht wiedersehn, / Als bis ich sie zu meiner Braut gemacht, / Und sie, *die Stirn bekränzt mit Todeswunden,* / Kann durch die Straßen häuptlings mit mir schleifen" (my emphasis, 342). Odysseus also desires to see Achilles mark her with his trace: "[. . .] gern möcht ich, / Gesteh ich dir, *die Spur* von deinem Fußtritt / Auf ihrer rosenblütnen Wange sehn" (my emphasis, 339). Both Odysseus and Achilles want to scar Penthesilea, to inscribe her with some visual representation. Achilles desires to wound her forehead, to symbolically brand her as his. Through his branding of her forehead, he desires to take (*im Arm zu nehmen* [my emphasis, 342]) her not only as his wife (*Weib*), but also metaphorically as a tangible (*begreiflich*) concept (*Begriff*). Nehmen is defined as "in die Hand greifen,"[19] and greifen is defined as "in die Hand nehmen."[20] Thus, Achilles' act of taking (*nehmen*) can be read as a physical act of possessing and as a metaphysical act of comprehending (*begreifen*). This association between Penthesilea and a concept (*Begriff*) recalls Anilochus' earlier statement, when he discussed the incomprehensibility of a messenger's brief, relating Penthesilea's words and actions (*Doch keiner in dem ganzen Griechenlager, / Der ihn begriff* [325]). Moreover, Achilles directly refers to Penthesilea as an ungraspable, incomprehensible concept: "Unbegreifliche, wer bist du?" (384). The German word for "concept," *Begriff,* conveys more so than English, the physical act of possession, holding, or grasping. Certainly, this definition reflects Achilles' dual intention of "taking" Penthesilea.

Furthermore, Penthesilea's *Kranz,* with which Achilles desires to scar her, suggests an act of writing. Duden defines *Kranz* in terms of weaving: "In der Form eines Rings *geflochtene* oder gebundene Blumen, Zweige" (my emphasis, 893). *Flechten* is an act of weaving similar to the Latin *texere*. Ironically, this is the one occasion where Achilles' means for controlling or binding is described with floral metaphors. Usually, his mode of "binding" is defined in terms of burdensome iron. Normally the Amazon bonds are organic, woven from rose stems and twigs: "Die Ketten noch, die Rosenblüten, / Von ihren Gliedern reißen und die unsern / Mit erzgegoßner Fessel Last bewuchten" (345). Figuratively, Achilles wants to bind and define Penthesilea with scars, in order to possess her as an understandable concept, a concept that will lead to effective cognition. He wants to write her as a concept into the visual structure of his epistemological system of understanding and knowledge with a binding, linguistic wreath (*bekränzen*) that literally scars her forehead with a visual reference.

Until now Penthesilea is either invisible to the eye (*das Aug erkennt nichts*) or completely unreadable: "Hier diese flache Hand, versichr' ich dich, / Ist *ausdrucksvoller als ihr Angesicht*" (my emphasis, 324). Confronting Penthesilea, who has no lines, indentations (*Drücke*), cuts, or scars (i.e., no representation), the Greeks find themselves with no means of reading Penthesilea; she is an empty text. The lack of expression (a sign without a signifier, *Bezeichnung*)[21] causes an inability to read. The image of Penthesilea as *von-Ausdruck-leer* suggests she is unreadable, because she has no scars or indentations. Standing opposite this empty image, the Greeks find themselves ironically frozen in stone: "als ob in Stein gehaun wir vor ihr stünden" (324). The Greeks appear as literal works of art. They are frozen in artistic representation. Whereas Penthesilea is a boundless empty text, the Greeks appear overburdened with an aesthetics of paralysis. Their frozen aesthetic state mirrors their mental stagnation, a failure of cognition. Achilles and Odysseus hope to remedy this mental stagnation by inscribing Penthesilea's expressionless (*ausdruckslos*) persona with visual scars—a violent visual representation.

Acts of scarring and ripping flesh can be read as writing in *Penthesilea*. Chaouli introduces an interesting juxtaposition between *Riß* and *Bisse* to illustrate this argument. By tracing the etymological meaning of *Riß* to earlier meanings, Chaouli discovers that the word is related to furrowing, marking the land, and related to *ritzen*, meaning to cut and etch. He applies this etymological connection between *Riß* and *ritzen* to argue Penthesilea's tearing of Achilles (*ich zerriß ihn* [425]) is an act of writing: "[. . .] she inscribes him [. . .] with the marks of her desire" (139). However, Chaouli does not examine Achilles' acts of ripping (writing / *reißen*) Penthesilea. She, not Achilles, is the first character to endure the etchings of language.

Penthesilea's first linguistic inscription occurs during a heated battle when Achilles succeeds in knocking Penthesilea to the ground. Ironically, when Penthesilea falls, Achilles stops fighting and begins calling out to the gods and to Penthesilea. Essentially he attempts to interpellate her into language:

> DIE OBERSTE. Die Lanzen, *schwächer* als die Brüste, splittern:
> Er, der Pelide, steht, Penthesilea,
> Sie sinkt, die Todumschattete, vom Pferd.
> Und da sie jetzt, der Rache preisgegeben,
> Im Staub sich vor ihm wälzt, denkt jeglicher,
> Zum Orkus völlig stürzen wird er sie;
> Doch bleich selbst steht der *Unbegreifliche*,
> Ein Todesschatten da, ihr Götter! *ruft* er,
> Was für ein Blick der Sterbenden traf mich!
> Vom Pferde schwingt er eilig sich herab;
> Und während, von Entsetzen noch gefesselt,
> [..........................]
> Dreist der Erblaßten naht er sich, er beugt
> Sich über sie, *Penthesilea! ruft er*,
> In seinen Armen *hebt er sie empor*. (my emphasis, 359)

Like the Greeks at the play's beginning, Achilles is defined as *der Unbegrifliche*. Caught in a state of confusion, Achilles first calls out to the gods, beseeching their assistance, and then cries out "Penthesilea!". This is the first time Achilles directly addresses her in the vocative case. He essentially interpolates Penthesilea, recognizing her subjectivity. After he interpolates Penthesilea, identifying her within his linguistic register, he enacts a metaphorical *Aufhebung*[22] and lifts Penthesilea (*hebt er sie empor*). His lifting of Penthesilea metaphorically elevates her from the chthonian depths of the sublime and Dionysian formlessness into an Apollonian linguistic form. Immediately following this *Aufhebung*, Penthesilea is literally wounded. Importantly, her wound is a rip: "man führt sie röchelnd, mit *zerrißner* Brust" (my emphasis, 360). He completely tears her apart. Penthesilea's wound is directly caused by Achilles' act of calling out her name. Achilles has permanently marked her by tearing (*reißen*) her with a representation, a name. Ironically, he does not use a weapon or any other *literal* tool for naming or inscribing Penthesilea. In fact, the scene emphasizes that literal weapons are weaker than human breasts (*die Lanzen schwächer als die Brüste*). The true power to inscribe the breast resides in language, not in literal weaponry. Penthesilea is aware of this, and she clearly states it was his whispering, his words, which tore her breast: "Mir diesen Busen zu *zerschmettern*, Prothoe! / — Ists nicht, als ob ich eine Leier zürnend / Zertreten wollte, weil sie still für sich, / Im Zug des Nachtwinds, *meinen Namen flüstert*" (my emphasis, 161). Achilles' language is the weapon that tears.

Not surprisingly, following this scene, Penthesilea becomes obsessed with Achilles. He had whispered her name, like a lyre in the wind, and inscribed her with his desire. Now he is the only thought that defines her consciousness: "Sie denkt nichts, als den einen nur" (361). Once Achilles inscribes Penthesilea with that single whisper of a name, she begins to take on his aesthetic features. She reflects Achilles' thoughts and desires. For example, Achilles' earlier plan to drag Penthesilea back to Greece, crowned with scars on her forehead, has now become Penthesilea's own desire:

> Laßt ihn kommen.
> Laßt ihn den Fuß gestählt, es ist mir recht,
> Auf diesen Nacken setzen. Wozu auch sollen
> Zwei Wangen länger, blühnd wie diese, sich
> Vom Kot, aus dem sie stammen, unterscheiden?
> Laßt ihn mit Pferden häuptlings heim mich schleifen,
> Und *diesen Leib* hier, frischen Lebens voll,
> Auf offnem Felde schmachvoll hingeworfen,
> *Den Hunden mag er ihn zur Morgenspeise,*
> *Dem scheußlichen Geschlecht der Vögel, bieten.*
> Staub lieber, als ein *Weib* sein, das nicht *reizt*. (my emphasis, 363)

Foreshadowing the gruesome act of cannibalism in the final scene, Penthesilea states she would rather allow her body be ripped, torn, and eaten by dogs than be a wife, a woman, without charm (*das nicht reizt*). Evoking all the imagery of ripping and tearing, and now the specter of cannibalism that concludes the play, Penthesilea adopts Achilles' own desire to inscribe and write with an aesthetic charm (*reizen*). The word *reizen* is related to *reißen* and *ritzen*.[23] This suggests that the type of charm (*reiz*) she prefers is the act of literally inscribing a body with wounds. It seems she would rather be fed to the dogs than be a wife without charm, a woman without inscription. However, her desire also implies authorial agency: "Staub lieber, als ein Weib sein, das nicht reizt" (363). More than wanting to be inscribed (a passive symbol), *she* wants to charm (*reizen*), she wants to inscribe (to actively create). She wants to scar and name like Achilles. In wanting to enact Achilles' act of inscription, she has come to reflect his image. By inscribing Penthesilea with the name, "Penthesilea!", Achilles has essentially created his mirror image.

Although Penthesilea reflects Achilles' image, she is not a complete subject, a perfect image of Achilles. She exhibits only aspects of Achilles' reflection. In other words, she becomes a fractured subject. Fittingly she states, "Und jeder Busen ist, der *fühlt*, ein *Rätsel*" (my emphasis, 365). Whereas earlier she had no emotion, no expression for the Greeks to read (*von Ausdruck leer*), her breast is now torn and inscribed with an image (a visual sense) that reflects Achilles. Most importantly, her breast now *feels*. Significantly, the word "aesthetics" is related to the senses or "feeling." Her breast is aestheticized (readable), but her breast is also the locus of a paradox, a puzzle (*ein Rätsel*). Prothoe emphasizes this paradoxical definition when she compares Penthesilea to an arch that has been split down the center:

> PROTHOE. So *hebst* du dich *empor*? — Nun, meine Fürstin,
> So seis auch wie ein Riese! *Sinke* nicht,
> Und wenn der ganze Orkus auf dich drückte!
> *Steh, stehe fest, wie das Gewölbe steht,*
> *Weil seiner Blöcke jeder stürzen will!*
> Beut deine Scheitel, einem Schlußstein gleich,
> Der Götter Blitzen dar, und rufe, trefft!
> Und laß dich bis zum Fuß herab zerspalten,
> Nicht aber wanke in dir selber mehr,
> Solang ein Atem Mörtel und Gestein,
> In dieser jungen Brust, zusammenhält. (my emphasis, 367)

Like the paradox of the arch which stands because every block wants to fall, Penthesilea has become a representation that stands because it is on the verge of collapsing. Her breast has become the locos of a conflict between two dichotomous forces: to fall (*stürzen*) and to rise (*heben*). Half of her wants to rise (*erheben*) like a giant, a remnant of her past as a cipher of the sublime (*das Erhabene*), and the other half wants to fall (*stürzen*), to be grounded in a limited, linguistic sense. In other words, she has become a type of negative representation akin to Kant's *negative Darstellung,* which is also a figure of irony, a paradox:

> According to Kant, this separation is a presentation of the infinite, a presentation that can only be negative, yet that paradoxically expands the soul (*die aber doch die Seele erweitert*). Thus, *negative Darstellung* seems to be composed of two related components: a drawing of limits or a drawing into question of limits and an expansion of the "soul": that is, of morality. (Helfer 43)

Similarly, Prothoe defines Penthesilea as a paradox caught between two "related components." The "drawing of limits" is the *stürzen,* the crashing fall instigated by Achilles' *Ruf*—his inscription upon Penthesilea's breast. The "expansion of the soul" is symbolized by Penthesilea's *erheben,* her giant persona that expands outward, supporting the arch's inclination to fall in upon itself. However, Penthesilea does not stay standing for long. As this scene closes, Penthesilea collapses into herself, like a robe.

Penthesilea's collapsing like a robe functions like a visual allegory of Idealist aesthetics. As she gazes into her reflection in a river, she is entranced and wants to jump in. Prothoe and Meroe stop her, but she faints and falls like a garment in their hands:

> PENTHESILEA. [. . .] Da liegt *er* mir zu Füßen ja! Nimm mich —
> *Sie will in den Fluß sinken, Prothoe und Meroe halten sie.*
> PROTHOE. Die Unglückselige!
> MEROE. Da fällt sie leblos,
> Wie ein *Gewand,* in unsrer Hand zusammen. (my emphasis, 368)

Penthesilea's description as falling like a *Gewand* is reminiscent of the aesthetic veil, a topos common throughout the *Goethezeit. Gewand* does mean robe, not a veil, but its meaning is derived from *Tuch.*[24] Moreover, like a veil, a *Gewand* or a *Tuch* is a piece of woven fabric, and as such refers to the topos of a text's construction as weaving (*texere*), a metaphor that also constitutes the image of the aesthetic veil. Certainly Goethe's poem *Zueignung* presents an enduring image of a *Schleier* as a symbol of *Poesie*: "Nun sah ich sie den reinsten Schleier halten, / Er floß um sie und schwoll in tausend Falten. / [. . .] Aus Mordenduft gewebt und Sonnen Klarheit, / Der Dichtung Schleier aus der Hand der Wahrheit" (Goethe 152). Penthesilea's image as a *Gewand* is also similar to Kant's comparison of the sublime to the "veiled" goddess at the temple of Isis:

> Vielleicht ist nie etwas Erhabneres gesagt, oder ein Gedanke erhabener ausgedrückt worden, als in jener Aufschrift über dem Tempel der Isis (der Mutter Natur): 'Ich bin alles, was da ist, was da war, und was da sein wird, und meinen *Schleier* hat kein Sterblicher aufgedeckt." (my emphasis, Kant 250)

Kant's example of the veiled goddess is an example of the aesthetic idea, a type of artistic (specifically poetic) *negative Darstellung.*[25] Thus, Penthesilea's image as a *Gewand* arguably suggests, within an Idealist framework of aesthetics, that she has become some type of aesthetic idea, a work of poetic art. Moreover, she reflects not an image of herself, but rather an image of Achilles, her author. Her reflection of Achilles, her author, also recalls Romantic aesthetic theory, where an author essentially creates an image of himself through his text: "und doch gibt es noch keine Form, die so dazu gemacht wäre, den Geist des Autors vollständig auszudrücken: so daß manche Künstler, die nur auch einen Roman schreiben wollten, von ungefähr sich selbst dargestellt haben" (Schlegel 182). Significantly, Penthesilea sees a male object, rather than herself, reflected in the water: "Da liegt *er* mir zu Füßen ja!" (my emphasis, 368). She has become an aesthetic reflection of Achilles.

Achilles as Author: Apollo

In many ways Achilles' inscription of Penthesilea expands his own definition from demigod to god. He becomes a metaphor for Apollo. In Amazon law, Mars, the symbolic father of the Amazons, appears to the Amazons in the form of a *Verstellung*. Male warriors become substitutions for the god himself: "Der Gott zeigt uns, durch seine Priesterin, / Ein Volk an, keusch und herrlich, das, statt seiner, / Als Stellvertreter, uns erscheinen soll" (391). However, Penthesilea's mother has usurped Amazon law by *naming* Achilles as Penthesilea's chosen mate: "geh, mein süßes Kind! Mars ruft dich! / Du wirst den *Peleiden* dir bekränzen" (my emphasis, 394). Instead of allowing Mars to present himself through a substitution, Penthesilea knows beforehand whom she must choose. In other words, Achilles cannot be a representation of Mars. Mars must *appear* to her, not be chosen by her, and certainly not be explicitly named: "Es schickt sich nicht, daß eine Tochter Mars' / Sich ihren Gegner sucht, *den* soll sie wählen, / *Den* ihr der Gott im Kampf *erscheinen läßt*" (my emphasis, 394). Irreverently, Penthesilea actively seeks out her opponent (her reflecting other), testing the limits of Amazon law. Penthesilea may not search for a representation of Mars, but she is fixated on Achilles. Moreover, through solar-like metaphors, Achilles does appear to be a substitution for a god, but not for Mars. Achilles is a substitution for Apollo, the god of song and poetry—aesthetics.

Achilles is frequently compared with the sun, giving him the metaphorical importance of the sun god Helios, who is also identified as Apollo.[26] He is like the rising sun: "Jetzt, auf dem Horizonte, steht das ganze / Kriegfahrzeug da! So geht *die Sonne prachtvoll / An einem heitern Frühlingstage auf*!" (my emphasis, 333). And just as the sun illuminates the moon, the moon occasionally eclipses the sun. Penthesilea, who has a giant's shadow and who is associated with the moon (Artemis), threatens to eclipse both the sun and Achilles: "Hilf! Zeus! / An seiner Seite fliegt sie schon! *Ihr Schatten*, / Groß, wie ein Riese, *in der Morgensonne*, / Erschlägt *ihn* schon!" (my emphasis, 335). Then, in an allusion to defeating Achilles, Penthesilea exclaims she wants to bring down the sun: "PENTHESILEA. Blödsinnige! / Bei seinen goldnen Flammenhaaren zög ich / Zu mir hernieder ihn — PROTHOE. Wen? / PENTHESILEA. *Helios*, Wenn *er* am *Scheitel* mir vorüberfleucht!" (my emphasis, 368). Later, she narcissistically gazes at the sun's reflection in a river, identifying the reflection as Achilles: "Da liegt *er* mir zu Füßen ja! Nimm mich — *Sie will in den Fluß sinken, Prothoe und Meroe halten sie*" (my emphasis, 368). Undoubtedly, the sun or a reflection of the sun illuminates Penthesilea, providing her with a specular image to define herself. Moreover, the image of the sun shining down on Penthesilea's head (*mir am Scheitel* [368]) recalls Achilles' initial desire to mark Penthesilea's forehead: "die Stirn bekränzt mit Todeswunden" (342). Through his literal presence as Achilles and his metaphorical presence as the sun (Apollo), Achilles engraves Penthesilea's forehead twice: once literally and once metaphorically. Through their textual interchangeability Achilles and the sun (Apollo) become synonymous. More precisely, Achilles becomes a cipher for Phoebus Apollo—the god of poetry, song, and illusion.

From the beginning, the Greeks and Achilles have been closely associated with aesthetics and representation. Greek vision supports the teichoscopy that begins the play's narrative (scenes 1–4). And whereas the Amazons are defined by blindness and disorder, the Greeks are defined as a work of art (*als ob in Stein gehaun* [324]). Undoubtedly, Achilles emphasizes the artistic sense of the Greeks. He exhibits several attributes Idealism uses to define *Darstellung* and artistic representation: language, reflection, and deception. Unlike Penthesilea, who appears at times nameless, unreadable, unnamable, and, most importantly, unrecognizable (*das Auge erkennt nichts*), Achilles is readable: "Er ist es, Königin; / An diesem Schmuck hier kannst du ihn *erkennen*" (my emphasis, 384). His readability places him in a close relationship with language that Penthesilea does not share. For example, when Penthesilea and her Amazons crash early in the play's action, she is defined as invisible chaos and formlessness, but when Achilles crashes in a similar chaotic situation, textual metaphors define his fall: "allen *Knoten* rings" (my emphasis, 330), "die Schenkel, die *verwickelten*, gelöst" (my emphasis, 331), and "die Beute, die im *Garn* liegt" (331). The word "text" is derived from the Latin texere, meaning to weave. Appropriately, the language used to describe Achilles evokes imagery of threads, tangles, and yarn, imagery which subtextually conveys linguistic significance. Although Achilles is "verworren" (330), his entangled state only emphasizes his affinity with linguistic signification. He is so closely associated with language that he occasionally weaves himself into a textual knot.

Along with language, Achilles also personifies reflection, a key component in the Kantian model of *Darstellung*.[27] His association with the sun and illumination is directly linked to his function as a source of reflection. He becomes a source of light: "Auf einem Hügel *leuchtend* steht er da / In Stahl geschient sein Roß und er, der Saphir, / Der Chrysolith, wirft solche Strahlen nicht!" (my emphasis, 356). And, as a source of light, he reflects an image of Penthesilea: "Ist das die Siegerin, die schreckliche, / Der Amazonen stolze Königin, / Die seines Busens erzne Rüstung mir, / Wenn sich mein Fuß ihm naht, *zurückespiegelt*?" (my emphasis, 343). Essentially, Achilles' light enables reflection and, subsequently, representation—a means for self-definition. Conversely, Penthesilea is associated with the moon, whose own source of light is dependent upon the sun. Only through her encounter with Achilles or his symbolic metaphor, the sun, does she radiate light: "Bis jetzt ihr Aug auf den Peliden trifft: / Und Glut ihr plötzlich, bis zum Hals hinab, / Das Antlitz färbt, als schlüge rings um ihr / Die Welt in helle Flammenlohe auf" (324–5). Penthesilea adopts Achilles' sun-like glow and burns as bright as the sun, but without his light Penthesilea is invisible and has no reflection.

In his metaphorical signification as the sun god Apollo, Achilles represents perhaps the most important aspect of "art," deception. In classical mythology, dream and illusion also define Apollo. Moreover, the key element in Idealist definitions of *Darstellung* and aesthetic representation is deception.[28] Thus, it is not surprising that deception thoroughly informs Achilles' persona. His deception causes the massive crash of Amazons: "er betrog sie —" (335). More importantly, during the fifteenth scene, he utilizes Penthesilea's semi-conscious dream state (*Penthesilea! O du Träumerin!* [375]) and deception to effect a linguistic definition of Penthesilea:

ACHILLES. O du, die eine *Glanzerscheinung* mir,
Als hätte sich das Ätherreich eröffnet,
Herabsteigst, Unbegreifliche, wer bist du?
Wie nenn ich dich, wenn meine eigne Seele
Sich, die Entzückte, fragt, wem sie gehört?
PENTHESILEA. Wenn sie dich fragt, so nenne diese *Züge*,
Das sei der Nam, in welchem du mich denkst. —
Zwar diesen goldnen Ring hier schenk ich dir,
Mit jedem Merkmal, das dich sicher stellt;
Und zeigst du ihn, so weist man dich zu mir.
Jedoch ein *Ring vermißt sich, Namen schwinden*;
Wenn dir der Nam entschwänd, der Ring sich mißte:
Fändst du *mein Bild in dir* wohl wieder aus?
Kannst dus wohl mit *geschloßnen Augen denken*?
ACHILLES. Es steht so fest, wie *Züg in Diamanten*.
PENTHESILEA. Ich bin die Königin der Amazonen,
Er nennt sich mareszeugt, mein Völkerstamm,
Otere war die große Mutter mir,
Und mich begrüßt das Volk: *Penthesilea*.
(my emphasis, 384–5)

Once it is obvious a veil of deception is drawn (*eine Glanzerscheinung*), Penthesilea reveals her name and transcends her otherwise unnamable essence into the signifier "Penthesilea." Yet at first, Penthesilea is skeptical of any form of signification. She appears to prefer nonlinguistic signifiers (*Züge*), but simultaneously questions the lasting validity of all symbolic and linguistic signification: "ein Ring vermißt sich" (384) and "Namen schwinden" (384). The ring, a tautological symbol of reflection (self-definition), is sometimes lost, and names disappear. Then Penthesilea questions Achilles' ability to imagine her without using his eyes. In other words, she questions his faculties of imagination, his ability to create an a priori *Darstellung* without sensory aid. Achilles responds by saying he can, like a facet in a diamond. However, this statement, like all his statements in this scene, is grounded in deception. A diamond distorts and bends light as light passes through it, creating an illusory rainbow. Ironically, immediately following the diamond example, Penthesilea reveals how she is named. A deceptive context creates the possibility for her self-definition. However, this definition, born of deception, proves to be problematic and ultimately dangerous for Achilles. This deceptive context, permitting Penthesilea's self-definition, transforms Penthesilea into a realm of aesthetics where she not only becomes readable, but where she also becomes an author—a self-defining subject with all the rights and privileges of authorship, including the ability to inscribe.

This transition occurs in the middle of the play, marking it as the structural *Wendepunkt* of the text. Thematically, it is significant that the characters cross a bridge at this point: "er führt sie *über die Brücke*" (my emphasis, 372). It is at this point that the play's main discourses also become intertwined: metaphor and literal language, the sublime and the beautiful, the Apollonian and the Dionysian, and most importantly, Achilles and Penthesilea. The play's two opposing protagonists speak face to face for the first time in mutual subject / object reflection. However, this textual integration is only an illusion destined to fade. Already, Penthesilea has begun to turn the tables on Achilles by symbolically writing her own definition. Under the guise of the illusory context that Achilles provides for this scene, Penthesilea becomes a storyteller, telling the history of her Amazon state (*Die ungeheure Sage* [390]). Moreover, her language is not entirely devoid of the Dionysian elements Achilles' Apollonian definition tries to veil. Her fiction entails imagery Achilles' Apollonian sensibility finds unnatural and inhuman: "Sie sind beraubt, unmenschlich, frevelhaft —?" (390). Imbued with an aesthetic agency that is indelibly tainted by inhuman vulgarity, Kleist's tragic female protagonist is a paradox of competing discourses that anticipates Nietzsche's definition of tragedy:

> In der Gesamtwirkung der Tragödie erlangt das Dionysische wieder das *Übergewicht;* sie schließt mit einem Klange, der niemals von dem Reiche der apollinischen Kunst her tönen könnte. Und damit erweist sich die apollinische Täuschung als das, was sie ist, als die während der Dauer der Tragödie anhaltende Umschleierung der eigentlichen dionysischen Wirkung: die doch so mächtig ist, am Schluß das apollinische Drama selbst in eine Sphäre zu drängen, wo es mit dionysischer Weisheit zu reden beginnt und wo es sich selbst und seine apollinische Sichtbarkeit verneint. So wäre wirklich das schwierige Verhältnis des Apollinischen und des Dionysischen in der Tragödie durch einen Bruderbund beider Gottheiten zu symbolisieren: *Dionysus redet die Sprache des Apollo, Apollo aber schließlich die Sprache Dionysus.* (my emphasis, Nietzsche 119–20)

As in Nietzsche's definition of tragedy, Penthesilea's Dionysian elements will eventually drown out Achilles' Apollonian signification. The veil of Apollonian representation Achilles has inscribed upon Penthesilea gives her the illusion of Apollonian aesthetic symmetry and form. More importantly, Penthesilea learns to speak the language of Apollo, but she will soon speak it with a vulgar Dionysian accent.

Penthesilea as Author

As an author, Penthesilea functions similarly to Achilles: when she speaks, she cuts. Coincidentally, Achilles finds himself wounded, cut in the arm, as the scene begins: "PENTHESILEA. Diana, meine Herrscherin, er ist / Verletzt! / ACHILLES. *Geritzt* am Arm, *du siehst, nichts* weiter" (my emphasis, 382). Achilles plays down the importance of the wound (*nichts weiter*), but the repercussions of Penthesilea's transcendence from a formless mass of chaos to an agent of language is not as benign as Achilles first imagines. Achilles suggests his wound is due to Penthesilea's ability to see: "du siehst" (382).

Penthesilea's gaze has become as dangerous as the sword. Throughout the play, seeing is directly related to cutting (*wie scharf es [das Auge] sieht*). Here the proximity of yet another visual act (*du* siehst) to an act of cutting (*geritzt am Arm*) emphasizes the textual importance of seeing as a metaphor for inscription. Significantly, vision's blade has changed hands from Achilles (a masculine gaze) to Penthesilea (a feminine gaze). This transfer of visual potency is underscored by an allegory of a suppressed masculine vision in Penthesilea's story about the Amazon state: "der Mann, des Auge diesen Staat erschaut, / Der soll das Auge gleich auf ewig schließen" (389). This imperative that men should not witness the Amazon state is similar to Kant's citing the warning at Isis' temple admonishing mortals not to lift her veil. Kant uses this example to elucidate a type of *negative Darstellung*, the aesthetic idea. Essentially, the veil of *negative Darstellung* enables the subject to experience a sublime feeling. Without the veil, the subject loses his life as he stares into infinite chaos. The Amazons' law that no man shall live once he has gazed upon the Amazon state functions similarly. No man can look directly at the Amazon state without a veil, without the veil of aesthetic illusion. Unfortunately for Achilles, this aesthetic illusion *is* unveiled: "du mußt dich *augenblicklich* ihr erklären" (my emphasis, 396). Significantly, this process of unveiling (*erklären*) is logically a reassertion of the visual (*augenblicklich*).

As the Greeks storm back into the scene, they destroy the scene's illusive context Achilles had constructed. Without this context, Achilles has no other choice but to tell Penthesilea her victory was only a deception; his humble surrender, a ruse: "Doch durch der Waffen Glück gehörst du mir; / Bist mir zu Füßen, Treffliche, gesunken, / Als wir im Kampf uns trafen, nicht ich dir" (397). However, the metaphysical boundaries are not as fluid as the consistently shifting political boundaries appear to be. Once Achilles imbues Penthesilea with his reflection, she, in turn, adopts his Apollonian ability to inscribe and represent aesthetically, and she does not yield this position. Ironically, Achilles loses the ability to read and see and no longer functions as a metaphor for the sun for the remainder of the play. Conversely, Penthesilea appears as the moon, stepping out of the sky: "[. . .] du mir aus dem Monde niederstiegst?" (391). Figuratively, Achilles' loss of metaphorical signification is caused by Penthesilea's eclipsing moon. Once Achilles stands engulfed by Penthesilea's lunar shadow, all his Apollonian attributes also fade.

Most importantly, he loses the ability to read, to intuit sensible information. His mistake to confront Penthesilea on the battlefield one last time in order to surrender to her—i.e., become her beau for a month and then drag her back to Greece as his wife—is presented as the epitome of misinterpretation. His failure to correctly read Penthesilea's intentions is a fatal failure of language:

> ACHILLES. Beim wolkenrüttelnden Kroniden,
> *Sie tut mir nichts*, sag ich! Eh wird ihr Arm,
> Im Zweikampf gegen ihren Busen wüten,
> Und rufen: "Sieg!" wenn er von Herzblut trieft,
> Als wider mich! — Auf einen Mond bloß will ich ihr,
> Indem, was sie begehrt, zu Willen sein;
> Auf einen oder zwei, mehr nicht: das wird
> Euch ja den alten, meerzerfreßnen Isthmus
> Nicht gleich zusammenstürzen! — Frei bin ich dann,
> *Wie ich aus ihrem eignen Munde* weiß,
> Wie Wild auf Heiden wieder; und folgt sie mir,
> Beim Jupiter! ich wär ein Seliger,
> Könnt ich auf meiner Väter Thron sie setzen.
> (my emphasis, 407).

Achilles believes she will do no harm to him (*sie tut mir nichts*), and he places all his faith, knowledge, and, in fact, his life in Penthesilea's mouth: "wie ich aus ihrem *eignen Munde weiß*" (my emphasis, 407). Unfortunately, the language coming from Penthesilea's mouth is fraught with irony, and what he knows (*weiß*) is tragically incorrect. What Achilles fails to recognize is that Penthesilea's word, upon which he relies for his safety, is produced under false pretenses. Achilles' entire conversation with Penthesilea takes place under the illusion that he is her captive and not the other way around, as truth would have it. This would not be a problem had the Greeks not disrupted this illusory context. However, he is forced to forfeit that illusion, which creates a void where there is no mediating representation to delimit what is or is not truth. This imperceptibility between "truth" and "illusion," the crux of Kleist's *Kantkrise*, triggers a total collapse of the epistemological structures governing Achilles' and

Penthesilea's modes of perception. Both figures are thrown into an interpretive hall of mirrors.

This proves to be especially dangerous for Achilles, whose ability to reflect has been overshadowed by Penthesilea. He appears metaphorically as a blank "white" page (*weiße Brust* [413]), and he is now sensibly imperceptible (*Unempfindlich* [403]). Essentially, he has assumed Penthesilea's expressionless image at the play's beginning (*von Ausdruck leer* [324]). Therefore, as the final battle unfolds, Penthesilea fails to both read and correctly interpret his illusory surrender: "Doch jetzt, da sie [Penthesilea] mit solchen Greulnissen / Auf ihn herangrollt, ihn, der nur *zum Schein* / Mit einem Spieß sich *arglos* ausgerüstet: / Stutzt er, und dreht den schlanken Hals, und horcht, / Und eilt entsetzt, und stutzt, und eilet wieder" (my emphasis, 412). Achilles appears both guileless (*arglos*) and under the pretense of illusion (*Schein*). This paradox (guilelessly deceiving) underscores the ironic fact that the epistemological limits responsible for differentiating one concept from another have been removed and replaced by a structure of knowledge that equates illusion with truth and truth with deception. This linguistic paradox enacts Kleist's *Kantkrise*: "Wir können nicht entscheiden, ob das, was wir Wahrheit nennen, wahrhaft Wahrheit ist, oder ob es uns nur so scheint" (34). Placed in such a paradoxical context, Penthesilea is unable to read Achilles' figurative declaration of war as a disguise for his surrender, and she fatally misinterprets his intent:

> [Penthesilea] stürzt — stürzt mit der ganzen Meut, o Diana!
> Sich über ihn, und *reißt—reißt* ihn beim Helmbusch,
> [....................................]
> Sie schlägt, *die Rüstung ihm vom Leibe reißend,*
> Den Zahn schlägt sie in seine weiße Brust,
> Sie und die Hunde, die wetteifernden,
> Oxus und Sphinx den Zahn in seine rechte,
> In seine linke sie. (413–14)

Penthesilea begins her fatal inscription of Achilles' body by ripping and tearing him into fragmented pieces: "die Glieder des Achills reißt sie in Stücken!" (411). Moreover she tears him twice (*reißt, reißt*): she tears him literally and metaphorically. Literally, her teeth cut his flesh, killing him. Metaphorically, her teeth, in close proximity to her mouth (her tool for linguistic communication) imprints him with her linguistic signature. Through this act, she defines herself not only as murderess, but also as author: "als ich an deinem Halse hing, hab ichs wahrhaftig *Wort für Wort* getan; ich war nicht so verrückt, als es wohl schien (my emphasis, 426). What one may perceive as crazy is Penthesilea functioning as an author, writing as it were "word for word," an act that fuses literal ripping and tearing with metaphorical signification. Unfortunately for Achilles, Penthesilea's aesthetic resolves not in Apollonian form, but rather in Dionysian dissolution.

Penthesilea's aesthetic writes Achilles into oblivion, because her Dionysian aesthetic erases representation as it writes. In a symbolic gesture to permanently deprive Achilles of his previous authorial control over representation, Penthesilea rips away his armor, the same glimmering armor that once reflected Penthesilea's image: "die seines Busens erzne Rüstung mir, / Wenn sich mein Fuß ihm naht, zurückespiegelt" (343), and stains and obstructs his reflection with dripping blood. She not only imprints him with her aesthetic, but she actually consumes him. In consuming Achilles, Penthesilea extinguishes the representative figure of representation itself; Penthesilea effectively consumes representation.

As if to underscore this representational lacuna, the scene ends with Penthesilea described as staring into infinite space, looking at an empty page: "Jetzt steht sie lautlos da, die Grauenvolle, / Bei seiner Leich, umschnüffelt von der Meute, / Und *blicket starr*, als wärs ein *leeres Blatt* [. . .]" (my emphasis, 414). The "empty page" (*ein leeres Blatt*) is none other than Achilles. The depiction effectively characterizes the textual state of affairs. Achilles is reduced from a signifier of art, reflection, representation, and language to an empty signifier, an empty text. Ironically, his self-dissolution into textual oblivion was indirectly attributed to Apollo, his former metaphor: "Doch ein *Verräter* ist die *Kunst der Schützen*; / Und gilts den Meisterschuß ins Herz des Glückes, / So *führen tücksche Götter uns die Hand*" (my emphasis, 422). The god who reigns over the art of archery is, ironically, Apollo. Thus, Apollo is not so much a *Verräter* to Penthesilea, but more so to Achilles. Achilles' own metaphorical representation (Apollo) was the hand that guided Penthesilea's linguistic arrow. It is the ultimate form of Romantic self-reflexivity and self-criticism. As indicated earlier, Penthesilea learned to speak the language of the Apollonian (*Kunst der Schützen*), and now Apollo guides her pen.

Achilles' own artistic language, his act of ripping, and tearing representational meaning upon Penthesilea's expressionless page, turns back on himself and effectively undermines his own subjectivity. Unlike an experience of the Kantian sublime that ends in the definition of the subject as a moral subject of reason, Achilles' representation of a sublime figure (Penthesilea) leads to his own self-deconstruction.

The play enables precisely that which Kant's figure of *negative Darstellung* is designed to prevent: "seeing" beyond all moral and sensible limits.[29] In *Penthesilea,* the linguistic limits between metaphorical and literal language are confused and dissolved, if not entirely removed. The subject does see beyond sensible limits. Her language becomes corporeal, literal: "Wort für Wort" (426). Indeed, she literally loves her partner to death:

> Wie manche, die am Hals des Freundes hängt,
> Sagt wohl das Wort: sie lieb ihn, o so sehr,
> Daß sie vor Liebe gleich ihn essen könnte;
> Und hinterher, das Wort beprüft, die Närrin!
> [..............................]
> Sieh her: als ich an deinem Halse hing,
> Hab ichs wahrhaftig *Wort für Wort* getan;
> Ich war nicht so verrückt, als es wohl schien. (my emphasis, 426)

The word no longer has metaphorical significance. The word does not refer to another word, another linguistic representation. It is immediately presented; the word has become actual.

This literalization of the word also leads to the fatal linguistic confusion between Küsse und Bisse: "PENTHESILEA. So war es ein *Versehen,* Küsse, Bisse, / Das reimt sich, und wer recht von Herzen liebt, / *Kann schon das eine für das andre greifen*" (my emphasis, 425). Penthesilea's mistake (*Versehen*) is not so much a visual error (*sehen*), an oversight, but rather a written error, a typo. In fact Penthesilea suggests she is aware of this when she states her killing of Achilles was a "slip of the tongue": "Ich habe mich, bei Diana, bloß *versprochen,* / Weil ich der raschen Lippe *Herr* nicht bin" (my emphasis, 426). *Versprechen* is certainly closer than *versehen* to the physical nature of Penthesilea's ironic "kiss of death," her mouth, her lips. The passage also indicates Penthesilea is asserting her female agency as author, consciously opposing it to masculine discourse (*Herr nicht bin*). She is not a male, but she may be a feminine master over language (*Lippe*). *Lippe,* meaning "lips," evokes not only a linguistic metaphor, but also a sexual metaphor of female genitalia. Like Irigaray's notion of "lips" in "The Sex Which is Not One,"[30] Penthesilea's language consists of a plurality within a single unit. In Penthesilea's discourse words are both literal and metaphorical. That is why she claims her act of misspeaking was not as crazy as it may appear: "Ich war nicht so verrückt, als es wohl schien" (426). Her linguistic plurality is further illustrated when she admits *Bisse* and *Küsse* are conceptually identical: "das eine für das andere *greifen*" (my emphasis, 425). In German, the word "concept" is *Begriff*. For Penthesilea there is no single limit to distinguish difference and meaning, concepts not only become immediate, but they also become indistinguishable, identical.

This collapse of linguistic boundaries allows Penthesila to commit suicide without weapons. She forges a metaphorical knife from the depths of her imagination, brings this metaphor out from its figurative context into the literal one and plunges it into her soul, literally killing herself:

> Denn jetzt steig ich in meinen Busen nieder,
> Gleich einem Schacht, und grabe, kalt wie Erz,
> Mir ein vernichtendes Gefühl hervor.
> Dies Erz, dies läutr' ich in der Glut des Jammers
> Hart mir zu Stahl; tränk es mit Gift sodann,
> Heißätzendem, der Reue, durch und durch;
> Trag es der Hoffnung ewigem Amboß zu,
> Und schärf und spitz es mir zu einem Dolch;
> Und diesem Dolch jetzt reich ich meine Brust:
> So! So! So! Und wieder! — Nun ists gut.
> *Sie fällt und stirbt.* (427)

The removal of the limits between metaphor and the literal creates a situation where the word is deadlier than daggers and arrows. Significantly, right before Penthesilea kills herself, she empties out her quiver and hands over all her weapons to Prothoe, as if they no longer contain the literal potency metaphor has now assumed: "Hier ist der Dolch. / *Sie löst sich den Dolch aus dem Gurt, und gibt ihn der Prothoe.* / Willst du die Pfeile auch? / *Sie nimmt den Köcher von der Schulter.* / Hier schütt ich ihren ganzen Köcher aus! / *Sie schüttet die Pfeile vor sich nieder* (427). Penthesilea's suicide reveals there is no mediation, no metaphorical linguistic representation to bridge the gap between intellectual imagination, concepts, and a priori ideas and the outside physical world. Here an internal representation akin to the Kantian model of *negative Darstellung*, which is produced mentally and supersensibly (internally), also destroys from within. Metaphorical linguistic representation fades away into complete negativity and leaves a void where there is no guiding moral or ethical façade. Thus Kleist collapses the limits Kant assigns *negative* Darstellung to guard and maintain (*Sittlichkeit* and *Sinnlichkeit*) and enables metaphor, a representation, to extend beyond the limits of both morality and sensibility.

This collapse of limits appears to enable a "pure representation," the goal of Idealism. In *Die Marquise von O . . .* and in *Das Käthchen von Heilbronn*, Kleist uses the metaphor of a swan to convey purity, a "pure representation." In *Die Marquise von O . . .*, a swan, who is associated with the Marquise, repeatedly submerges below an intangible plane of water to cleanse herself of earthly, sensible bile. When she emerges, she is pure and unblemished, "rein aus der Flut" (116). A similar scene is presented in *Das Käthchen von Heilbronn*, as Käthchen emerges from a grotto where she had been bathing. Like the Marquise, she emerges from a "Kristallsees blauen Fluten" (512), sparkling clear and pure. Contrasted with Kunigunde's lack of physical veracity as an artificial work of art, "mosaische Arbeit" (520), Käthchen's "sparkling" appearance is presented as "pure." In *Penthesilea*, a similar scene portrays the title figure submerging herself, like a swan, in a marble urn of water, washing herself of Achilles' blood: "Das Haupt ganz unter Wasser, Liebe! So! Und wieder! So, so! *Wie ein junger Schwan*!" (my emphasis, 420). Penthesilea's health is restored, although only momentarily. In each example, water symbolizes a medium that washes away blemishes and stains, making way for a pure representation, a swan. Therefore, as Penthesilea becomes synonymous with yet another image of a bathing swan—appropriating all the symbolical importance of that image in Kleistean aesthetics—it appears "pure representation" is achieved. However, as in the other two texts where the swans' representational veracity proves to be artificial, contrived, and influenced by sensible perception, Penthesilea's representational veracity also reverts into sensible representation. There is no transcendence of the subject into an a priori ideal of "pure representation."

The play's final lines undermines Penthesilea's "pure representation" by reinstating her as a metaphor for the text itself. Unlike Achilles, whose death resembles an empty page or "leeres Blatt," Penthesilea's death is comparable to an oak in full bloom—an oak blooming with an abundance of live "Blätter." *Blatt* means page as well as leaf. Metaphorically, Penthesilea's image as a tree full of "blooming" *Blätter* symbolizes a text full of written words—pages. As a metaphorical tree, she has become the metaphorical support of the text's aesthetic, its leaves. As such she has achieved self-definition as a cipher for the text itself, *Penthesilea.*

In an act of Romantic self-criticism, Penthesilea's linguistic abundance (*Blätter*) ultimately invites a clearly masculine force "er," to usurp her and uproot the text's very own supporting structure: "Sie sank, weil sie zu stolz und kräftig *blühte*! / Die abgestorbne Eiche steht im *Sturm,* / Doch die gesunde stürzt *er* schmetternd nieder, / Weil *er* in ihre Krone *greifen* kann" (my emphasis, 428). In this final passage there are two trees: a dead oak void of leaves, void of words (Achilles), and a living oak full of leaves, full of language (Penthesilea). Ironically, both trees as metaphorical structures of language, linguistic discourses, are feminine. It seems Kleist is employing the Romantic topos of women as signifiers of aesthetic language. Both stand against the force of a masculine storm. The lifeless, empty tree remains untouched, ungrasped; however, Penthesilea's linguistic abundance (*Blätter*) creates a conceptual friction, a means to grasp (*greifen*) deep within her crown, and uproot her symbolic structural support. This image creates a hermeneutic enigma. By reading the storm's ability to grasp (*greifen*) as an allegory of producing concepts (*Begriffe*), the storm's destruction of Penthesilea becomes clear. Achilles' image as an empty page and a dead feminine tree withstands the storm's grasps: his barren discourse is not at odds, presents no friction, with the currents of a masculine storm. It remains standing at the text's closure. However, Penthesilea as a living metaphor of a feminine discourse cannot remain standing in the midst of a masculine storm of conceptuality; she cannot permanently exist within a patriarchal structure of knowledge. Penthesilea momentarily infiltrates the text's semiotic system; yet she ultimately is unable to escape the force of the text's epistemological atmosphere, which is masculine. She is forcibly subjugated (*doch die gesunde stürzt er schmetternd nieder*).

When critics interpret *Penthesilea* and *Das Käthchen von Heilbronn* together as a textual continuity, they focus on the juxtaposition of Käthchen's *Hingebung* versus Penthesilea's *Handeln*. However, "submission" is not unique to these two plays. Kleist's female figures frequently express a certain level of submission either to patriarchy or to some higher authority. In the four texts I analyze in my thesis, every female title character eventually submits to an inescapable patriarchy, its language and / or its social law. In *Das Bettelweib von Locarno* the Bettelweib submits to the Marquis' order that she reposition herself in the corner of a room, rather than the center of the room, ultimately resulting in her death; in *Die Marquise von O . . .*, the Marquise eventually surrenders to the Graf's unrelenting courtship and marries him; in *Das Käthchen von Heilbronn* Käthchen's entire persona is characterized by her submission to Graf vom Strahl's will, culminating in a less than blissful marriage; and, contrary to Kleist's statement, Penthesilea ultimately surrenders herself to patriarchal law. Right before Penthesilea commits suicide she renounces Amazon law and autonomy and says she will "follow" Achilles, follow him into death: "Ich sage vom Gestz der Fraun mich los, und folge diesem Jüngling hier" (426). Because Penthesilea's act of submission occurs in a context of fierce feminine independence, action, and authorial agency, her submission is less apparent than initially appears. Yet, she does renounce her feminine independence and follow a male's (Achilles') example. Ironically, Penthesilea is textualized the moment she submits to Achilles' corpse, "diesem Jüngling hier"—a text she had just inscribed with her teeth. In this Hegelian-like act of submission, Penthesilea is recognized by a masculine force (*weil er in ihre Krone greifen kann*), and subjugated (*stürzt er schmetternd nieder*). However, she still functions as a signifier (the title) for the text. According to Hegel's "master / slave dialectic," the subject comes to recognize itself as a subject through its work: "Through this rediscovery of himself by himself, the bondsman realizes that it is precisely in his work, wherein he seemed to have only an alienated existence, that he acquires a mind of his own" (119). Penthesilea achieves textual signification, self-definiton, through her final authorial act of free will (suicide) and submitting to masculine signification (*[ich] folge diesem Jungling hier*). In submitting to Achilles' corpse, her textual creation, Penthesilea enacts a symbolic *Aufhebung*, lifting herself to "des Lebens Gipfeln" (428), and becomes *Penthesilea*, the text. The storm's final act of forcibly subjugating her (*die gesunde stürzt er schmetternd nieder*) only reaffirms her metaphorical "self-certainty"[31] as the text's aesthetic "being-for-self"—its self-definition.

Epilogue

Subjugation and Subversion: The Power of Absence

As Hegel states: "The truth of the independent consciousness is accordingly the servile consciousness of the bondsman." In other words, the bondsman achieves independent self-consciousness through his subjugation to the lord, who in turn reflects the independent consciousness, or what Hegel calls the "being-for-self." By unveiling a crisis of reflection, or representation, within the philosophical structure of authority, Hegel challenges the traditional relationship between "master and slave." Ironically, this inversion of authority occurs due to the bondsman's surrender, a surrender of his will.

Throughout my study I have argued Kleist's female title characters employ a similar act of subjugation to manipulate and subvert Idealist discourse—in particular the figure of representation that grounds that discourse. The Bettelweib's obedience to the Graf's order that she reposition herself transforms her into a Kantian *negative Darstellung,* effecting a reversal of master and slave. The Marquise's refusal to identify the one "true" father of her child ignites a paternal conundrum at the heart of representation, severing representation's relationship with truth. Käthchen's unwavering subjugation fails to provide the Graf vom Strahl with a pure representation of woman, an epitome of the eternal feminine, and reflects instead the narcissistic male's own gaze as he defines himself through an "I," not a valid "other" or "not I" in the Fichtean sense of self-definition. Penthesilea's surrender (*[ich] folge diesem Jüngling hier* [426]) marks a major shift in the discourse on representation that distorts the limits between the literal and the figurative. In this manner, she undermines not only representation, but also the binary logos upon which Idealism and western philosophy are based. Ultimately all four females undergo a process of subjugation, self-negation and dissolution that consequently questions the truth-potential of representation, the cornerstone of Idealist discourse.

At the heart of this critique lies each character's transcendence from a figurative existence as character to a metaphoric presence as work, as the aesthetic project itself. Each character becomes synonymous with a work in progress, or what Kristeva might call a subject-in-process.[1] Moreover, Hegel also states work (creation) is the process through which the bondsman achieves self-certainty.[2] In Kleist's female-titled texts, a similar process unfolds as each female character assumes the combined role of character, author, and text.[3] However, there are important distinctions between Hegel and Kleist. First, Kleist chooses a female voice of alterity to confront male discourse—his own authorial voice, itself a medium of Idealist discourse. Second, despite the act of subjugation, there is no synthesis or sublation that resolves into a new juxtaposition of thesis and antithesis—which would only reify the paradigm of Idealist discourse. Rather, these four females strive to completely negate themselves, their work, and ultimately their own self-certainty before it becomes static, defined, or certain.

In this manner the characters appear to epitomize Lacoue-Labarthe and Nancy's notion of the Romantic "literary absolute"—the auto-production of the text producing itself, its own theory and criticism, and ultimately its complete self-dissolution. In their discussion of the fragment, Lacoue-Labarthe and Nancy remark: "[the work] abandons or excises the work itself—and thus is transformed in an almost imperceptible manner into the 'work of the absence of work'" (57). Moreover, Lacoue-Laberthe and Nancy also emphasize the importance of "process" or development that was essential to the Romantic program.[4] Similarly each title heroine undermines herself and the aesthetic theory she represents as a means to defer an Idealist static definition. The Bettelweib's hauntings are similar, yet always slightly different and seemingly endless; the Marquise produces an endless line of "little Russians"—nascent, but developing, representations; Käthchen's literal and metaphoric essence is in a constant state of flux; and similarly Penthesilea's persona constantly vacillates, leaving the logocentric Greeks unable to fix one definition upon her.

However, there is a drawback to the females' instability. Despite having a dynamic, fluid, and amorphous essence, their subversive efforts seem transitory. Their self-destruction appears to encourage the return of the dominant discourse, Idealism. Like Butler's critique of Kristeva, which criticizes her strategy of subversion because "her theory appears to depend upon the stability and reproduction of precisely the paternal law that she seeks to displace" (102), Idealist discourse (a guarantor of paternal law) repeatedly reasserts its dominance in each work I examine. Ephemeral female essence and the general displacement of linear organization she effects are supplanted by the subsequent return of the dominant status quo. This return to "normalcy" certainly questions the subversive import of each character's aesthetic.

One only needs to examine the ending of each text to appreciate this contradiction. In the final lines of *Das Bettelweib von Locarno*, the Bettelweib exists as a sign. She and her haunting are absent, only her name refers back to the text's beginning and defines the "alte kranke Frau," whose entrance instigates the course of events, the text itself. In other words, the Bettelweib's absence as character enables her presence as the work, *Das Bettelweib von Locarno*. Ultimately, however, she appears dependent upon male discourse for her presence as text. The male "[hatte] das Bettelweib von Locarno aufstehen heißen" (198). Male discourse essentially calls her into existence.

The Marquise's omnipresence as character throughout the novella is juxtaposed by the complete absence of her child, who functions as a cipher for the "work of the absence of work." The Marquise's penchant for negation (*nichts*) first negates her own will, and then excises her child, its origins and corporeal tangibility, in order to give birth to the presence of the figurative, the aesthetic project. However, like the Bettelweib, the text's presence is dependent on a male "Erscheinung" or representation for the story's plot: "er würde ihr damals nicht wie ein Teufel erschienen sein, wenn er ihr nicht, bei seiner ersten Erscheinung, wie ein Engel vorgekommen wäre" (143).

Similar to the Bettelweib, Käthchen also suffers a fall that results in her self-negation. Throughout the play an independent Käthchen fades away as she aggressively adopts the male projection of the ideal passive female with such exaggerated fervor that she becomes an incorporeal image redirecting masculine discourse back upon itself in a paradic fashion. But again her disruption ends with a commodity-like exchange between males, her father Theobald and the Graf vom Strahl. Her transient essence, epitomized by her own fleeting wanderings, end as patriarchal law supplants her own will: "wohlan, so nehmt sie, Herr Graf vom Strahl, und führt sie zur Kirche" (531). She is forcefully led to the church, the symbolic guarantor of patriarchal law.

Penthesilea's surrender inaugurates the total dissolution of figurative and literal limits, whereby she gains control of textual language. This control culminates in her twofold death, a hyperbolic exaggeration of her self-destructive tactics. She first surrenders and dies as the character, Penthesilea, and then she expires as the text, *Penthesilea*—a blooming "tree" of "Blätter" (pages) too dense to withstand the maelstrom of masculine "hot air": "Doch die gesunde [Eiche] stürzt [der Sturm] schmetternd nieder / Weil er in ihre Krone greifen kann" (428). Although she momentarily seizes and controls the authorial project through her anthropophagic defeat of the Apollo-God-Poet figure Achilles, she is unable to escape the very discourse she undermines.

However, it is possible that escaping is not the goal, or that the notion of "goal" itself (a teleological or linear destination connoting "good" in phallocentric discourse) is an inappropriate judgment of their "defeat." For in each work the female encourages, welcomes, her own destruction, and metaphorically, the deconstruction of her namesake, the text (discourse) she re-presents. The irony in her self-destruction is the subsequent undermining of Idealist discourse, the very discourse within which she exists as character and text. What appears as defeat and empty absence welcoming the return of the dominant discourse is, ironically, a willful avoidance, or suspension, of masculine recognition. It is like Irigaray's notion of an "elsewhere," a transcendental space of unrepresentability or inarticulation that allows the female to disrupt the "phallocentric economy" of masculine representation.

To explain this paradox it is helpful to examine the conflict within Kleist's own aesthetic discourse. His works are born of Idealism, albeit negatively, and his method for critiquing that discourse draws upon Idealist theories of representation. He masks his discourse and its disconcerting import, like his female characters, in a surrender to Kantian aesthetics. Kristeva argues a similar paradox exists for female discourse and its potential to subvert sexist or patriarchal language. She views female discourse as being simultaneously a subject and a subversive dissident within Male discourse. Irigaray presents an even stronger critique stating:

> Women's social inferiority is reinforced and complicated by the fact that woman does not have access to language, except through recourse to "masculine" systems of representation which disappropriate her from her relation to herself and to other women. (85)

Her statement provides a powerful analogy to the problem of female discourse in Kleist's works. His female characters find themselves excluded and dependent upon employing "masculine" systems of representations for their subversive practices. However, like Iragaray's female subject, Kleist's women only mimic male discourse. They do not demand "to speak as a (masculine) subject" (Irigaray, 124); rather they only wish to don the tenor of male voice to disrupt the system through burlesque. In this manner they not only subvert and subject themselves to Idealist (patriarchal) discourse, but they also develop a means to "appropriate" themselves for themselves, albeit negatively. The Kleistian female subject's demise subverts discourse without asserting another "master-discourse,"[5] for what she presents, as the Marquise emphatically states, is absence or *nichts*. To provide a viable (i.e. phallically visible) "other" discourse that completely usurps and replaces Idealist discourse would merely reify the power structure of Idealism's patriarchal discourse. It is a paradoxical answer to Kleist's own paradox of trying to subvert Idealism with Idealistic (mimetic) aesthetics—an aesthetics culminating in negation and loss.

Explaining Kleist's contradictory female figures with feminist readings enables alternative interpretations of self-negation and absence as a viable mode of subversion—even if that subversion is only transient, or a work-in-process. Yet my argument also engenders a subsequent complication that must be addressed. As a basis for my analysis of Kleist's female title characters I assume the existence of a female voice within a canonical male author, a theoretical position that is potentially controversial. However, feminist readings of canonical male authors certainly exist and identifying female voice in canonical male texts is not entirely new. In her article "Notorious Signs, Feminist Criticism and Literary Tradition" Anrienne Munich argues critics can and should locate various voices in male-authored texts. She states: "one cannot neatly equate a work with the sex of its author, the identity of an individual writer may not necessarily be coterminous with her or his sexual organs." She then emphasizes that to limit textual interpretation based solely on the "sex" of the author "identifies with dominant (patriarchal) thinking" (244). Moreover, feminist theory is hotly divided along essentialist and non-essentialist lines, debating whether gender is equal to "sex" or culturally influenced; or, in fact, if sex and gender are both cultural constructs either imposed by an imperious culture or willfully chosen.

Butler's seminal work *Gender Trouble* directly addresses this question. In her study Butler argues gender is not a fixed designation, and states:

> The presumption of a binary gender system implicitly retains the belief in a mimetic relation of gender to sex whereby gender mirrors sex or is otherwise restricted by it. When the constructed status of gender is theorized as radically independent of sex, gender itself becomes a free–floating artifice, with the consequence that *man* and *masculine* might just as easily signify a *female* body as a *male* one, and *woman* and *feminine* a *male* body as easily as a *female* one. (10)

One could state Kleist was afflicted with an especially acute form of "gender confusion." Questions concerning his own gender and sex certainly give currency to this possibility. His curious surgery in 1800, purportedly undertaken in Würzburg to "fix" a problem interfering with his suitability for marriage to his fiancée, and his highly erotic letters to his friend Ernst von Pfuel suggest his own notions of "sex" and gender were, at the least, under professional and self-scrutiny, and that these problems proceeded to manifest themselves in "atypical" expressions. I am not simply equating physical conditions or homoerotic tendencies with the necessary presence of a "female" voice; however, these examples do imply Kleist's own persona consisted of competing voices vying for expression in his equally controversial prose. It is a theme ironically analogous to Kleist's own status within the circle of the literary giants of his day. After all, Kleist's work is defined by its peripheral existence lying just beyond Goethe's, the great poet-patriarch's, loving embrace. For Kleist, this devastating expression of misrecognition and absence came to define his own poetic *oeuvre*.[6]

Notes

Introduction

1 *Heinrich von Kleist,Sämtliche Werke und Briefe,* vol. 1 (Munich: DTV, 1994). 796.

2 Unless otherwise stated, all parenthetical page numbers in Kleist citations refer to *Heinrich von Kleist,Sämtliche Werke und Briefe,* ed. Sembdner, vol. 2 (Munich: DTV, 1994).

3 This summary about Ulrike is influenced by MacLeod's incisive analysis. Catriona Macleod, "The 'Third Sex' in an Age of Difference: Androgyny and Homosexuality in Winckelmann, Friedrich Schlegel, and Kleist," *Outing Goethe and His Age,* ed. Kuzniar (Stanford: Stanford, 1996). 210.

4 *Heinrich von Kleist,Sämtliche Werke und Briefe,* vol. 1 (Munich: DTV, 1994).

5 Joachim Pfeiffer analyzes the discourse of "sentimental friendship" and how this discourse becomes entrenched in Kleist's own homoerotic aesthetic. Pfeiffer also mentions several critics who focus on the January 7, 1805 letter to Pfuel, and use this letter as an impetus to read Kleist's texts from a homosexual viewpoint: Isidor Sadger, Fritz Wittels, Lilian Hoverland, and Gerhard Weinholz. Joachim Pfeiffer, "Friendship and Gender: The Aesthetic Construction of Subjectivity in Kleist," *Outing Goethe and his Age,* ed. Kuzniar (Stanford: Stanford University Press, 1996) 217.

6 "Du stelltest das Zeitalter der Griechen in meinem Herzen wieder her, ich hätte bei Dir schlafen können, Du lieber Junge; so umarmte Dich meine ganze Seele! Ich habe Deinen schönen Leib oft, wenn Du in Thun vor meinen Augen in den See stiegest, mit wahrhaft *mädchenhaften* Gefühlen betrachtet. Er könnte wirklich einem Künstler zur Studie dienen. Ich hätte, wenn ich einer gewesen wäre, vielleicht die Idee eines Gottes durch ihn empfangen. Dein kleiner, krauser Kopf, einem feisten Halse aufgesetzt, zwei breite Schultern, ein nerviger Leib, das Ganze ein musterhaftes Bild der Stärke, als ob Du dem schönsten jungen Stier, der jemals dem Zeus geblutet, nachgebildet wärest. [. . .] Ich heirate niemals, sei Du die Frau mir, die Kinder, und die Enkel!" 749–50.

7 In Kuzniar's introduction of *Outing Goethe and his Age*, ed. Kuzniar (Stanford: Stanford University Press, 1996) 7.

8 After reading Marie's comments about *Penthesilea*, Kleist declared she read his soul like a seer: "Unbeschreiblich rührend is mir alles, was Sie mir über die Penthesilea schreiben. Es ist wahr, mein innerstes Wesen liegt darin, und Sie haben es wie eine Seherin aufgefaßt" (797). Later he entrusted Marie to read and critique his next text: "Jetzt bin ich nur neugierig, was Sie zu dem Käthchen von Heilbronn sagen werden" 797.

9 Robert Helbling, "A Peripatetic Writer without a Biography," *The Major Works of Heinrich von Kleist* (New York: New Directions, 1975) 3–20.

Chapter I

1 The definition of "novella" used here is Goethe's definition: "an event which is unheard of but has taken place." Quoted in J. A. Cuddon, *A Dictionary of Literary Terms* (Garden City: Doubleday and Company, 1976) p. 453. Cuddon also defines the novella as a "genre of epic quality with restriction to a single event, situation or conflict" (453).

2 *Heinrich von Kleists Lebensspuren: Dokumente und Berichte der Zeitgenossen*, ed. Helmut Sembdner (Bremen: Carl Schünemann, 1957) 434.

3 In this respect, the text presents a type of *Antibildungsroman* that directly challenges the aesthetic construction of the subject as presented throughout the *Goethezeit*.

4 "Kleist's use of vision in relationship to incomplete or incorrect knowledge forms a unique paradigm within what Michael Titzmann has identified as a visually coded notion of knowledge in philosophy and literature in the Age of Goethe, where sight is generally linked positively to cognition." Martha B. Helfer, *The Retreat of Representation: The Concept of 'Darstellung' in German Critical Discourse* (Albany: State University of New York Press, 1996) 122.

5 "Diese reine, seelenerhebende, bloß negative Darstellung der Sittlichkeit, bringt dagegen keine Gefahr der Schwärmerei, welche ein Wahn ist, über alle Grenzen der Sinnlichkeit hinaus etwas *sehen*, d. i. nach Grundsätzen träumen (mit Vernunft rasen) zu wollen; eben darum, weil die Darstellung bei jener bloß negativ ist. [. . .] Das moralische Gesetz aber ist an sich selbst in uns hinreichend und ursprünglich bestimmend, so daß es nicht einmal erlaubt, uns nach einem Bestimmungsgrunde außer demselben umzusehen." Immanuel Kant, *Kritik der Urteilskraft*, ed. Gerhard Lehmann (Stuttgart: Reclam, 1963) 183.

6 Kant states: "Also ist das Gefühl des Erhabenen in der Nature Achtung für unsere eigene Bestimmung, die wir einem Objekte der Natur durch eine gewisse

Subreption (Verwechselung einer Achtung für das Objeckt statt der für die *Idee der Menschheit in unserem Subjekte*) beweisen, welches uns die Überlegenheit der Vernunftbestimmung unserer Erkenntnisvermögen über das größte Vermögen der Sinnlichkeit gleichsam anschaulich macht" (my emphasis, Kant154). Also: "[. . .] Jene Absonderung ist also eine Darstellung des Unendlichen, welche zwar ebend darum niemals anders als bloß negative Darstellung sein kann, die aber doch *die Seele erweitert*" 182. Helfer also identifies Kant's figure of *negative Darstellung* as a method of self-definition: "[. . .] The *Critique of Judgment* does offer a partial explanation of how the subject can present itself to itself as it is rather than just as it appears. The beautiful and the sublime are aesthetic judgments that offer sensible presentations of the subject, yet both judgments involve a moment in which the imagination transcends sensibility and paradoxically creates a presentation of the supersensible subject. In the case of the beautiful it is an indirect presentation (*indirekte Darstellung*) of the moral good, which is 'originally determining' for the subject, and for the sublime it is a negative presentation (*negative Darstellung*) of the 'idea of humanity in our subject'" (35).

7 See Kant 182.

8 Emil Staiger, "Heinrich von Kleist, 'Das Bettelweib von Locarno'. Zum Problem des dramatischen Stils. *Meisterwerke deutscher Sprache aus dem 19. Jahrhundert* (Zürich: Atlantis Verlag, 1961), pp. 100–117; Egon Werlich, "Kleists 'Bettelweib von Locarno'. Versuch einer Aufwertung des Gehalts. *Wirkendes Wort*, 15 (1965): 239–57; R. Leroy and E. Pastor, "Die Brüchigkeit als Erzählprinzip in Kleists 'Bettelweib von Locarno,'" *Etudes Germaniques*, 2 (1979):164–175.

9 Patstor and Leroy state: "Staiger, der doch unseres Wissens als erster auf eine solche Ungereimtheit aufmerksam wurde, diese bagatellisierend 'Kleists Nachlässigkeit bei allem, was keine Folgen hat' zuschrieb" (165).

10 This is a quotation frequently cited from Kleist's novelle *Die Marquise von O . . .* used to support the argument that Kleist's often chaotic, incomprehensible texts correlate to his own existential dilemma that began with his infamous "Kantkrise."

11 Gerhard Schulz, "Kleists 'Bettelweib von Locarno': Eine Ehegeschichte?," *Jahrbuch der deutschen Schiller Gesellschaft* 18 (1974): 431–40.

12 Detoit also references Hamacher's analysis of *Das Erdbeben in Chile* as a precedence for a comparison between Kant's sublime and Kleist. Thomas Dutoit, "Ghost Stories, the Sublime and Fantastic Thirds in Kant and Kleist," *Colloquia Germanica: Internationale Zeitschrift für Germanistik*. 27.2 (1994): 225–54.

13 See Dutoit 225.

14 Leroy and Pastor also stress this anomaly: "Wenn man also von St. Gotthard kommt, sieht man das Schloß in Schutt und Trümmern liegen; sonst nicht? Was heißt das? Wenn man von anderswoher kommt, sieht man dann das Schloß überhaupt nicht? oder liegt es dann unversehrt vor den Augen des Reisenden?" (169). However, they do not attribute any sublime significance to the name or the castle itself.

15 "Kühne überhangende gleichsam drohende Felsen, am Himmel sich auftürmende Donnerwolken, mit Blitzen und Krachen einherziehend, Vulkane in ihrer ganzen zerstörenden Gewalt, Orkane mit ihrer zurückgelassenen Verwüstung, der grenzenlose Ozean, in Empörung gesetzt, ein hoher Wasserfall eines mächtigen Flusses u. dgl. machen unser Vermögen *zu widerstehen*, in Vergleichung mit ihrer Macht, zur unbedeutenden Kleinigkeit. Aber ihr Anblick wird nur *um desto anziehender*, je furchtbarer er ist, wenn wir uns nur in Sicherheit befinden; und wir nennen diese Gegenstände gern erhaben, weil sie die Stellenstärke über ihr gewöhnliches Mittelmaß erhöhen, und ein Vermögen zu *widerstehen* von ganz ander Art in uns entdecken lassen, welches uns Mut macht , uns mit der scheinbaren Allgewalt der Natur messen zu können" (my emphasis, Kant 160–1).

16 All translations of Kant are from Immanuel Kant, *Critique of Judgment*, trans. J. H. Bernard (New York: Hafner, 1951) 102.

17 See *Critique of Judgment* 102.

18 In *Die Marquise von O . . .*, Kleist uses metaphors of weapons and war to create a sexual subtext: "Bald darauf kehrte er auf den *Waffenplatz* zurück, gab Befehl, der Flamme, welche wütend um sich zu greifen anfing, Einhalt zu tun, und leistete selbst hierbei Wunder der Anstrengung, als man seine Befehle nicht mit dem gehörigen Eifer befolgte. Bald kletterte er, *den Schlauch in der Hand*, mitten unter brennenden Giebeln umher, und regierte *den Wasserstrahl*; bald *steckte* er, die Naturen der Asiaten mit Schaudern erfüllend, in den Arsenälen, und wälzte Pulverfässer und gefüllte Bomben heraus" (my emphasis,106). In *Das Käthchen von Heilbronn*, Käthchen's cleansing of a rusted blade is a sexual innuendo: "[ich] tröste ihn und führ ihn, um ihm das Mädchen zu übergeben, in den Stall hinunter, wo sie steht, und mir *eine Waffe* von Rost *säubert*" (my emphasis, 439). Throughout *Penthesilea* weaponry is completely intertwined with a sexual subtext. Dirk Grathoff identifies all weapons in *Penthesilea* as phallic symbols: "Er [Achill] legt den Phallus ab. Er begegnet Penthesilea *unbewaffnet*, hat alle *phallischen Gewaltinstrumente* wie Schwerter, Dolche, Pfeile abgelegt und will sich ihr hingeben" (my emphasis). Dirk Grathoff is quoted in *Heinrich von Kleist "Penthesilea": Erläuterungen und Dokumente* , ed. Hedwig Appelt and Maximilian Nutz (Stuttgart: Reclam, 1992) 149.

19 Duden identifies *verschieden* , which is also equivalent to "sich getrennt habend" (*scheiden*) as the participle form of *verscheiden* (*sterben*). Duden, *Deutsches Universalwörterbuch*, ed. Günther Drosdowski (Mannheim: Dudenverlag, 1996) 1660.

20 See Friedrich Kluge, *Etymologisches Wörterbuch der Deutschen Sprache*, ed. Walther Mitzka (Berlin: de Gruyter, 1967) 640.

21 See Duden 431.

22 *Verfahren* means "process." However, the prefix *ver* is frequently used to indicate an error. Duden mentions that *ver*: "drückt in Bildungen mit Verben aus, dass eine Person etw. falsch, verkehrt macht," p. 1630. Thus, I read *verfahren* here as a "mistake."

23 *Gleichgültig* means "indifferent," yet, literally, it means "equally (*gleich*) valid (*gültig*)."

24 Kuzniar emphasizes the audible nature of woman's voice which opposes masculine voice, originating in the symbolic--the visual: "Cixous and Irigaray oppose woman's voice, issuing from the mouth, to male discourse, which, arising in the Lacanian symbolic, marks a repression of the body. Cixous specifically links woman's voice with song and breath and contrasts it with codified male language [. . .]. Hence for Irigaray, who plays on the sexual ambiguity of the word *lips* in *This Sex Which Is Not One*, the voice, articulated by the lips, suggests woman's sexual difference. Further encoding the voice as female is the source of its production; the vocal chords, like woman's sexual organs, remain hidden from view. Expressing the unseen, the sensualized voice promises to signify woman's interiority. Her body may be heard in the singing voice." Alice A. Kuzniar, "Hearing Woman's Voices in *Heinrich von Ofterdingen*," *PMLA* 107.5 (1992): 1196–207.

25 Throughout Kleist's works the act of falling (*stürzen* and *fallen*) is often synonymous with sex and a subject's fall from innocence. In *Der Zerbrochne Krug*, Helfer argues a jug's fall and subsequent shattering is synonymous with the female characters, p.163; The Marquise's fainting fall in *Die Marquise von O . . .* is interpreted by Dorrit Cohn as a subconscious surrender to sexual desire. Dorrit Cohn, "Kleist's 'Marquise von O . . .': The Problem of Knowledge". *Monatshefte* 67.2 (1975): 129–43. Paglia interprets Penthesilea's and Achilles frequent stumbles and crashes to sexual desires to dominate and be dominated. Camille Paglia, *Sexual Personae* (New York: Vintage, 1991) 261. In Chapter III, I argue that Käthchen throws herself out a window, falling and breaking both legs, out of apparent devotion and love for the Graf Wetter vom Strahl in *Das Käthchen von Heilbronn*. Other texts where *stürzen* or *Fall, fallen* occur within the context of sex are *Das Erdbeben in Chile, Die Verlobung in St. Domingo, Der Findling,* and *Prinz Friedrich von Homburg*.

26 Paul Derks. *Die Schande der heiligen Päderastie. Homosexualität und Öffentlichkeit in der deutschen Literatur, 1750–1850* (Berlin: rosa Winkel, 1990) 87.

27 The *erkünstelte Heiterkeit* reveals another level of deception, namely an aesthetic deception. *Erkünstelt* means "feigned," but the word is originally derived from the root word *Kunst*, "art" (Duden 452). This aesthetic dimension of the word refers back to the "Florentine" knight and the homoerotic scene. In Romanticism, some male subjects go through a process of self-effemination in their attempt to gain a poetic ability, a talent portrayed as inherent in women. See Martha B. Helfer, "Confessions of an Improper Man": Friedrich Schlegel's *Lucinde*," *Outing Goethe and His Age*, ed. Alice A. Kuzniar (Stanford: Stanford University Press, 1996). That the Marchese's feigning is described as *erkünstelt* corresponds to this romantic topos of homoeroticism, self-effeminism, and an appropriation of an aesthetic ability. Most importantly, in Idealism, representation is dependent upon a subreption of the senses, a subreption that is dependent upon the illusive qualities of aesthetics, poetry, and rhetoric: see Helfer, *Retreat of Representation*, pages 16 (Klopstock), 19 (Herder), 21 (Kant), 42, 48, 70 (Fichte), and 81 (Novalis).

28 This is in reference to my earlier argument that his offer to spend the night with the Knight (*er wolle sogleich aufstehen*) is an attempt to represent himself as a substitute for the Bettelweib.

29 Repeatedly, the female characters, Andrea, Amalia, and Camilla, rein in their male counterparts whose linguistic dialogues, theories, and ideas repeatedly come close to over-extending the limits of comprehensibility, and falling into tautological dogmatism. "Amalia. Wenn das so fortgeht, wird sich uns, ehe wirs uns versehen, eins nach dem andern in Poesie verwandeln. Ist denn alles Poesie? [. . .] "Camilla. Es ist gut, daß Ihr endlich ein Ende macht. Ihr wollt eben alles in die Schule nehmen und seid nicht einmal Meister über die Redensarten, die Ihr führt; so daß ich nicht übel Lust hätte, mich zur Präsidentin zu konstituieren und Ordnung im Gespräch zu schaffen." Friedrich Schlegel, "Gespräch über die Poesie," *Charakteristiken und Kritiken I*, ed. Hans Eichner (Munich: Schöningh,1967) 304 and 311.

30 "Ver- drückt in Bildungen mit Verben aus, dass eine Person etw. falsch, verkehrt macht" (Duden 1630).

31 The chances that the Marchese would remove actual guns and knifes from a closet is also doubtful after the narrator explains that the Marchese always places his weapons in the corner in which the Bettelweib previously slept.

32 "Das Bettelweib von Locarno verdankt seinen Ursprung einem Abenteuer, einer Art Spukgeschichte, die dem Bruder von Ernst [Friedrich v. Pfuel] in Gielsdorf bei dem alten Onkel, dem Ritterschaftsdirktor von Pfuel, passiert war" (*Lebensspuren* 358).

33 See Helfer, *Retreat of Representation*.

34 Nietzsche refers to metaphors as a form of currency that has lost its value: "die Wahrheiten sind Illusionen, von denen man vergessen hat, daß sie welche sind,

Metaphern, die abgenutzt und sinnlich kraftlos geworden sind, Münzen, die ihr Bild verloren haben [. . .]." He then compares man's construction of truths and notions of reality to that of a web: "Man darf hier den Menschen wohl bewundern als ein gewaltiges Baugenie, dem auf beweglichen Fundamenten und gleichsam auf fließendem Wasser das Auftürmen eines unendlich komplizierten Begriffsdomes gelingt--freilich, um auf solchen Fundamenten Halt zu finden, muß es ein Bau wie aus Spinnefäden sein, so zart, um von der Welle mit fortgetragen, so fest, um nicht von jedem Winde auseinandergeblasen zu werden." Finally, his idea of the intuitive intellect "plays" with this web of concepts, tearing and restructuring them to form new meanings through irony: "Jenes ungeheure Gebälk und Bretterwerk der Begriffe, an das sich klammernd der bedürftige Mensch sich durch das Leben rettet, ist dem freigewordnen Intellekt nur ein Gerüst und ein Spielzeug für seine verwegensten Kunststücke: und wenn er es zerschlägt, durcheinanderwirft, ironisch wieder zusammensetzt, das Fremdeste paarend und das Nächste trennend, so offenbart er, daß er jene Notbehelfe der Bedürftigkeit nicht braucht und daß er jetzt nicht von Begriffen, sondern von Intuitionen geleitet wird." Friedrich Nietzsche, "Über Wahrheit und Lüge im aussermoralischen Sinn," *Werke in Drei Bänden* (Munich: Carl Hanser Verlag, 1954) 314, 315, and 321.

Chapter II

1 Unless otherwise stated, all parenthetical page numbers in Kleist citations refer to *Heinrich von Kleist,Sämtliche Werke und Briefe*, ed. Helmut Sembdner, vol. 2 (München: DTV, 1994) 104–143.

2 "The mystery with which [*The Marquise of O--*] deals is domestic and psychological rather than cosmic. In it Kleist refers to what he was fond of calling *die gebrechliche Einrichtung der Welt*, the faulty or imperfect or unstable structure of ordering of the world, the flaw in the scheme of things. [. . .] The heroine thinks of the 'order of the world' as not only 'inexplicable' (*unerklärlich*) but also 'great and sacred' (*gross und heilig*), and we are told that she 'wholly submits' to it, intellectually at least. She has still to learn the full facts of her particular situation, and to face her own fellings." David Luke and Nigel Reeves, Introduction, *The Marquise of O- And Other Stories*, trans. Luke and Reeves (London: Penguin, 1978) 18.

3 For an in-depth analysis of Kleist's concept of paternity see Silke-Maria Weineck, "Kleist and the Resurrection of the Father".

4 Gerhard Neumann argues Kleist's use of the taboo-breaking scene is just one in a series of "Tabudurchbrechungen" that potentially reveal hidden truths; Vinken and Haverkamp call the scene a visualization of the sexual act hidden by the infamous dash: "Wie das Positiv zum Negativ" (137); John Ellis analyzes the incestuous scene, comparing the father's violation of accepted social morals with the Graf's violation/rape of the Marquise. However, he does not argue

the commandant represents any paternal potential (34). Joachim Pfeiffer offers another view of the incest scene through a psychoanalytical approach. He focuses on the Oedipal implications of the father's authority within the Marquise's familial structure. Pfeiffer also does not consider the commandant as the child's father (54–60). In "Jenseits von Oedipus: Vaterkörper und Vaterschrift in Kleists Erzählungen" Weineck argues the reconciliation scene between the Marquise and her father reveals other paternal possibilities that draw into question the novella's "Happy End": "nicht nur, weil sowhol der Vater der Marquise als auch Leopardo, der Jäger, plausible Kandidaten für die Vaterschaft des Kindes sind . . . ." (144).

5 Unless otherwise stated, all textual translations are from *Heinrich von Kleist: The Marquise of O- And Other Stories,* trans. Luke and Reeves (London: Penguin, 1978).

6 In his discussion of hypotyposis in paragraph 59 of *Critique of Judgment,* Kant proposes that ideas are rendered symbolically through analogy. There is no sensible intuition capable of rendering pure ideas, thus analogy becomes the representational tool enabling cognitive reflection thereof. Within Kleist's story the ad is likewise an analogy, an analogy of *a* father. The ad does not directly name the father, but rather indirectly enables cognitive process to define *a* father.

7 See Robert Helbling, "The Kant Crisis," *The Major Works of Heinrich von Kleist* (New York: A New Directions Book, 1975); Martha B. Helfer,*The Retreat of Representation* (Albany: SUNY, 1996); Ernst Cassirer, *Heinrich von Kleist und die Kantische Philosophie* (Berlin: Reuther and Reichard, 1919); John H.Smith, "Dialogic Midwifery in Kleist's 'Marquise von O' and the Hermeneutics of Telling the Untold in Kant and Plato," *PMLA* 100.2 (1985): 203–19.

8 The following analysis of *Darstellung* is derived from Helfer's interpretation in *The Retreat of Representation.*

9 "*Negative Darstellung* is a moral imperative that guards against the 'illusional belief in our capacity to *see* beyond all bounds of sensibility. . . .It does not permit us to look around at and ground of determination external to itself" (Kant qtd. in Helfer 49).

10 For examples see Kleist's "Empfindungen vor Freidrichs Seelandschaft," or "Unwahrscheinliche Wahrhaftigkeiten."

11 The English translation reads: "Based on a true incident, the setting of which has been transposed from the north to the south" (Luke and Reeves 68).

12 "From the moment the narrator appears in the guise of a witness and recounts the events as a faithful imitation, it takes another witness to vouchsafe for the reliability of the first and we are caught at once in *an infinite regress*" (my emphasis). Paul de Man, "Aesthetic Formalization: Kleist's *Über das*

Marionettentheater." *The Rhetoric of Romanticism* (New York: Columbia University Press, 1984) 275.

13 Duden defines the negative implication of "ver" as follows: "Drückt in Bildungen mit Verben aus, dass eine Person etw. falsch, verkehrt macht." Duden, *Deutsches Universalwörterbuch*, ed. Günther Drosdowski (Mannheim: Dudenverlag, 1996) 1630.

14 Recent scholarship tends to emphasize the rape and the Graf's guilt therein in an attempt to offset past scholarship (Frühoff, Cohn, and Schmidhäuser), which has, according to Kunzel, like the story itself trivialized the actual rape. For example, see Kunzel, Raihala, and Winnett. In her study Susan Winnett argues strongly that the Marquise is raped. She reads the dash as "the most delicately accomplished rape in our literature" (68). She also maintains that the narrative works to suppress the rape by representing it through the dash, which ironically founds the narrative itself—it is the impetus for its "publication." In citing the text's subtitle, Winnett focuses on the ambiguity surrounding the verb *verlegen*, which also can mean "to publish" and well as "to move." Whereas I agree with Winnett's analysis of the dash as the locus of the "publication," I argue the narrative does not offer conclusive proof about the Marquise's "rape." In fact I argue the contrary. There is more evidence suggesting the Marquise seeks sexual gratification "willingly" (*wo sie eben . . . zu Boden sinken* ***wollte*** [my emphasis, 105]), and that she is not a passive victim of aggressive male violence, but rather a complex character with a determined will (*ich* ***will*** *nichts wissen* [my emphasis, 129]). For example, see Neumann's analysis of the Marquise's sexual persona.

15 All emphasis mine.

16 Barbara Vinken and Anselm Haverkamp make a similar argument about the divine status of the child's father. They argue the Marquise's vehement rejection of the Graf stems from the fact that she wants to believe the child's father is himself a god: "Was die Marquise dem Grafen nicht verzeihen kann, ist nicht eine menschliche Schwäche, in der er sich wie ein Tier benommen hat, sondern: daß er kein Gott war" (146). Ultimately, however, they accept the Graf's claim of culpability and self-definition as *the* father.

17 In Kluge *geheim* is traced back to the concept "Zum Haus gehörig." Friedrich Kluge, *Etymologisches Wörterbuch der Deutschen Sprache*, ed. Walther Mitzka (Berlin: de Gruyter, 1967) 241.

18 For an analysis on the biblical symbolism in Kleist see Thomas Friedrich.

19 Christine Kunzel interprets the final scene ironically and finds a degree of self-determination in the Marquise's behavior. She argues the Marquise's eventual embrace of the Graf as her "lover" enacts a metaphorical, or deferred, hanging, i.e. punishment for his earlier transgression: "In der besagten letzten Szene der Erzählung fällt die Marquise dem Grafen 'um den Hals' und verweist damit

meiner Meinung nach im Kontext der *Marquise von O ...* weniger auf eine Abhängigkeit der Frau von einem Mann . . ., sondern vielmehr auf das Motiv einer verhinderten bzw. verwechselten Hinrichtung" (78). Lorelle Raihala also argues the Marquise is an independent protagonist, who appears to "achieve a measure of emancipation" (95).

20 "Was ist also Wahrheit? Ein bewegliches Heer von Metaphern, Metonymien, Anthropomorphismen, kurz eine Summe von menschlichen Relationen, die, poetisch und rhetorisch gesteigert, übertragen, geschmückt wurden, und die nach langem Gebrauche einem Volke fest, canonisch und verbindlich dünken: die Wahrheiten sind Illusionen, von denen man vergessen hat, dass sie welche sind, Metaphern, die abgenutzt und sinnlich kraftlos geworden sind, Münzen, die ihr Bild verloren haben und nun als Metall, nicht mehr als Münzen in Betracht kommen." Friedrich Nietzsche, "Über Wahrheit und Lüge im aussermoralischen Sinn," *Werke in Drei Bänden*, ed. Karl Schlechta, vol. 3 (Munich: Hanser Verlag, 1954) 314.

21 Helfer identifies weaving as a metaphor for literary production in Kant, Novalis, and Kleist. Helfer also emphasizes that the Latin verb for weaving (*texere*) is etymologically related to the German and English noun for a written work: text / *der Text*.

22 Romantic texts are replete with examples of protagonists symbolically usurping authorial control, instigating the Romantic motif of auto-production. In their analysis of Romanticism and the notion of "autopoiesy" Lacoue-Labarthe and Nancy argue that Romantic literature (*Poiesy*) and the theory of literature is self-productive: "in other words, literature producing itself as it produces its own theory" (12). Martha Helfer also identifies examples of Romantic auto-production in Schlegel's *Lucinde*: "Hence, read against the grain, the 'Dithyramb' amounts to little more than Julius inscribing his own sexual prowess in an autoerotic act of aesthetic intercourse. The product of this masturbatory writing is the text *Lucinde*, which Julius loves and Schlegel calls 'my son'" (178).

23 "Jenes ungeheure Gebälk und Bretterwerk der Begriffe, an das sich klammernd der bedüftige Mensch sich durch das Leben rettet, ist dem freigewordnen Intellekt nur ein Gerüst und ein Spielzeug für seine verwegensten Kunststücke: und wenn er es zerschlägt, durcheinanderwirft, ironisch wieder zusammensetzt, das Fremdeste paarend und das Nächste trennend, so offenbart er, daß er jene Notbehelfe der Bedürftigkeit nicht braucht und daß er jetzt nicht von Begriffen, sondern von Intuitionen geleitet wird" (my emphasis, Nietzsche 321).

24 *Aufbürden*, which literally means to lay a burden upon someone, originates from *Bürde*, which is related to *gebären* to give birth to. See Kluge 111.

25 See Edward Tripp's definition of Morpheus, Phantasus, and Somnus in *The Meridian Handbook of Classical Mythology* (New York: Meridian, 1974) p. 534.

For a complete picture of Morpheus and Phantasus see Ovid, "Ceÿx and Alcyon," *Metamorphoses*, trans. Rolfe Humphries (Bloomington: Indiana University Press, 1969) 377–90.

26 In Kleist's play *Amphitryon* there is a similar episode where a sexual encounter involving Zeus creates a state of confusion and ambiguity. Zeus deceives Alkmene into believing he is her husband, Amphitryon, sleeps with her, and fathers the half-god child, Hercules.

27 "Now, quick to leave the cave, Morpheus flies on his noiseless wings across the darkness" (Ovid 387)

28 In Hank and Hodge's *A Dictionary of Surnames*, Juliette is related to Julia, a feminized form of Julius or Julio. These are in turn traced back to a Roman clan iulius, "possibly an adj. deriv. of Iuppiter, gen. Iovis, the supreme god . . . ." Patrick Hanks and Flavia Hodges, *A Dictionary of Surnames* (Oxford: Oxford University Press, 1988) 285. In *The Facts on File Dictionary of First Names*, Dunkling and Gosling also link Julius to Jove: a "Roman clan name which the Romans themselves derived from Greek ioulos 'downy (bearded)' but which probably derived from Jovilios 'descended from Jove.'" Leslie Dunkling and Wiliam Gosling, *The Facts on File Dictionary of First Names* (New York: Facts On File, 1984) 147.

Chapter III

1 Brentano stated after a rumor had spread that Kleist died: ". . . nachdem ich nun seine übrigen im Phöbus zerstreuten Arbeiten, besonders den Anfang des Käthchens von Heilbronn und der schönen Erzählung Kohlhaas gelesen, war ich recht erfreut, ihn lebendig zu wissen und zu sehn," and "Von seinen Arbeiten habe ich den Phöbus mit ungemeinem Vergnügen die zwei ersten Akte des Trauerspiels Käthchen von Heilbronn . . . gelesen." *Heinrich von Kleists Lebensspuren: Dokumente und Berichte der Zeitgenossen*, ed. Helmut Sembdner (Bremen: Carl Schünemann, 1957) 314–15. E.T.A. Hoffmann mentioned: "Sie können denken, wie mich das "Käthchen" begeistert hat; nur drei Stücke haben auf mich einen gleichen tiefen Eindruck gemacht - das "Käthchen", "Die Andacht zum Kreuze" und "Romeo und Julie" - sie versetzten mich in eine Art poetischen Somnambulismus, in dem ich das Wesen der Romantik in mancherlei herrlichen leuchtenden Gestaltungen deutlich wahrzunehmen und zu erkennen glaubte!" Quoted in Anthony Stephens, *Heinrich von Kleist: the Dramas and Stories* (Oxford/Providence: Berg, 1994) 129.

2 "Als Goethe das Kleistsche Käthchen von Heilbronn, was ihm sein treuer Sekretär Kräuter [Riemer?] zubrachte, da es in Weimar viele entzückte, unter andern Falk und Schulz[e], und viele es auf der Bühne zu sehen wünschten, gelesen hatte, sagte er: 'Ein wunderbares Gemisch von Sinn und Unsinn! die verfluchte Unnatur!' und warf es in das lodernde Feuer des Ofens mit den

Worten: 'Das führe ich nicht auf, wenn es auch halb Weimar verlangt'" (*Lebensspuren* 343)

3 A critic stated in *Der Sammler* 22. März 1810: "Man sieht es dem Ganzen an, daß dieses Schauspiel nichts anders als ein ziemlich unzusammenhängendes Gerippe einer Rittergeschichte sei, bei dem man sehr oft von der Kette der Ideen Verbindung losgerissen wird. . . . Auch die Sprache ist hier und da nicht anständig genug, z. B. der Ausdruck: *Geh', Narr! der du bis*t - und da, wo der Graf dem Bürgermädchen seine Gefühle aufdeckt, versteigt er sich so sehr in das Gebiet der Mythologie, daß er gewiß nicht verstanden werden konnte. . . .Der gebildetere Teil [des Publikums] wünschte dem Dichter einen solidern Geschmack, Konsequenz, und Studium des Horaz'schen Briefes an die Pisonen" (*Lebensspuren* 323).

4 In an announcement in his literary journal *Phöbus*, Kleist challenges all writers and poets to a competition for an unobtainable prize: "Unter dem Schutze des daherfahrenden Gottes eröffnen wir einen Wettlauf; jeder treibt es, soweit er kann, und bleibt unüberwunden, da niemand das Ziel vollkommen erreichen, aber dafür jeder neue Gemüter für den erhabenen Streit entzünden kann, ohne Ende fort." Quoted in Katharina Mommsen, *Kleists Kampf mit Goethe* (Heidelberg: Lothar Stiehm, 1974) 69. Kleist couches his competition in the Romantic imagery of "Unendlichkeit"; however, rather than remaining within the Romantic school, Kleist announces that the real adversary are those authors of "long established literary fame": "Aber wie wir selbst bewaffnet sind, werden wir keinen anderen Unbewaffneten oder auch nur Leichtbewaffneten auf dem Kampfplatz, den wir hierdurch eröffnen, neben uns leiden. Große Autoren von längst begründetem Ruhm werden mit uns sein" (qtd. in Mommsen 69). As Mommsen points out, the author who received the greatest fame in his day was Goethe. For Kleist, Goethe was the literary establishment.

5 Böttiger stated in regards to the play: "Romantisch ist die Anlage des Ganzen gewiß, wenn man darunter unbegreiflich versteht" (*Lebensspuren* 239); and Fouque declared: "Bei Lesung der ersten Blätter dieser Ritter-Tragödie glaubten wir, eine Parodie auf den romantischen Schnickschnack unsrer Zeit zu finden. Bald aber ward es uns gewiß, daß es dem Hrn. v. Kleist barer, brenender Ernst sei" (*Lebensspuren* 338). Stephens mentioned: "Just as *Die Familie Schroffenstein* is, superficially, a chivalric melodrama in the popular style, so *Das Käthchen von Heilbronn* presents itself first as a variation of the same convention, enriched by many elements which had since become popularly 'Romantic.' Contiguous to this is the level on which some, but not all, of these modish elements are exaggerated into parody. " Anthony Stephens, *Heinrich von Kleist: the Dramas and Stories* (Oxford/Providence: Berg, 1994) 129. Brown noted: " . . . he [Kleist] was writing to a formula aimed at the popular end of the market rather than exploring issues which concerned him deeply. The question that arises is whether the assumption of this style is deliberate or mocking and parodistic." Hilda Meldrum Brown, *Heinrich von Kleist: The Ambiguity of Art and the Necessity of Form.* (New York : Oxford University Press, 1998) 321; and finally, Ueding remarked: "Ein Großteil der Ritterszenen hat mit Parodie zu

tun." Gert Ueding, "Zweideutige Bilderwelt: *Das Käthchen von Heilbronn.*" *Kleists Dramen: Neue Interpretationen*, ed. Walter Hinderer (Stuttgart: Phillip Reclam, 1981) 174.

6 "Aus dieser Hermetik folgt ja die Zweideutigkeit der Bilderwelt, und auch die Traumbilder haben an ihr teil: darin steht Kleist in krassem Gegensatz zur romantischen Schule" (Ueding 175).

7 See Cullens and von Mücke 491. Chris Cullens, and Dorothea von Mücke, "Love in Kleist's *Penthesilea* and *Käthchen von Heilbronn*," *Deutsche Viertel Jahrsschrift für Literaturwissenschaft und Geistesgeschichte* 63.3 (1989): 461–93.

8 In *Die Familie Schroffenstein* identities and genders are switched, resulting in death, not self-definition. In *Der Findling* Nicolo inserts himself into the persona of Colino, his stepmother's secret lover, and attempts to orchestrate a self-definition of himself through his stepmother's recognition of him as (re)presenting Colino. The definition fails, resulting in Nicolo's own violent death.

9 Like Kant's notion of pure concepts or ideas --God, Freedom, and Immortality-- Käthchen's father, the court, and the Graf all describe Käthchen as if she were a god and immortal. Moreover, the male figures' repeated inability to physically and mentally grasp Käthchen reveals another feature akin to Kant's notion of the idea: Käthchen's apparent freedom.

10 "Herr Friedrich Wetter Graf vom Strahl, du bist einstimmig von der Vehme losgesprochen" (451).

11 According to Duden, *Urkunde* is etymologically related to the old high German word *urchundi* which is equal to *Erkenntnis.* Duden. *Deutsches Universalwörterbuch.* ed. Günther Drosdowski (Mannheim: Dudenverlag, 1996) 1624.

12 This summary of Fichte's self-positing subject, a subject defining itself as *Darstellung*, is taken from Martha B. Helfer, *The Retreat of Representation: The Concept of 'Darstellung' in German Critical Discourse* (Albany: State University of New York Press, 1996) 60–68.

13 In her article "Kleist's 'Penthesilea' Geschlechterparadigmen. Die Frau als Projektionsfigur männlicher Identität--oder doch nicht?," Sigrid Lange identifies Käthchen's role as a response to classical images of women: "*Amphitryon* und *Das Käthchen von Heilbronn* sind Liebesgeschichten mit einem brachialen Happy-End. Die darin enthaltene Provokation trifft, wie man bei Kleist fast vermuten sollte, nichts weniger als einen der unantastbaren Topoi der klassischen Ästhetik: den Mythos von der erlösenden Fähigkeit des Weiblichen. Man erinnere sich: von Goethes *Pandora* bist zum Schluß der *Faust,* von Schillers *Jungfrau von Orleans* bis zu Hölderlins *Diotima,* in ihren poetischen Versionen wird der Mythos vom **Ewigweiblichen** über die

alltägliche triviale Konkretion hinaus transzendiert" (my emphasis). Sigrid Lange, "Kleists 'Penthesilea,'" *Weimarer Beiträge: Zeitschrift für Literaturwissenschaft, Ästhetik und Kulturwissenschaften* 37.5 (1991): 706–7.

14 Duden 1630.

15 Duden 1630.

16 The paradigmatic examples of Romantic self-reflexivity are Schlegel's statements: "ein Roman ist ein romantisches Buch" and "manche Künstler, die nur auch einen Roman schreiben wollten, von ungefähr sich selbst dargestellt haben." Friedrich Schlegel, *Charakteristiken und Kritiken I*, ed. Hans Eichner (Munich: Schöningh, 1967) 182 and 335.

17 Helfer 151.

18 Although the Graf is not the typical "Bildungsroman" protagonist searching for an aesthetic for self-definition, the Graf's relationship with women is presented as a search for an aesthetic: "Käthchen! Warum kann ich es nicht? Du Schönere, als ich singen kann, ich will eine eigene Kunst erfinden, und dich weinen [. . .]. Doch wenn ich jemals ein Weib finde, Käthchen, dir gleich: so will ich die Länder durchreisen, und die Sprachen der Welt lernen, und Gott preisen in jeder Zunge, die geredet wird" (455).

19 Reeve identifies the metaphorical substitution of the Graf's horse in place of the Graf himself, and also suggests that the stables in which Käthchen sleeps reveal more sexual activity than the superficial storyline intends. "Kleist supplies a strong inducement to connect Käthchen with the noble horse and the horse, a stallion with all its sexual connotations, with Strahl." William C. Reeve, *Kleist's Aristocratic Heritage and "Das Käthchen von Heilbronn"* (Montreal and Kingston: McGill-Queen's University Press, 1991) 34. Here I emphasize the homoerotic imagery of the Graf moving the androcized Kunigunde down from the horse, metaphorically, off himself, as a sexual act that places Kunigunde in a dominant position.

20 See Reeve 34.

21 The word "text" is derived from the Latin "texere" meaning "to weave." *Webster's New Universal Unabridged Dictionary* (New York: Barnes and Noble Books, 1996) 1963

22 My reading of Novalis is based on Helfer's analysis of Novalis. Helfer argues Novalis rewrites Fichte's theory of the "self-positing subject" into a poetical mode she calls "visual-verbal Poesie," epitomized by fluid in general and most specifically the fluid mirror in Klingohr's fairy tale that reflects truly. "The mirror contains an eternal "original image" that counteracts the necessary deception of *Darstellung* Novalis had identified in the *Fichte-Studies*" (Helfer 102).

[23] "Daß er aber nicht im Stande gewesen wäre, sie an sich zu locken . . ." (*Die Marquise von O . . .* 116).

[24] "Mhd. antlize, ahd. antlizzi, eigtl. = das Entgegenblickende" (Duden 128).

[25] In *Heinrich von Ofterdingen* woman's language is epitomized by fluid, and Kuzniar defines Novalis' theory of language as a "concept of poetry, which is, like woman, fecund, fluid, and inventive, ever changing and pointing beyond itself." Alice A. Kuzniar, "Hearing Woman's Voices in *Heinrich von Ofterdingen*," *PMLA* 107.5 (1992): 1203.

[26] Fluidity is the cornerstone of Novalis' theory of a "visual-verbal Poesie" that transcends illusion and enables "true" represntation.

[27] Perhaps this is because Käthchen is herself a product of male production. She has two fathers; however, her mother is textually absent and appears only as a figure of fiction. The Kaiser, Käthchen's real father, tells this story about Kitchen's mother, as he remembers the events leading up to their encounter. Moreover, the Kaiser uses a showpiece with a male's image, Pope Leo, to identify Käthchen as his daughter, a definition that overshadows all maternal importance."Käthchen's Mutter heißt Gertrud! Ich weiß, daß ich mir, als sie sehr weinte, ein Schaustück, mit dem Bildnis Papst Leos, von der Brust los machte, und es ihr als ein Andenken von mir, den Sie gleichfalls nicht kannte, in das Mieder steckte; und ein solches Schaustück, wie ich eben vernehme, besitzt das Käthchen von Heilbronn!" (519). Käthchen's maternal history is defined by male imagery. Therefore, Käthchen fails to provide the Graf with a Romantic-like aesthetic language, *Poesie*. Thus he is unable "to speak the languages of the world and to praise God in every tongue that is spoken": " [. . .] die Sprachen der Welt lernen, und Gott preisen in jeder Zunge, die geredet wird" (455). In other words, he is left unable to define himself through an aesthetic medium of *Poesie*, which is typically, in Romanticism, provided by a female, because Käthchen is herself a product of patriarchy.

Chapter IV

[1] *Xena: Warrior Princess Official Site*, Feb. 2001, <http://www.studiousa.com>.

[2] In *Nordissche Miszellen*, a critic accused Kleist of creating "unnatürliche Bilder" in his *Penthesilea*. *Lebensspuren*, ed. Helmut Sembdner (Bremen: Carl Schünemann, 1964) 252.

[3] In *Miszellen für die Neueste Weltkunde*, a critic claims Penthesilea is disgusting and therefore aesthetically untenable: "Penthesilea ist im Wahnsinn eine Furie, die Abscheu erweckt, statt Grausen [. . .]. Er [Kleist] beleidigt den Geschmack und empört das Zartgefühl, wo er nur Entsetzen hervorbringen wollte. Das Ekelhafte ist niemals Object der schönen Kunst" (*Lebensspuren* 254).

4 Jost Hermand mentions the tendency for scholars to fixate on Kleist's personal comments about *Penthesilea*. Jost Hermand, "Kleist's Penthesilea im Kreuzfeuer geschlechtsspezifischer Diskurse," *Monatshefte* 87.1 (1995): 34.

5 Textual page references are to Heinrich von Kleist, *Sämtliche Werke und Briefe*, ed. Helmut Sembdner. vol. 1 (Munich: Hanser, 1984) 321–428.

6 Kleist's epigrams often reveal an ironical, self-parodical intent. In the epigram, "Die Marquise von O . . ." Kleist cynically states: "Dieser Roman ist nicht für dich, meine Tochter. In Ohnmacht! Schamlose Posse! Sie hielt, weiß ich, die Augen bloß zu" (22). And in the epigram dedicated to *Penthesilea*, "Dedikation der Penthesilea," Kleist sarcastically parodies his drama: "Zärtlichen Herzen gefühlvoll geweiht! Mit Hunden zerreißt sie, welchen sie liebet, und ißt, Haut dann und Haare, ihn auf" (20).

7 V.C. Hubbs argues the two plays should be interpreted as a textual whole: "From the above passages it can be inferred that Penthesilea and Kätchen should be considered as two parts of a single entity and that they are undoubtedly, inasmuch as Kleist conceived them as a polarization, extreme examples of one single basic force or phenomenon." V. C. Hubbs, "The Plus and Minus of Penthesilea and Käthchen," *Seminar: A Journal of Germanic Studies* 6.3 (1970): 187.

8 Linda Hoff-Purviance develops the compelling argument that Kleist structurally and thematically modeled his play after the 24 books in Homer's *Iliad*. Linda Hoff-Purviance,."The Form of Kleist's *Penthesilea* and the *Iliad*." *The German Quarterly* 55 (1982): 39–48.

9 Michel Chaouli describes the play's motif of eating as a critique of Kantian aesthetics where the distance between the aesthetic and the literal is consumed. Distance becomes a metaphor for representation. The loss of distance, according to Chaouli, is the loss of representation. Michel Chaouli, "Devouring Metaphor: Disgust and Taste in Kleist's *Penthesilea*." *The German Quarterly* 69.2 (1996): 125–143.

10 See Katharina Mommsen 43.

11 In her reading of Goethe's *Faust I*, Paglia identifies sex as "a mode of western knowledge and control. Gretchen, the lamb-like feminine innocent, is physically and morally ruined, ending in infanticide. Her illicit intercourse with Faust implants her with western aggression. Seduction is an intellectual game. It is the invasion of one hierarchy by another." Camille Paglia, *Sexual Personae* (New York: Vintage Books, 1991), here 254. I suggest Kleist employs metaphors of sex in a similar manner. Both Achilles and Penthesilea struggle to infect the other with their social framework, ideology, and sexual dominance. However, unlike Gretchen, Penthesilea is never passive or sexually invaded. Rather, she literally invades Achilles and his masculine discourse with an arrow, a frequent

substitute for language throughout the play (e.g., *[. . .] aus Köchern mir die Antwort senden* [325]).

12 For example, in the other three texts I analyze in my thesis, the theme of a fall is paramount to a subtextual discussion of representation: *Das Bettelweib von Locarno* (*Die Frau, das sie sich erhob, glitschte mit der Krücke auf dem glatten Boden aus* [196]) this passage becomes a repeted scene, a re-presentation; *Die Marquise von O . . .(sie auch völlig bewußtlos niedersank. Hier - traf er* [106]) the infamous dash becomes a symbol for trying to create a truthful re-presention of the "true" father; and *Das Kätchen von Heilbronn* Kätchen's devotion to the Graf represents the Romantic ideal "idea" of female representation.

13 "Auch ist das letztere der Art nach von dem ersteren Wohlgefallen gar sehr unterschieden: indem dieses (das Schöne) direkt ein Gefühl der Beförderung des Lebens bei sich führt, und daher mit Reizen und einer spielenden Einbildungskraft vereinbar ist; jenes aber (das Gefühl des Erhabenen) eine Lust ist, welche nur indirekt entspringt, nämlich so daß sie durch das Gefühl einer augenblicklichen Hemmung der Lebenskräfte und darauf sogleich folgenden desto stärkern Ergießung derselben erzeugt wird, mithin als Rührung kein Spiel, sondern Ernst in der Beschäftigung der Einbildungskraft zu sein scheint." Immanuel Kant, *Kritik der Urteilskraft*, ed. Gerhard Lehmann (Stuttgart: Reclam, 1963) 134.

14 Duden, *Deutsches Universal Wörterbuch* (Mannheim: Dudenverlag, 1996) 221.

15 See Kant 181–2.

16 "Man darf nicht besorgen, daß das Gefühl des Erhabenen durch eine dergleichen abgezogene Darstellungsart, die in Ansehung des Sinnlichen gänzlich negativ wird, verlieren werde; denn die Einbildungskraft, ob sie zwar über das Sinnliche hinaus nichts findet, woran sie sich halten kann, fühlt sich doch auch eben durch diese Wegschaffung der Schranken derselben unbegrenzt: und jene Absonderung is also eine Darstellung des Unendlichen, welche zwar ebendarum niemals anders als bloß negative Darstellung sein kann, die aber doch die Seele erweitert" (Kant 182).

17 In German *erkennen* (to recognize) is directly related to cognition (*Erkennung, Erkennt-nis*). See Duden 451.

18 By tracing the etymological development of *Darstellung* in aesthetic philosophy from the 16th to the 18th century and later into the early 19th century with Novalis and Kleist, Helfer identifies vision as a crucial element in the philosophical definition of *Darstellung*. "[. . .] It is remarkable that post-Kantian theories of *Darstellung* capitalize on the visual, a fact noted by Jean Paul as early as 1804." Martha B. Helfer, *The Retreat of Representation: The Concept of 'Darstellung' in German Critical Discourse* (Albany: State University of New York Press, 1996) 49.

[19] Duden 1068.

[20] Duden 631.

[21] Duden defines *Ausdruck* as a *Bezeichnung,* which can be translated as a "sign." See Duden 173.

[22] Achilles' interpellation of Penthesilea is a mode of self-definition akin to Althusser's notion of *interpellation* and akin to a Hegelian definition of subject. Both theories demand the subject be subjugated to become a subject. Literally, Penthesilea is subjugated, beaten down by Achilles. Thus Achilles' lifting of Penthesilea visually signifies Penthesilea's symbolical definition as subject through a Hegelian *Aufhebung*. Coincidentally, the next time the two speak again, his first words are: "in jedem schöneren Sinn, *erhabne* Königin!" (my emphasis, 378). *Erhaben* refers not only to her sublime presence, but also to her elevated definition as an *Aufhebung,* an absolute subject.

[23] According to Duden *reizen* is related to *reißen*. See Duden 1239.

[24] Duden identifies *Gewand* as originating from *gewendetes, gefaltetes Tuch*. Duden 605.

[25] "Mit einem Worte, die ästhetische Idee ist eine einem gegebenen Begriffe beigesellte Vorstellung der Einbildungskraft, welche mit einer solchen Mannigfaltigkeit der Teilvorstellungen in dem freien Gebrauche derselben verbunden ist, daß für sie kein Ausdruck, der einen bestimmten Begriff bezeichnet, gefunden werden kann, die also zu einem Begriffe viel Unnennbares hinzu denken läßt, dessen Gefühl die Erkenntnisvermögen belebt und mit der Sprache, als bloßem Buchstaben, Geist verbindet" (Kant 250).

[26] This interpretation is indebted to Chaouli's identification of Achilles as an interchangeable metaphor for the sun. See Chaouli 137.

[27] "Das Schöne kommt darin mit dem Erhabenen überein, daß beides für sich selbst gefällt. Ferner darin, daß beides kein Sinnes- noch ein logisch-bestimmendes, sondern ein *Reflexionsurteil* voraussetzt" (my emphasis, Kant 133).

[28] In her examination of *Darstellung* in *Retreat of Representation,* Helfer argues deception is the consistent element within various interpretations of *Darstellung*. See her interpretation of Klopstock (15), Herder (19), Kant (42 and 48), Fichte (70), and Novalis (81).

[29] Ironically, Kant varies his wording in the discussion of the guardian role of *negative Darstellung*. In the 1790 edition he uses "Sittlichkeit" instead of "Sinnlichkeit" : "Diese reine, seelenerhebende, bloß negative Darstellung der Sittlichkeit, bringt dagegen keine Gefahr der Schwärmerei, welche ein Wahn ist, über alle Grenze der Sinnlichkeit ([1790 edition] Sittlichkeit) hinaus etwas sehen, d. i. nach Grundsätzen träumen zu wollen" (Kant 183).

30 See Luce Irigaray, *This Sex Which is Not One*, trans. Catherine Porter (Ithaca: Cornell University Press, 1985).

31 See G. W. F. Hegel, *Phenomenology of Spirit*, trans. A. V. Miller (Oxford/New York: Oxford University Press, 1977) 118.

Epilogue

1 See Toril Moi's introduction to Kristeva, Julia, *The Kristeva Reader*, ed. Toril Moi, New York: Columbia University Press, 1986.

2 "Through this rediscovery of himself by himself, the bondsman realizes that it is precisely in his work, wherein he seemed to have only an alienated existence, that he acquires a mind of his own" (Hegel 119).

3 The exception to the four texts I examine is *Die Heilige Cäcilie*. Here the female figure is completely absent as character and functions only as a linguistic signifier of the spirit or idea of Cäcilie. Therefore she does not embody all three states as a physical as well as metaphysical character, author, and text, like the others do. However, the text is conceivably the "apotheosis" of Kleist's theory of female representation, where the figure is completely transfigured into the work itself.

4 "To borrow a term from a later tradition not unrelated to romanticism, that of Schopenhauer and Nietzsche, one is tempted to say that the essence of the fragment is individuation. As an indicator of a process rather than a fixed state, this term is in agreement with the important *Athenaeum* fragment 116, where the 'particular essence' of romantic poetry is 'that it should forever be becoming and never be perfected'" (Lacoue-Labarthe and Nancy, 43).

5 Kristeva's term.

6 For an excellent study of Kleist's troubled relationship with Goethe see Mommsen, Katharina, *Kleists Kampf mit Goethe*, Heidelberg: Lothar Stiehm, 1974.

Bibliography

Adelung, Johann Christoph. Grammatisch-kritisches Wörterbuch der Hochdeutschen Mundart. 2. Auflage. Hildesheim: Georg Olms, 1970.

Agge, Joel. Introduction. *Penthesilea: A Tragic Drama.* by Heinrich von Kleist. Trans. Joel Agee. New York: Michael di Capua Books, HarperCollins, 1998.

Allan, Seán. *The Stories of Heinrich von Kleist.* Ed. James Hardin Rochester: Camden House, 2001.

Arens, Katherine M. "Kleist's *Bettelweib von Locarno*: A Propositional Analysis." *Deutsche Vierteljahrsschrift für Literaturwissenschaft und Geistesgeschichte* 57.3 (1983): 450-68.

Brown, Hilda Meldrum. *Heinrich von Kleist: The Ambiguity of Art and the Necessity of Form.* New York : Oxford University Press, 1998.

Butler, Judith. *Gender Trouble: Feminism and the Subversion of Identity.* New York: Routledge, 1990.

Cassirer, Ernst. *Heinrich von Kleist und die Kantische Philosophie.* Berlin: Verlag von Reuther and Richard, 1919.

Chaouli, Michel. "Devouring Metaphor: Disgust and Taste in Kleist's *Penthesilea.*" *The German Quarterly* 69.2 (1996): 125-143.

Cohn, Dorrit. "Kleist's *Marquise von O . . .*: The Problem of Knowledge." *Monatshefte* 67 (1975): 129-44.

Cullens, Chris, and Dorothea von Mücke. "Love in Kleist's *Penthesilea* and *Käthchen von Heilbronn.*" *Deutsche Vierteljahrsschrift für Literaturwissenschaft und Geistesgeschichte* 63.3 (1989): 461-93.

Cuddon, J. A. *A Dictionary of Literary Terms.* Garden City: Doubleday and Company, 1976.

De Huszar Allen, Marguerite. "Denial and Acceptance. Narrative Patterns in Thomas Mann's *Die Betrogene* and Kleist's *Die Marquise von O.*" *The Germanic Review* 64.3 (1989): 121-28.

de Man, Paul. "Aesthetic Formalization: Kleist's *Über das Marionettentheater.*" *The Rhetoric of Romanticism.* New York: Columbia University Press, 1984. 263-290.

Derks, Paul. *Die Schande der heiligen Päderastie. Homosexualität und Öffentlichkeit in der deutschen Literatur, 1750-1850* . Berlin: Rosa Winkel, 1990.

Duden. *Deutsches Universalwörterbuch.* Ed. Günther Drosdowski. Mannheim: Dudenverlag, 1996.

Dunkling, Leslie, and William Gosling. *The Facts on File Dictionary of First Names.* New York: Facts On File, 1984.

Dutoit, Thomas. "Ghost Stories, the Sublime and Fantastic Thirds in Kant and Kleist." *Colloquia Germanica: Internationale Zeitschrift für Germanistik* 27.2 (1994): 225-54.

Eagleton, Terry. *Literary Theory: An Introduction*. Minneapolis: University of Minnesota Press, 1991.

Ellis, John. *Heinrich von Kleist: Studies in the Character and Meaning of his Writings*. Chapel Hill: U of North Carolina Press, 1979. 21-35.

Erläuterungen und Dokumente: Heinrich von Kleist "Penthesilea." Ed. Hedwig Appelt and Maximilian Nutz. Stuttgart: Reclam, 1992.

Fichte, Johann Gottlieb. "An Attempt at a New Presentation of the *Wissenschaftslehre*." *Introductions to the Wissenschaftslehre, and Other Writings (1797-1800)*. Ed. and Trans. Daniel Breazeale. Indianapolis: Hackett Publishing, 1994. 7-9, 106-18.

Fricke, Gerhard. *Gefühl und Schicksal bei Heinrich von Kleist: Studien über den inneren Vorgang im Leben und Schaffen des Dichters*. Darmstadt: Wissenschaftliche Buchgesellschaft,1963.

Friedrich, Thomas. "Ein Scandalum durch Anspielung auf das Mysterium [...] Erklären: Zur Mariensymbolik in Heinrich von Kleists *die Marquise von O ....* " *Beiträge zur Kleist-Forschung*. 16 (2002) 259-82.

Furst, Lilian R. "Begging an Answer: Kleist's *The Beggarwoman of Locarno*."*Countercurrents:On the Primacy of Texts in Literary Criticism*. Ed. Raymond Adolph Prier. Albany: State University of New York Press, 1992. 98-111.

———. "Double-Dealing: Irony in Kleist's *Die Marquise von O . . ..*" *Echoes and Influences of German Romanticism*. Ed. Michael S. Batts, Anthony W. Riley, and Heinz Wetzel. New York: Peter Lang, 1987. 85-95.

Goethe, Johann Wolfgang. "Zueignung." *Werke (Hamburger Ausgabe)*. Ed. Erich Trunz. Vol. I. Munich: Beck, 1988. 149-52.

Hamacher, Werner. "Das Beben der Darstellung." *Positionen der Literaturwissenschaft: Acht Modellanalysen am Beispiel von Kleists "Das Erdbeben in Chili."* Ed. David E. Wellbery. Munich: Beck, 1987.

Hanks, Patrick, and Flavia Hodges. *A Dictionary of Surnames*. Oxford: Oxford University Press, 1988.

Hegel, G. W. F.. *Phenomenology of Spirit*. Trans. A. V. Miller. Oxford and New York: Oxford University Press, 1977.

Heinrich von Kleists Lebensspuren: Dokumente und Berichte der Zeitgenossen. Ed. Helmut Sembdner. Bremen: Carl Schünemann, 1957.

Helbling, Robert E. *The Major Works of Heinrich von Kleist*. New York: New Directions, 1975.

Helfer, Martha B. "Confessions of an Improper Man": Friedrich Schlegel's *Lucinde*." *Outing Goethe and His Age*. Ed. Alice A. Kuzniar. Stanford: Stanford University Press, 1996. 174-93.

———. "Dorothea Veit-Schlegel's *Florentin*: Constructing a Feminist Romantic Aesthetic." *The German Quarterly* 69.2 (1996): 144-60.

———. *The Retreat of Representation: The Concept of 'Darstellung' in German Critical Discourse*. Albany: State University of New York Press, 1996.

Hermand, Jost. "Kleists *Penthesilea* im Kreuzfeuer geschlechtsspezifischer Diskurse." *Monatshefte für deutschen Unterricht, deutsche Sprache und Literatur* 87.1 (1995): 34-47.

Hilliard, Kevin. "*Rittergeschichte Mit Gespenst*: The Narration of the Subconscious in Kleist's *Das Bettelweib von Locarno*." *German Life and Letters* ns 44.4 (1991): 281-90.

Hoff-Purviance, Linda. "The Form of Kleist's *Penthesilea* and the *Iliad*." *The German Quarterly* 55 (1982): 39-48.

Hubbs, V. C. "The Plus and Minus of Penthesilea and Käthchen." *Seminar: A Journal of Germanic Studies* 6.3 (1970): 187-94.

Irigaray, Luce. *This Sex Which is Not One*. Trans. Catherine Porter. Ithaca: Cornell University Press, 1985.

Jacobs, Carol. "The Rhetorics of Feminism." *Uncontainable Romanticism*. Baltimore: Johns Hopkins University Press, 1989. 85-114.

Kant, Immanuel. *Critique of Judgment*. Trans. J. H. Bernard. New York: Hafner, 1951.

———. *Kritik der Urteilskraft*. Ed. Gerhard Lehmann. Stuttgart: Reclam, 1963.

Kircher, Hartmut. *Heinrich von Kleist: 'Das Erdbeben in Chili, Die Marquise von O . . .'*. Munich: Oldenbourg, 1992.

Kleist, Heinrich von. *Heinrich von Kleist: The Marquise of O- And Other Stories*. Trans. David Luke and Nigel Reeves. London: Penguin, 1978.

———. *Penthesilea: A Tragic Drama*. Trans. Joel Agee. Illus. Maurice Sendak. New York: Michael di Capua Books, HarperCollins, 1998.

———. *Sämtliche Werke und Briefe*. Ed. Helmut Sembdner. 2 vols. Munich: DTV, 1994.

Kluge, Friedrich. *Etymologisches Wörterbuch der Deutschen Sprache*. Ed. Walther Mitzka. Berlin: de Gruyter, 1967.

Krüger-Fürhoff, Irmela Marei. "Epistemological Asymmetries and Erotic Stagings: Father-Daughter Incest in Heinrich von Kleist's *The Marquise of O . . .*." *Women in German Yearbook: Feminist Studies in German Literature and Culture* 12 (1996): 71-86.

Kunzel, Christine. "Der Fall der Frau Marquise im 20. Jahrhundert oder: Die Unmöglichkeit einer Vergewaltigung in Ohnmacht oder Schlaf." *Gewalt und Geschlecht: Bilder, Literatur und Diskurse im 20. Jahrhundert*. Ed. Hanno Ehrlicher. Köln: Böhlau, 2002. 131-44.

———. "Heinrich von Kleists die Marquise von O; Anmerkungen zur Repräsentation von Vergewaltigung." *Figurationen; Gender, Literatur, Kultur*. 1:1. (2000): 65-81.

Kuzniar, Alice A.. "Hearing Woman's Voices in *Heinrich von Ofterdingen*." *Publications of the Modern Language Association of America* 107.5 (1992): 1196-207.

———. Introduction. *Outing Goethe and His Age*. Ed. Alice A. Kuzniar. Stanford: Stanford University Press, 1996.

Lacoue-Labarthe, Philippe, and Jean-Luc Nancy. *The Literary Absolute: The Theory of Literature in German Romanticism*. Trans. Philip Barnard and Cheryl Lester. Albany: State University of New York Press, 1988.

Lange, Sigrid. "Kleists 'Penthesilea'." *Weimarer Beiträge: Zeitschrift für Literaturwissenschaft, Ästhetik und Kulturwissenschaften* 37.5 (1991): 705-722.

Leroy, R. and Pastor, E. "Die Brüchigkeit als Erzählprinzip in Kleists *Bettelweib von Locarno*." *Etudes Germaniques* 34.2 (1979): 164-75.

Munich, Adrienne. "Notorious signs, feminist criticism and literary tradition". *Making a Difference: Feminist Literary Criticism*. Ed. Gayle Green and Coppelia Kahn. London and New York: Methuen, 1985.

MacLeod, Catriona. "The 'Third Sex' in an Age of Difference: Androgyny and Homosexuality in Winckelmann, Friedrich Schlegel, and Kleist." *Outing Goethe and His Age*. Ed. Alice A. Kuzniar. Stanford: Stanford University Press, 1996. 194-214.

Mahlendorf, Ursula R. "The Wounded Self: Kleist's *Penthesilea*." *The German Quarterly* 52 (1979): 252-72.

Mommsen, Katharina. *Kleists Kampf mit Goethe*. Heidelberg: Lothar Stiehm, 1974.

Müller-Seidel, Walter. "*Penthesilea* im Kontext der deutschen Klassik." *Kleists Dramen: Neue Interpretationen*. Ed. Walter Hinderer. Stuttgart: Phillip Reclam, 1981. 144-71.

———. "Die Struktur des Widerspruchs in Kleists 'Marquise von O.'" *Heinrich von Kleist: Aufsätze und Essays*. Ed. Walter Müller-Seidel. Darmstadt: Wissenschaftliche Buchgesellschaft, 1967. 244-68.

Neumann, Gerhard. "Skandalon: Geschlechterrolle und soziale Identität in Kleists *Marquise von O....* " *Heinrich von Kleist: Kriegsfall—Rechtsfall—Sündenfall*. Ed.Gerhard Neumann. Freiburg: Rombach, 1994. 149-92.

Nietzsche, Friedrich. *Werke in Drei Bänden*. Ed. Karl Schlechta. 3 vols. Munich: Hanser Verlag, 1954.

Novalis. *Monolog, Die Lehrlinge zu Sais, Die Christenheit oder Europa, Hymnen an die Nacht, Geistliche Lieder, Heinrich von Ofterdingen*. Ed. Ernesto Grassi. Hamburg: Rowohlt, 1988.

Ovid. *Metamorphoses*. Trans. Rolfe Humphries. Bloomington: Indiana University Press, 1969.

Paglia, Camille. *Sexual Personae*. New York: Vintage, 1991.

Pfeiffer, Joachim. "Friendship and Gender: The Aesthetic Construction of Subjectivity in Kleist." *Outing Goethe and His Age*. Ed. Alice A. Kuzniar. Stanford: Stanford University Press, 1996. 213-27.

———. "Die wiedergefundene Ordnung: Literaturpsychologische Anmerkungen zu Kleists *Die Marquise von O . . ..*" *Jahrbuch für Internationale Germanistik* 19.1 (1987): 36-53.

Prandi, Julie D.. *Spirited Women Heroes: Major Female Characters in the Dramas of Goethe, Schiller and Kleist*. New York: Peter Lang, 1983.

———. "Woman Warrior as Hero: Schiller's *Jungfrau von Orleans* and Kleist's *Penthesilea*." *Monatshefte* 77.4 (1985): 403-414.

Raihala, Lorelle. "Who Has Control of the Marquise's Life?" *Kleists Erzählungen und Dramen: neue Studien*. Ed. Paul-Michael Lutzeler. Würzburg: Königshausen & Neumann, 2001. 93-106.

Reeve, William C. *Kleist's Aristocratic Heritage and "Das Käthchen von Heilbronn."* Montreal and Kingston: McGill-Queen's University Press, 1991.

Schlegel, Friedrich. *Charakteristiken und Kritiken I*. Ed. Hans Eichner. Munich: Schöningh, 1967.

Schmidhäuser, Eberhard. "Das Verbrechen in Kleists *Marquise von O . . .*: Eine nur am Rande strafrechtliche Untersuchung." *Kleist Jahrbuch* (1986): 156-175.

Sembdner, Helmut. *In Sachen Kleist: Beiträge zur Forschung*. Munich: Hanser Verlag, 1974.

Seyhan, Azade. *Representation and Its Discontents: The Critical Legacy of German Romanticism*. Berkeley: University of California Press, 1992.

Smith, John H.. "Dialogic Midwifery in Kleist's *Marquise von O* and the Hermeneutics of Telling the Untold in Kant and Plato." *Publications of the Modern Language Association of America* 100.2 (1985): 203-19.

Staiger, Emil. *Meisterwerke Deutscher Sprache: aus dem neunzehnten Jahrhundert*. Zürich: Atlantis Verlag, 1961.

Stephens, Anthony. *Heinrich von Kleist: The Dramas and Stories*. Oxford and Providence: Berg, 1994.

Stipa, Ingrid. "Kleist's *Penthesilea*: from Misapprehension to Madness." *Seminar: A Journal of Germanic Studies* 27.1 (1991): 27-38.

Tripp, Edward. *The Meridian Handbook of Classical Mythology*. New York: Meridian, 1974.

Ueding, Gert. "Zweideutige Bilderwelt: *Das Käthchen von Heilbronn*." *Kleists Dramen: Neue Interpretationen*. Ed. Walter Hinderer. Stuttgart: Reclam, 1981.

Vinken, Barbara and Haverkamp, Anselm. "Die zurechtgelegte Frau: Gottesbegehren und transzendentale Familie in Kleists *Marquise von O ....* " *Heinrich von Kleist: Kriegsfall—Rechtsfall—Sündenfall*. Ed.Gerhard Neumann. Freiburg: Rombach, 1994. 127-47.

Webster's New Universal Unabridged Dictionary. New York: Barnes and Noble Books, 1996.

Weineck, Silke-Maria. "Jenseits von Oedipus: Vaterkörper und Vaterschrift in Kleists Erzählungen." *Beiträge zur Kleist-Forschung*. 16. (2002): 139-54.

———. "Kleist and the Resurrection of the Father." *Eighteenth-Century-Studies*. 37:1. (2003): 69-89.

Werlich, Egon. "Kleists *Bettelweib von Locarno*." *Wirkendes Wort* 15 (1965): 239-57.

Wilpert, Gero von. "Der Ausrutscher des Bettelweibes von Locarno." *Seminar: A Journal of Germanic Studies* 26.4 (1990): 283-93.

Winnett, Susan. "Marquise's "O" and Mad Dash of Narrative," *Rape and Representation*, Ed. Lynn A. Higgins and Brenda R. Silver. New York: Columbia University Press, 1991. 67-86.

Index

N

R

S

T

U

V

W

X

Z

Studies on Themes and Motifs in Literature

The series is designed to advance the publication of research pertaining to themes and motifs in literature. The studies cover cross-cultural patterns as well as the entire range of national literatures. They trace the development and use of themes and motifs over extended periods, elucidate the significance of specific themes or motifs for the formation of period styles, and analyze the unique structural function of themes and motifs. By examining themes or motifs in the work of an author or period, the studies point to the impulses authors received from literary tradition, the choices made, and the creative transformation of the cultural heritage. The series will include publications of colloquia and theoretical studies that contribute to a greater understanding of literature.

For additional information about this series or for the submission of manuscripts, please contact:

Dr. Heidi Burns
Peter Lang Publishing
P.O. Box 1246
Bel Air, MD 21014-1246

To order other books in this series, please contact our Customer Service Department:

800-770-LANG (within the U.S.)
212-647-7706 (outside the U.S.)
212-647-7707 FAX

Or browse online by series at:

www.peterlangusa.com